MARCUSE AND FREEDOM

Grateful acknowledgment is made for permission to quote from the following:
Negations Herbert Marcuse 1968 and *Five Lectures* Herbert Marcuse 1970.
Reprinted for the British market by permission of Penguin Books Ltd.
Permission for other markets granted by Beacon Press.
One Dimensional Man Herbert Marcuse 1964, reprinted for UK and Commonwealth markets by permission of Routledge and Kegan Paul PLC. Reprinted for other markets by permission of Beacon Press.
Eros and Civilisation Herbert Marcuse 1955, *Soviet Marxism* Herbert Marcuse 1958 and *Counterrevolution and Revolt* Herbert Marcuse 1972 reprinted by permission of Beacon Press.
Reason and Revolution Herbert Marcuse 1941 reprinted by permission of Humanities Press Inc. Atlantic Highlands, New Jersey.
Studies in Critical Theory Herbert Marcuse 1972 reprinted by permission of New Left Books Ltd.

MARCUSE AND FREEDOM

PETER LIND

CROOM HELM
London & Sydney

© 1985 Peter Lind
Croom Helm Ltd, Provident House, Burrell Row,
Beckenham, Kent BR3 1AT
Croom Helm Australia Pty Ltd, First Floor,
139 King Street, Sydney, NSW 2001, Australia

British Library Cataloguing in Publication Data

Lind, Peter
   Marcuse and freedom.
   1. Marcuse, Herbert   2. Liberty
   I. Title
   323.44'092'4   B945.M2984
   ISBN 0-7099-1684-1

Printed and bound in Great Britain
by Billing & Sons Limited, Worcester.

CONTENTS

TABLES

Tables

PREFACE

        This book is about Marcuse as a political phi-
losopher. It concerns the least known, yet most
inspiring aspect of his work, namely his conception
of freedom. This conception of freedom has much to
offer in terms of an alternative to dominant liberal
views on freedom.
        This conception of freedom constitutes the
positive philosophy of a writer often decried for
his pessimism.
        The image of a free society of co-operation,
mutual understanding and all round individual development forms the core of this conception of freedom.
        From this idea of freedom Marcuse develops his
critique of modern philosophical or scientific currents, of which his critique of Freud, Sartre and
technological rationality are good examples.
        Ten years after the events of the late sixties
which almost overnight made his name known world
wide, this aspect of his philosophy was still ill
understood even by gifted political opponents. This
is best illustrated by the following article by
Maurice Cranston, which in other respects conveys
well the sentiment of many fellow academics (The
Guardian, July 31st, 1979). It also conveys typical
misapprehensions, which this study hopes to dispel.

        Herbert Marcuse, who died in West Germany
on Sunday at the age of 81, was a neo-Marxist
political philosopher who became suddenly
world-famous, at the age of seventy, as the
"theorist" of student revolts. In his writings
he offered students a fairly modest share in
the formation of a new revolutionary proletariat, but his bitter critique of existing society, his intense utopian aspiration, and his

frank advocacy of violence and intolerance, won him an enthusiastic following among the more extreme elements of the Student Power movement. He became correspondingly unpopular with the American Right, and various threats were uttered against his life. Nevertheless he was allowed to retain his chair at the State university of California at San Diego well beyond retirement age.

Many of his former disciples in the student movement rejected his views in the early 1970s. He was howled down by students of the "New Left" in Germany during a visit there in 1971.

Two years earlier, he was attacked by Daniel Cohn-Bendit at a noisy lecture in Rome. "Why did you accept dirty bourgeois money to talk about revolution?"

Marcuse was born in Germany in 1898 into a cultivated bourgeois Jewish family, and received a typically thorough German education in philosophy and history. As a young man he fell under the influence of Rosa Luxembourg's Marxism, and later became one of the founders of the "Frankfurt" school of sociology, which cultivated, on Marxist lines, the sociology of knowledge. The rise of Nazism drove Marcuse and the other Frankfurt sociologists into exile, first to Paris and Geneva, then to America. Marcuse himself put forward at this time a "sociological" explanation of the Nazi system, namely that it was the characteristic ideology of capitalism at its monopoly stage.

He argued further that liberalism, which belonged to the earlier competitive phase of capitalism, must be considered outmoded, so that the only alternative to fascism was the introduction of socialism.

Marcuse never changed his mind on this subject. He was equally fixed in his belief that Stalinism was a perverted form of socialism.

His first work in English was Reason and Revolution, a defence of Hegel and of German metaphysics against the attacks both of empirically-minded Marxists and scientifically-oriented liberals. The book appeared in 1941 when German metaphysics was decidedly unfashionable, but nevertheless earned the author a certain academic reputation, and he was invited to become a professor at several of the leading

American universities.

In 1955 he published his most original and perhaps his best book: Eros and Civilisation. In this he turned his attention from the old socialist idea of an economic revolution to the more anarchistic and utopian idea of emotional revolution.

He attacked Freud's notion that civilisation depends on the regression of instincts and the sublimation of sexual drives, and argued that while this was true of known, class-dominated civilisations, it need not be true of civilisation as such. "Surplus repression", as he called it, could and should be dispensed with. Men's need for discipline in existing societies was the consequence of the perversion of men's nature by those societies. In a society without repression, very little discipline would be needed.

In Marcuse's next important book, One Dimensional Man, the optimistic, humanistic spirit gave way to a note of impatience and intolerance. Here he attacked the affluent society, and especially American society, as an unmitigated evil, not only because it corrupted the working classes into accepting capitalism, but because it distorted the will of men by introjecting false desires. Marcuse concluded that democracy, understood as accepting the decisions of the majority, was an unacceptable system while the majority remained mentally enslaved.

In a later essay A Critique of Pure Tolerance he made a further attack on the liberal-democratic values of freedom and toleration. Such values could have no place, he argued, in a society of manipulated majorities. The Non-violence preached by people like Gandhi and Luther King was a doctrine of submission.

Marcuse favoured the use of violence on behalf of humanity, even though real men in the present world might not understand that violence was being used on their behalf. Despairing of the willingness of the working class in advanced bourgeois societies to enact the revolutionary role, Marcuse suggested that coloured people, rebellious students, hippies and other such alienated minorities might discharge at least a part of this historic mission.

Maurice Cranston is professor of political

science at the London School of Economics.

The following letter was published a few days later.

Sir, - If Herbert Marcuse was alive today to read the exceedingly unfair presentation of his views by Professor Cranston (Guardian, July 31), he would probably say that such latter-day liberalism as Prof. Cranston's (in contrast to the true liberalism of John Stuart Mill) stands condemned out of its own mouth by its very unfairness; and he would not be wrong.

Prof. Cranston is entitled to challenge Marcuse's conception of freedom, but it ill befits a professor of politics to write as though the liberal democratic conception of freedom to which he himself subscribes were the only tenable one. And it ill befits a liberal to portray a conception of freedom which differs from his own as being no conception of freedom at all.

Marcuse in fact believed, as his writings make plain, that the central terms of political discourse - such terms precisely as "tolerance, "democracy", and "freedom" are vacuous unless they are referred to the socio-political system in which they are employed, and that they may well be part of the political vocabulary of a system which practises the opposite of what is preaches.

It was Marcuse's view that both Stalinist Russia and the American-led "West" purported to be "free" and "democratic" and opposed to violence, while in fact, in different ways, entrenching unfreedom and domination and purveying violence. One may agree with this view or not. But one should be able to distinguish it from the frank advocacy of violence and from outright opposition to freedom
- Yours faithfully,

Heinz Lubasz,
Department of History,
University of Essex,
Wivenhoe Park, Colchester.

The conception of freedom to which Lubasz alludes is what this book is about.

Peter Lind

ACKNOWLEDGEMENTS

This study would not have been possible without
the help of many people. This has taken many forms.
My most important debt goes to the staff and students of the university of Essex. They provided
intellectual stimulation, needed encouragements and
much in terms of human relationships.

I have debts of gratitude to individual departments, first of all to the Department of Government,
but also to the Departments of Philosophy and History, as well as to sociologists. I wish in particular
to thank Jean Blondel for his always inspiring commitment to Political Science, Bo Särlvik for kind
interest and support, Ivor Crewe for sympathetic
advice and encouragement and Ian Budge, whose help
has been invaluable.

I also wish to thank David Robertson, John
Gray, Ernesto Laclau and Robert Bernasconi for many
ideas and impulses. I am indebted to Colin Phillips,
Harry Lubasz, Erik Tannenbaum, Bob Goodin David
McKay, and to many other members of the staff. I
wish to thank Joanna Brunt for always being herself
and especially Majorie MacGlasham for being it too,
and an angel as well. I am most grateful to the
typists, in particular Inge Sunnesen and Bente Ib-
sen, for their patience and care with the various
versions of this book. I recall with pleasure animated discussions with Derek Hearl on the manuscript
and wish to thank Lone Molbjerg for her kind help.

I must also thank Steve Klein, Carol Piper,
Mark Taylor, Moira Crawley, Agnete Glavind, Vibeke
Geyer, Jacques Lheureux and Connie Solbjerg for
being such good friends while this book was under
way.

Peter Lind

Chapter One

INTRODUCTION

1.1 The Question of Freedom

Freedom - personal, political, religious or economic - is a pervasive ideal in our societies. It is best comprehended as a series of questions almost without answers. What should we understand by freedom? How important is this ideal for our daily lives? What role should it play in the establishment or improvement of the social institutions structuring our existence? How can freedoms of all kinds be promoted? That freedom is unquestionably good and valuable is the most fundamental tenet of the wider liberal ethic which has progressively emerged during the last four or five centuries. This took place in the context of the complex economic, social and political transformations that marked the end of feudalism in Europe, and to these processes liberalism itself, as a political doctrine, was to contribute (1). The range of questions and ideals evoked by the notion of freedom is what constitutes - in an often confused, vague and yet very real sense - the most distinctive trademark of Western political and social institutions, and more clearly still, that of Western philosophy and culture.

The following considerations should help to clarify the context for the present work. These considerations are banal enough. It seems intuitively fair to say that the present age has seen a hitherto unprecedented increase in freedom for many people, be it in terms of their spare time, their ability to travel, or in relation to the sort of job and existence they and their children can aspire to. Yet at the same time there are too many disquieting signs that not all these achievements have genuinely promoted freedom. The imperative of the work place, the demands in time and energy of the once cosy middle class career have increased considerably, and

the impenetrability of complex economic and social
systems seems greater than ever. This is perhaps
more true of politics than in any other sphere of
life, where we see many traditional liberties e-
roded, not so much by the perversity of man or the
cunning of the political rulers as by what, by all
accounts, appears as the force of events. There no
longer seems to be clear-cut and certain answers for
either the larger options or for detailed, technical
and yet important policy issues such as pollution or
local government. This appears to be true at all
levels, and in such a context, it can be difficult
to see how the traditional ideals of democracy,
parliamentarism and individual rights can be retained as valid, possible, or useful. The end of
ideology has not yet arrived, but many signs suggest
that the ideal of freedom based on the rational and
conscious choice of man the elector-citizen is perhaps obsolete, if it ever was a solution (2).
  The question of freedom occupies a singular
place within the literature of political theory (3).
It is often treated as a technical problem, requiring either conceptual clarification (4) or some
futher reflection on the place of democracy or elections in liberal capitalist countries or elsewhere
(5). Yet freedom is not a technical term alone, and
cannot be treated as such. Any such attempt (6) will
be up against the manifold and powerful connotations
which we associate with the term, however much we
may want to ignore them for the purpose of peaceful
research(7).
  The question of freedom, however intractable,
is central to political theory, and appears there
mostly under three headings. One is the question of
individual rights, including the whole series of
difficulties such ideals may generate theoretically,
conceptually and practically (8). Secondly there is
the question of democracy, which shapes our entire
attitude toward our own institutions as well as
those of other political systems (9). The third,
less easily identifiable and no less difficult, is
the matter of the degree of individual liberty provided by the various political and social institutions. The answers to such questions, of which Berlin's celebrated 1958 essay on "Two Concepts of
Liberty" is undoubtedly the most impressive, even
today, if less for its substance than for its almost
uncanny persuasiveness, are ones which necessarily
cut accross many disciplines; yet without such answers, however provisional, there can be no discussion of the good society (10). Not to take account

of such ideas, the debates they may engender, and the divisions they may reveal, can surely only mean that politics can only be a matter for technical answers and/or for the wheelings and dealings of (necessarily) unprincipled politicians.

The importance of the question of freedom for other areas of social research should need no emphasis. The concept of freedom is a most useful focal point for quite diverse enquiries in philosophy, sociology, history and political science (11). It thus allows for fruitful interdisciplinary encounters and limited comparative exercises. It cuts across many traditional boundaries with puzzling, yet stimulating consequences. If anything, it forces upon the searcher a sense of the comprehensive nature of many social problems and circumstances. The price for this highly integrative capacity is, not unexpectedly a high degree of complexity and indeterminacy. This indeterminacy and ambiguity has three main causes, all consequences of the comprehensiveness of the concept itself. The most obvious of these is the variety of linguistic and political connotations that the term has acquired in daily and theoretical discourse. As soon as we leave the terrain of evocative generalities, the usage of term can be shown to be highly problematical - simple reflection shows that even expressions such as "free economy" or "free elections" are riddled with problems (12). A second important cause for this equivocal character of most statements about freedom in general comes from the range of problems, in relation to day to day situations or in terms of distinctive philosophical/scientific puzzles and approaches thereto, that the term can be taken to encompass. It is possible to speak of freedom in relation to education (13), when buying a beer (14), or with respect to the range of options open to individuals within a society (15). The third important cause for this almost constitutional ambiguity leads us to the host of problems raised by the largely undoubted, if restricted human capacity for free will and self-direction, and its potential consequences for both individual and human history (16).

The importance of Marcuse's work in this context is that it deals, at least implicitly, with all these aspects of freedom, and moreover, does so from an explicit marxist standpoint. The latter point is essential. There are surprisingly few marxist works dealing directly with the question of freedom, Garaudy's La Liberté and Raya Dunayevskaya's Marxism

Freedom being the only two obvious exceptions
(٠٠٠). Most other marxist works with a bearing on the
question will focus on the problem of alienation,
with a few to either elucidate what Marx may well
have meant by that phrase (18), or aim at broadening
Marx's intent to include every human aspiration
under the sun (19). Alternatively, we are stuck with
such much used phrases as Hegel's "freedom is necessity", which, for all the philosophical impetus it
may have given to generations of marxist scholars,
still seems unhelpful in the context of a wider
liberal tradition (20). There is of course the work
of Sartre or Merleau-Ponty, which, for all their
ingenuity, seem to my mind so remote from the marxist tradition as to lose any element of repre-
sentativeness in the present context: This is especially true of Sartre's major work, _Being and No-_
thingness which contains much good material on the
question of freedom and has virtually no relation
whatsoever with the marxism he displays in his other
writings (21).

Marcuse is one of the very few marxist thinkers
who explicitly addresses himself to the question of
freedom. Furthermore he does so in the context of a
vigorous critique of contemporary civilization, a
critique informed by Kant, Hegel, Marx and Freud.
Against the overwhelming liberal bent of much of the
literature on freedom, liberal here in the dual
sense of a specific political and philosophical
tradition, Marcuse opposes his own views on freedom,
views which are highly critical, if not unreservedly
so, of the complacency displayed by much of that
literature (22). Against the predominant view of
liberty as purely an individual matter, Marcuse
opposes an ideal of community and the reality of
profoundly collective human institutions. Against
the belief in piecemeal social engineering, gradual
changes and the priority of technical solutions,
Marcuse advances a view of the good society as an
integral whole, advocates the necessity of revolution and constantly stresses human will and human
reason as the lasting guarantees for a free society.
He attacks the romantic yearning for a better past
as well as the unquestioning acceptance of the ethos
of linear progress, challenges accepted views on the
nature of man, the role of art and of the constitution of society. He suggests that there may be a
freedom that is at once material and spiritual,
individual and communitarian, spontaneous and rational. That such a freedom exists echoes throughout
most of his work. That we may judge present freedoms

with respect to this more inclusive conception is perhaps nowhere more clearly stated than in One Dimensional Man, his most famous work.

The following passage from that work is particularly suggestive. The contrast between "Freedom" and freedoms is forcefully drawn, and the provocative underlying thesis is that of a "benevolent totalitarianism" where existing freedoms in contemporary "advanced industrial societies" contribute to a general and much more fundamental lack of freedom:

"Under the rule of a repressive whole, liberty can be made into a powerful instrument of domination. The range of choice to the individual is not the decisive influence in determining the degree of human freedom, but what can be chosen and what is chosen by the individual. The criterion for choice can never be an absolute one, but neither is it entirely relative. Free election of masters does not abolish the masters or the slaves. Free choice among a wide variety of goods and services does not signify freedom if these goods and services sustain social controls over a life of toil and fear - that is, if they sustain alienation. And the spontaneous reproduction of superimposed needs by the individual does not establish autonomy; it only testifies to the efficacy of the controls" (23).

This passage, along with the various arguments interwoven into its central thesis, would appear to justify classifying Marcuse's work as an important contribution to literature on freedom from the marxist (24) tradition, or from the more recent body of "Western Marxism" (25). Yet it would be futile to look further into One Dimensional Man for a better structured theory or more detailed considerations. There are a number of similar passages which suggest that such a structured conception of freedom may exist, or that some such theory may be found in Marx, or in some combination of Marx with Freud, or Hegel, or even Fourier, but that is all. Their is very little on Marx in that work and there is nothing more elaborate on freedom than obscure references or vague, if evocative, statements.

Yet there is a theory of freedom in Marcuse, and it is both detailed and fairly well structured, and it rests very firmly on a distinctively marxist reading of contemporary realities. It is not to be found in One Dimensional Man, which is most certain-

5

ly Marcuse's worst book and in many ways quite
unrepresentative of his other writings. It marks the
high point of a period where Marcuse was furthest
away from his basic marxist orientation (I shall
return to this point) and it is the only major work
of Marcuse not guided and informed by his wider
understanding of what constitutes human freedom.
Such an idea is present elsewhere in Marcuse, and it
serves as the underlying structure for virtually all
his works apart from the short period 1959-1966 marked by One Dimensional Man and his sudden access to
fame. That his other major works published in English, such as Reason and Revolution (1941), Eros
and Civilization (1955) and Soviet Marxism (1958)
also contributed to this fame, and to a more lasting
reputation both among students and fellow academics,
is all to often forgotten (26). Yet these works all
retain what the former had not namely a deep-seated,
if at times implicit, commitment to marxism (with
qualifications, to be sure) and, what is more, to a
distinctive idea of freedom which owes much to Marx,
but also something to Hegel, Kant, Freud and the
existentialist tradition. We shall consider this
idea in detail in the following chapter. In chapter
4, 7 and 8 we shall also discuss at some length the
relation between this idea and other notions of
freedom.

1.2 The Argument, the Difficulties, the Literature
The central argument of this study is that such an
underlying theory of freedom can be traced in virtually every one of Marcuse's works. A further contention is that this theory is squarely rooted in a
distinctive reading of Marx, which constitutes a
pivotal influence upon Marcuse. This theory of freedom, it is claimed, is what gives to Marcuse's work
its overall unity and originality. It is because and
in relation to this theory that Marcuse's varied
excursions into classical German philosophy, the
realm of culture, the interpretation of Freud or the
assessment of Soviet Marxism all fall within the
single framework of one central theoretical perspective. One final and subsidiary claim is that the key
to this theory of freedom, and thus to Marcuse's
work over five decades, is to be found in the earlier rather than in the later writings. To elucidate
this theory of freedom, and show how it relates to
the wider body of marxist literature and how in turn
it articulates a very diverse and yet sustained
critique of contemporary institutions and ideas

should itself constitute an important contribution to the literature on the question of freedom.

In order to deal with an author reputedly as difficult as Marcuse, it may be wise to consider with some care the particular difficulties of his work, the general methodological questions this raises and the existing secondary literature.

There is a number of immediately apparent difficulties in dealing with a political theorist such as Marcuse. Some of them are to be found in almost any original work going beyond the boundaries of a given discipline; some are specific to Marcuse. The common headline for these difficulties can be summarised under the question: "How to read Marcuse?" (27).

What is at stake here is not so much the Marcusian style or his "Hegelian" manner of presentation (28). These problems are aptly summarised by MacIntyre who states that his manner of writing is "both literary and academic; he is allusive and seems to presuppose in his readers not only a high degree of general culture, but a wide area of presumed agreement on academic matters" (29). Nor will we dwell upon the many ambiguities, vagueness or apparent inconsistencies which strike an academically trained mind at first reading. It would also be superfluous to expand on Marcuse's use of a whole battery of highly specialised philosophical terminologies which sends the student of political science back to such unlikely figures as Heidegger, Dilthey or Scheler. That his use is a highly idiosyncratic one is another matter to which we shall return.

Much more disquieting is the appearance of a profound disregard for any empirical material to support at least his more controversial statements. MacIntyre can, without much exaggeration, write that "Marcuse seldom, if ever, gives us any reason to believe that what he is writing is true. He offers incidental illustrations of his theses very often; he never offers evidence in a systematic way. Above all there is entirely absent from his writings any attempt on his own part to suggest or to consider the difficulties that arise for his position and hence no attempt to meet them " (30). Cotten is also quick to point out that the sociological material to which Marcuse refers in One Dimensional Man is of very unequal quality, and by no means representative of the available research (31).

At the same time, it has also been often noted that Marcuse is highly selective in the sources and authors he chooses to consider at some length. That his whole work is heavily biased in favour of the young Marx need not be expanded further upon at this stage. Likewise, his choice of Freud's metapsychology, the most speculative part of Freud's writings, runs counter to the prevalent opinion in both clinical and academic psychology, which for once agree in rejecting these more metaphysical aspects of Freud's legacy. Moreover, as if to make matters worse, Marcuse imposes his own interpretation on Freud, Marx and Hegel without necessarily seeking at least some justification in the original intentions or recent academic developments in the research concerning these authors and their ideas.

One more difficulty is worth mentioning in this context. It is the "essentially open-ended, probing, unfinished quality" of the critical theory of the Frankfurt School (32). Although Marcuse was less reluctant than some of the other members of the institute to express himself in completed books with an overall exposition of his ideas, he too spread his ideas in a number of articles and publications, making it almost impossible to grasp fully any of his works without at least some knowledge of his other publications.

Finally one more difficulty is to be found in Marcuse's insistence upon the historical dimension as the central one for any understanding of social sciences. Even without accepting the validity of this contention, such a dimension cannot easily be disregarded in an author who so closely relates his own writing to the overall evolution of recent or past history.

We need not go further into these difficulties. They only add to the more general problems raised by the interpretation of a body of text stretching over five decades. Should earlier or later texts be given more weight? What role should be given to the patent influence of the specific socio-historical context, for instance - the situation in late Weimar Germany or America in the fifties? What importance should be given to the philosophical or scientific antecedents? What kind of evidence should the interpretation itsef rest upon, at least primarily? How much can the secondary literature be relied upon for clarification, and to which extent have previous interpretations clouded central issues?

The last question is crucial. The secondary literature on Marcuse is now voluminous, often concerned to bring to light isolated aspects of Marcuse's work. It has considerable influence upon the way this controversial, multisided and at times

not unambiguous body of writings is approached. It
is therefore essential that the literature is considered, however briefly, and that the dominant earlier interpretations of Marcuse's work are discussed, before my own approach is further defined.

The secondary literature is of varying interest
and quality. Most of it is superficial - at some
stage every decent academic felt obliged to write
his article on the "spiritual father" of the "New
Left" - and on the whole concentrates on the more
famous (or infamous) texts of the late fifties and
sixties. Typical of this first generation of critical articles, reviews and books on Marcuse's work
was a tendency to be either entirely apologetic or
totally hostile. Marcuse was alternatively described
as nothing but a "totalitarian" (read "dirty com-
mie") or as being anything but a marxist, a revisio-
nist wolf in sheep's clothing. In both cases, with a
few notable exceptions, there was in this early
literature no serious attempt to clarify the broad
lines of Marcuse's thought, the nature of his relation to Marx and the marxist tradition and little,
if any, of the possible consequences of either for
his later theoretical endeavours.

The second generation of articles and works
about Marcuse is rather more balanced as regards
such simplistic overalll judgements. There have been
a large number of articles in the review Telos, some
in the Canadian Journal of Political Sciences, a few
in the New Left Review, and many others scattered
throughout various journals or readers. There has
also been a growing number of books which genuinely
contribute to our understanding of the man and his
work. Perry Anderson's Considerations on Western
Marxism provides an excellent background picture for
Marcuse's place among a variety of other marxist or
quasi-marxist scholars in Europe and in the Western
world (33). Trent Schroyder, in his Critique of Domination skilfully places Marcuse as one of the important figures in his ambitious, if somewhat incon-
clusive, reconstruction of a new type of social
theory starting from Marx's analysis of Hegel and
Kant and rounding out in Habermas's work (34). Sidney Lipshire's Herbert Marcuse: from Marx to Freud
and Beyond (35) offers a well informed and meticulous account of Marcuse's wok centered around a
balanced assessment of Eros and Civilization, which
is also the main subject of Robinson's less convincing, but philsophically well informed The Sexual
Radicals (36). MacIntyre's little book on Marcuse,
for all its strained logic and snap judgements,

INTRODUCTION

deserves to be placed in this group for its many
perceptive comments and its attention to the Marx-
Marcuse problem (37). More recent works include Phil
Slater's decidedly unconvincing <u>Origins and Significance of the Frankfurt School</u> (38).The newly published <u>The Essential Frankfurt School Reader</u> offers, together with the reprint of many articles and
essays otherwise dispersed in various journals or
books, many useful thoughts on the question of the
indebtedness of members of the Frankfurt School to
the prevailing intellectual and political climate of
the newly industrialized Germany of the turn of the
century . There is also much good discussion of
major themes and specific methodologies employed by
various members of the school. Among still more
recent books, two deserve mention. Vincent Geoghegan's <u>Reason and Eros - The Social Theory of Herbert
Marcuse</u> brings little new and is on the whole light.
Yet the book has occasionally pertinent observations
and remarks. The force of Barry Katz's <u>Herbert Mar-
cuse</u> lies in its interesting and hitherto unpublished biographical data on Marcuse's early life. The
book's weakness lies in the lack of critical distance to its subject, and the ensuing superficiality
of much of its analyses (39).

Yet, on the whole, even this more recent literature <u>assumes</u> rather than examines in detail a
relation of some sort between Marx and Marcuse. All
the interest focuses upon what makes Marcuse's brand
of marxism distinctive, peculiar or different from
that of classical marxism, the marxism of the Second
Internationale or that of the socialist block. As a
consequence, what we witness in this literature is
an <u>intensive</u> search for some overall key to Marcuse
or some magic formula which can explain and account
for all that is not marxist in his work. There is
little or no attempt to retrace what is marxist in
Marcuse, and how this may serve to articulate or
structure the various influences which are so mani-
festly at play in his work. As a result, for all the
intriguing discoveries and provocative reflections
of this research, the blanket interpretations which
usually direct it are at best partial, when not
misleading.

Three such partial interpretations deserve our
attention, however. This is so because they shed
valuable light on essential aspects of Marcuse's
work, the studies in which they appear are themselves informative or well argued, and they tend to be
decisive studies for the rest of the literature.
They will also serve to sketch the overall back-

ground for Marcuse's work.

1.3 Marcuse is a Young Hegelian

This is the thesis advanced by MacIntyre and, indirectly, by Althusser in his general broadside a-
gainst "humanist marxism", whose more specific attacks on "Feuerbachianism" Marcuse implicitly acknowledges in Counterrevolution and Revolt (40).
MacIntyre focuses on one particular and fairly obvious aspect of Marcuse's work, its indebtedness to
Hegel. This he thinks is best captured by using the
label "Young Hegelian" or "Left Hegelian". This for
literary purposes is evidently a real find. It is a
label which is witty, biting, suggestive. It is one
which allows MacIntyre to recall and echo in every
page of his little book the sarcasm and irony poured
out by Marx and Engels, more than one hundred and
thirty years ago, upon Hegel's immediate heirs, in
the devastating critiques of The Holy Family and
The German ideology (41). It is a label that MacIntyre handles with great dexterity, placing it here
and there in his analyses, dwelling upon it on
occasion and using it as the ultimate sword with
which to cut the Gordian knot in any problem.

The underlying assertion is very bold. It implies that there exist such deep affinities between
Marcuse's work and those of the philosophers of the
immediate post-Hegelian period, say the 1830s and
1840s, that we can safely ignore the events of the
intervening period of German history in so political
a writer as Marcuse. It means that we can ignore the
impact of Neo-Kantian positivism, or the work of
Nietzsche, Husserl or Heidegger, or again the influence of Darwin and Durkheim in shaping the history of ideas. It means that we can ignore the tremendous economic and social transformation that the now
republican and unified Germany underwent during that
period. It means that we can ignore as well, not
only Marx's own influence, but that of a new and
powerful Social Democratic Party, the many left-wing
groups and the workers' and soldiers' councils movement in the 1920s (in which Marcuse took an active
part) as well as the impact of the bolshevik revolution and of the rise of fascism in Germany and
elsewhere.

It is not an assertion which MacIntyre documents very well. Admittedly he does not mean to say
that Marcuse's work is identical or intimately founded upon that of Edward Bauer, Max Stirner, Ludwig
Feuerbach, David Strauss or the Bruno brothers (42).

But should not at least a few explicit references
have been included to usefully strengthen the case?
There are none in the whole of MacIntyre's ninety
pages of criticism and suggestive parallels. Nor is
there any attempt to relate Marcuse's writings to
the major themes of these authors, and this for good
reasons. It would be difficult to find anywhere in
Marcuse any of the liberal political ambitions of
the Young Hegelians, or of their aspiration toward a
progressive transformation of the Prussian state
into an enlightened monarchy (43). Nor would it be
easy to find in Marcuse any references to the theo-
logical questions which so preoccupied the Young
Hegelians (44).

The bulk of MacIntyre's argument, then, centres
upon four issues where Marcuse supposedly sides with
the Left Hegelians against Marx or the mainstream
marxist tradition. The first of these concerns the
style and terminology used by Marcuse. Marcuse, as
opposed to Marx, speaks of "Man" rather than "men",
talks of "human essence" instead of personality,
human nature or the interplay of social forces, and
on the whole appears to move within the domain of
philosophical abstractions instead of detailed economic or political analyses (45). This, it should be
added, is perhaps the most important point illumi-
nated by MacIntyre, even if he is not alone in doing
so. Yet as Morton Schoolman correctly points out,
even during the period 1928-33 (we hall see pre-
sently why this period is significant) it is important to ask why Marcuse embraces such philosophical
abstractions and what purpose they play in his work
as a whole (46). This question points to the whole
problem of the relation between philosophy and marxist theory in Marcuse's work. As it is not possible
to deal with this question adequately at this stage,
let me simply assert that Marcuse's deliberate use
of philosophical categories is never purely philosophical, but is, on the contrary, primarily political.

The second issue that MacIntyre raises in this
context is Marcuse's relation to Hegel's <u>Logic</u> and
the method he develops therein. Marcuse is there
attacked for being more abstract and even more concerned with absolute ontological certainties than
the left Hegelians; Marcuse there shows himself
close to the Right Hegelians, and opposed to the
left wing of Young Hegelianism, which took more
interest in <u>The Phenomenology of Mind</u> where they saw
a younger Hegel display both more philosophical
acumen and much greater attention to the empirical

realities of the surrounding world (47). MacIntyre
can feel reassured. Marcuse gives adequate prominence to the latter work in his Reason and Revolution,
and it is surprising that MacIntyre fails to note
that in the interpretation Marcuse gives of the
Hegel-Marx relation it is the Phenomenology rather
than the Logic which constitutes the most direct
influence upon Marx's own theoretical perspective.
As for the Logic - which does figure in good place
in Marcuse's discussion of Hegel, if not of that of
Marx - it is more doubtful that Marcuse alone in the
marxist tradition finds this work valuable. As Martin Nicholaus has pointed out recently, it is precisely to this most abstract discussion of dialectical
logic that Marx turns when he conceives the project
of a treatise of the capitalist mode of production
as a whole, a project whose original inception can
be retraced in the invaluable Grundrisse (48). From
this initial project, "only" the three volumes of
Capital were ever to be published in more or less
completed form. Yet the importance of the Logic for
the original design is nevertheless such that Lenin
could state "that it is impossible completely to
understand Marx's Capital, and especially its first
chapter, without having thoroughly studied and understood the whole of Hegel's Logic" (49).

The third issue that MacIntyre raises relates
to the whole controversy around the "young" versus
the "mature" Marx. What MacIntyre says of Marcuse in
this context is sensible enough, if somewhat simplistic. It is the interpretation of Marx which
appears curious. MacIntyre correctly points out that
Marcuse opposes any form of absolute determinism and
cites the famous passage from Reason and Revolution
where he argues that the logical implacability of
the economic laws governing capitalism does not imply the same inexorability in relation to the transformation of that order into a true socialist society (50). That Marcuse's interpretation of this point
is totally contradicted by Marx himself is amply
proven, according to MacIntyre, by a 15-word cita-
tion from Capital (51). The wider context of Marx's
revolutionary ideas, which Marcuse wants to re-
introduce into this equation, is to be dismissed as
"youthful aberrations" of the author of Capital. As
for Marx's economic determinism, it is real enough,
but it co-exists with an extraordinary voluntarism
and a very practical belief in the impact of political activities in helping to promote the "unavoidable" revolution. Even a cursory reading of Marx's
most famous texts reveals that there is very little

fatalism in Marx. The workers are constantly urged
to take their destinies into their own hands, and to
work, rage and battle to make this revolution a
reality. As for Marx himself, how else do we account
for the numerous letters, pamphlets and speeches on
almost every major political event in Europe that he
and Engels sent to supporters and potential allies?
Neither the creation of the First International, nor
the several attempts to influence, modify and encou-
rage the creation and evolution of a united Socialist party in Germany bears witness to the blind
faith in economic laws suggested by MacIntyre's
account (52).

The last important issue brought out by MacIntyre again points to something central in Marcuse
and shows a marked lack of understanding for precisely those aspects of Marx which Marcuse wants to
stress, when it does not directly misrepresent Marx.
Let us first consider MacIntyre's argument. Marcuse's reading of Marx as a whole, and especially
that concerning the idea of a truly classless society - not a subject, it may be noted, upon which Marx
is so terribly explicit - is simply unmarxist. Nor
can this interpretation of Marx be accepted as a
valid set of standards with which to judge the
achievements of Soviet marxism. This is so because,
as MacIntyre tells us, "Marx was throughout his
career a radical democrat, who believed that all
that was wrong with the liberties of bourgeois parliamentary regimes was that their enjoyment was
effectively restricted to a minority and who wished
all to enjoy the liberties of that minority" (53).
Against the utopian and idealistic strains in Marcuse's thinking MacIntyre opposes the "realism" of
Marx and his readiness to accept the social and
economic realities of his time as the point of
departure for any futher progress.

Just how adequate this (drastic) re-interpretation of Marx is, is perhaps best seen from a short
passage of the presumably authoritative "critique of
the Gotha Programme", written about 8 years after
the publication of the first volume of Capital. Marx
here writes in the context of a practical political
programme for the newly re-organised German Social-
Democratic party, and deals among other things with
detailed issues such as education or the length of
the working day. He also deals with the issue of
political liberties and rights: "I have dealt more
at length with the "undiminished proceeds of labour", on the one hand, and with "equal right" and
"fair distribution", on the other, in order to show

what a crime it is to attempt, on the one hand, to force on our party again, as dogmas, ideas which in a certain period had some meaning but have now become obsolete verbal rubbish, while again perverting, on the other, the realistic outlook, which it cost so much effort to instil into the Party, but which has now taken root in it, by means of ideological nonsense about right and other trash so common among the democrats and French Socialists" (54).

Marx, "a radical democrat", is here rejecting, as a matter of course, exactly the attitudes and intentions that MacIntyre attributes to him. When he refers to a realistic outlook, he does not understand the practical compromises or political necessities as imposed by a hostile political environment. No, he refers to the single-minded determination to cut through such diversions toward the only real solution, namely the "violent overthrow of the bourgeoisie" (55). It should be noted that in the same text, at the "mature" age of 57, Marx once more refers approvingly to the Manifesto of the Communist Party whose utopian dimension can hardly be ignored (56).

As for Louis Althusser, one must admire the amount of energy, time and space he devotes to his critique of "Humanist Marxism", even if most of his observations are singularly abstract and general. Such tenacity would be surprising if one were unaware of Althusser's difficult position within the French Communist Party, and remember that what he has written was never intended as being purely academic (57).

Althusser's sharp attacks on "Humanist marxism" and his characterization of it as idealistic, reformist and essentially private marxism are not entirely beside the point. One feature common to the writers which can reasonably be included under this particular heading, including Marcuse, is precisely a distinctive emphasis upon the ideal elements of marxist theory, together with a concern for the philosophical root of his research and an interest in the individual emancipatory effects of this research (58). These are worthy aims in themselves, and even when placed in their context, are necessary as complements or antidotes to a certain conception of marxism as a pure product of mechanical forces (59). Yet the distinction between these aims and so much essentially individualistic and liberal literature becomes easily blurred.

To be entirely fair, out of the confrontation between Marx or marxism and the flow of ideas these authors bring with them much of value has emerged in terms of literary interests, academic pursuits, a wider commitment to the community of men, and very honest efforts to better come to terms with the difficult business of living. But to the extent these writings are disconnected with the struggles and daily life of just those people Marx decided constituted the only "really revolutionary class" - when they cease to reflect in some way or another the aspirations and demands of the proletarian men and women, as shaped by their situation of proleta- rians and their history as proletarians - these writings lose the historical connection with Marx, with marxism, and with the practical impetus of that tradition (60). To that extent, and only to that extent, Althusser is right.

The distinction is a difficult one. The lines are blurred, imprecise, hard to define. Nevertheless it is a crucial distinction; it is what separates the call for a revolution from what is only a battle of ideas, practical ideals from mere generous ges- tures, collective emancipation from simple indivi- dual liberation. Where Marcuse stands in that res- pect we do not yet know. But before we put this or the other label on his life work, it may be worth our while to look at it seriously, to investigate his relation to Marx, and to see in which way it is reflected in the overall articulation of his work.

1.4 Marcuse is a Heideggerian

This thesis has received considerable attention in recent years, and for good reasons. As we shall consider this thesis in detail in the course of the following chapters, my exposition of it here will be brief. The various arguments which have been advan- ced in this context can be summarized around a few central points (61).

The first is that there are elements in Mar- cuse's thought which are clearly reminiscent of the existentialist tradition or of the particular pheno- menological approach of Heidegger (62). Some of these will be found in almost all his work. Thus Marcuse will often rely upon anecdotical knowledge, try to establish his position upon daily experiences or reflections, and attempt to appeal to an overall intuition of his readers or auditors, as well as present them with well constructed arguments. Simi- larly, he will always attempt to relate the wider theoretical constructions that he uses to the sense of the personal and the felt realities of individual experience. Moreover, the individual's intuition and his own experience of what Marcuse describes or evokes often appear as important criteria for the truth of a given statement, and, as we shall see, individual experience has as such a singular epistemological status in Marcuse's work (63). Finally, the subject matter of Marcuse's inquiries itself will often be such areas as private life and private emotions, the importance of culture in the life of the individual or the relation between philosophy and day-to-day attitudes.

These elements are fairly stable in Marcuse's writings. Then in addition there is a whole terminology and a series of positions in the years 1928-33, and to some extent thereafter, which clearly point to the influence of Heidegger. First among these is a concern for ontology, that is the difficult area of philosophy which concerns itself with the nature of the world prior to knowledge itself and with the fundamental attitudes of man toward life or towards the world. This is an area where Heidegger's own work in the twenties had momentous repercussions in German academic circles, something which until then had slowly slid into the background, mostly under the impact of positivism's onslaughts on much traditional philosophy.

There are also other aspects of Marcuse's work where this Heideggerian influence can be seen. Much of Heidegger's philosophy is informed by a latent, at times quite explicit, rejection of all that the accelerated process of industrialization had brought to Germany. There is in Heidegger a continuous attempt to explain and understand this new modernity, together with a ceaseless search for some foundation which will not be comprehended by this modernity, but precedes or includes it. Much of his work should probably be understood in this light: the continuing search for a different ontological foundation beyond Descartes to the ancient Greek texts, the bold reinterpretation of Greek thought aiming to bring up an essentially different world view, and the radical separation of ontology as a founding field of knowledge (from the mere ontic realm to which other disciplines and sciences were relegated). The emphasis on personal destiny to be recaptured and assumed by an awareness of both a personal past and the force of tradition also belongs, in different ways and to varying extent, to this general opposition to the new industrial Germany. Not all of these themes are necessarily unique to Heidegger and not all of them are to be found in Marcuse's own writings. Yet there is more than an echo of these themes in the deep, if by no means unqualified pessimism of <u>One Dimensional Man</u> and its explicit rejection of much of the more recent change in the American society in which Marcuse had chosen to live (64).

The second important point to remenber in this context is that Marcuse began his career with a long ambitious and imaginative review of Martin Heidegger's newly published <u>Being and Time</u> (1927) and went from Berlin to Freiburg to prepare his "Habilitationschrift" under the direction of Heidegger (65). Marcuse had received his doctorate from that same university some years earlier, in 1923, on the subject of "Der Deutsche Kunstlerroman", after successful studies in philosophy there and in Berlin, where his family lived and where he was born. The intervening year in publishing and book-selling, again in Berlin, must have afforded Marcuse some opportunities for study and reflection. The above-mentioned review of Heidegger - entitled "Contributions to a Phenomenology of Historical Materialism" (66) - is usually regarded as the earliest and certainly a very imaginative attempt to fuse Heideggerian ideas and terminology with a distinctive interpretation of marxism, prefiguring later and similar attempts by Sartre and Merleau-Ponty.

Marcuse stayed in Freiburg for four years, from 1929 to 1933. He completed in that time his "habilitationschrift", which would have meant a post at the university, but personal and perhaps political differences with Heidegger (who was to make an extraordinary pro-Hitler speech later that year) meant that this was never to be (67). The work itself was published in 1932 under the title <u>Hegel's Ontology and the Foundation of a Theory of Historicity</u> (68). It bears all the marks of Heidegger's own concerns with the metaphysical dimension of Hegel's philosophy, and in addition to a single overall acknowledgement of Heidegger, displays all the familiar philosophical categories of the latter. Marcuse also published more than a dozen articles, essays and book reviews in these years, and here too Heidegger's special terminology was evident for all to see. It is only after Marcuse left Freiburg, and especially after the famous rectoral speech of 1933 that this changed. Marcuse in the meantime had joined the "Institut für Sozialforschung" in Frankfurt, only to be sent directly from there to its Geneva office, and then to the institute's new home at Columbia University, New York.

There are two basic variations of the "Heideggerian marxism" argument. The first of these, and by far the most plausible, concentrates on the period just described. The gist of that argument is that Marcuse's work during that period is best understood as a continuous, if more or less successful attempt to integrate the philosophical teaching of Heidegger with a more or less orthodox interpretation of marxism. According to that version, while the influence of Heidegger was either waning or insignificant after 1933, the period between 1928 and 1933 can almost entirely be understod in terms of these two competing influences. This seems to be the position advanced by Habermas and Alfred Schmidt, and to a lesser degree by Goldmann (69). The second position is much more ambitious. Picking up what are real similarities between Marcuse and Heidegger, and to a great extent helping to make these influences clearer, this second version propounds that the whole of Marcuse's works can be understood in such terms. This version has been advanced most forcefully by Piccone and Delfini, but also finds echoes elsewhere (70).

My own position, one which I share to an extent with Schoolman (71), is that neither of these positions succeed in capturing Marcuse's own perspective even during the years in Freiburg. Whatever the merits of this interpretation it understates the fact that during these years Marcuse was vividly interested and concerned with the idea of promoting a better understanding of Marx, radically different from that of mainstream marxism, and this independently of Heidegger's revival of ontological philosophy. It also underemphasizes the degree to which Marcuse was critical of this philosophy, which comes across most clearly in the articles and essays he contributed to journals at that time. It furthermore fails to stress the variety of influences which were already at play in Marcuse's work - not only Marx and Heidegger, but also Dilthey, Hegel, Lukács, and even Mannheim.

As for the wider influence, it appears limited, outside of what has already been mentioned. There are a number of reasons for this, which we shall consider in detail in the following pages. There are also good reasons for not getting fixed upon 1933 as the magical breaking point. It certainly is a turning point between the final disillusionment with Heidegger, the acceptance as a full member in an institute committed to marxist studies and the exile to USA. Yet, as we shall see, there are good reasons for considering the earlier date of 1932 as an equally important turning point.

1.5 Marcuse is a Member of the Frankfurt School
This statement, or some variation thereof, would
appear to be a basic premise in several of the
better informed writings on Marcuse (72). It does so
tacitly or explicitly, with or without qualification
and applies with more or less force, depending upon
the author's perspective. The thrust of the underlying argument varies little, however. Marcuse's
work is best understood as part of a collective body
of work carried out under the name of "critical
theory" by the collaborators of the Frankfurt Institute for Social Research. The further implication of
this argument is that Marcuse's overall perspective
and the problems most central to his thought are
very largely shaped by the decisive leadership of
Horkheimer, as well as by Adorno and other major
figures of the Institute. Three recurrent elements
can be distinguished in all the variations of this
argument. Firstly, the statement "Marcuse is a member of the Frankfurt School" is purely descriptive.
Secondly, it is the short form of a thesis implying
a near identity of views between leading members of
the institute during the 1930s and 1940s. Thirdly,
it implies the much wider thesis that Marcuse's work
as a whole must be understood in this light.
    As a descriptive statement it is inaccurate. An
accurate statement would be as follows: in 1933
Marcuse joined the "Institut für Sozialforschung".
This institute was founded in 1923 by a group of
marxist scholars with the aim of furthering marxist-
orientated multidisciplinary research in a variety
of fields, outside of the traditional German academic structures, and financially as well as organiza-
tionally independent from state organizations and
parties or trade unions. The only such connection
was a rather loose relation to the newly-founded
University of Frankfurt whereby, by decree of the
Ministry of Education, the director of the institute
was to be a full professor at this University. The
first director, Carl Grünberg was followed in 1931
by Max Horkheimer who shifted the emphasis from the
orthodox marxism of his predecessor, toward more
theoretical and philosophically informed research,
and promoted the studies of Freud and of the whole
realm of superstructures for which the institute was
to become famous. Marcuse was a full member of the
institute only during 1933-41, when the institute
was located at Columbia University in New York City.

His progressive involvement with the OSS and the
State Department from this date onward meant a les-
sening of the links with the institute, as it did
with many other members engaged in war-time service
for the governmental agencies or departments. Unlike
others, however, Marcuse chose to remain in the OSS
after the war, and in fact until 1950. Only then did
he resume a full academic life. When he did so he
chose not to return to the Institute of Social
Research, newly re-established in Frankfurt with the
benediction of the Allied Forces and of the new
German government, but returned in an individual
capacity to Columbia University as a lecturer in
Sociology. He later moved to Harvard, Brandeis and
the San Diego campus of the University of California. Thus, strictly speaking, in the 50 years or so
since his first publictaion, Marcuse has been a full
member of the Institute of Social Research for not
more than 8 or 9 years, years in which the location
of the Institute was not Frankfurt, but New York.

These facts are not disputed, but it is as well
to keep them in mind, when examining the two theses
also implied by the phrase "Marcuse is a member of
the Frankfurt School".

The bluntest formulation of the first of these
theses is probably that of Phil Slater. In the
introduction to his Origin and Significance of the
Frankfurt School he states that: "Despite the role
of other figures in the institute (such as Friedrich
Pollock, Leo Lowenthal, Karl August Wittfogel) it is
essentially the work of Horkheimer, Marcuse, Adorno
and Fromm which constitutes the core of the Frankfurt School theory. And it was between 1930 and the
early 1940s (when the team split up) that the Frankfurt School took shape and produced its most original work on the problem of a 'critical theory of
society'" (73). Yet even this formulation is nowhere
as blunt as the subsequent treatment Slater gives
the varied and highly individual writings of the
core members of the institute. Books, essays, articles and private communications are all thrown into
a hodge-podge of equally-weighted fragments with
which Slater constructs a long list of supposedly
common positions toward figures or issues such as
Trotsky, Rosa Luxemburg, the KPD or the "death
drive" hypothesis in Freudian theory (74).

Not all commentators who adopt a perspective of
this kind assert, even implicitly, the same near
total identity of views among the various collaborators of the institute. The most interesting and
influential position is undoubtedly that of Martin

Jay, whose main work <u>The Dialectical Imagination</u>
offers a sympathetic picture of the people and the
research at the institute in the years 1923-50 (75).
Even his most forceful critics (see the reviews by
Jacoby, Kellner, Lubász, Piccone and Thomas) will
readily agree that Jay not only has recorded much
valuable material which would otherwise have been
lost, but that the work in which it is presented is
a brilliant piece of intellectual history, well
documented, eminently readable and masterfully organized (76).

All this makes his account of the main thesis -
namely that there existed from 1930 to 1950, not so
much an identity of views on precise questions as a
common outlook and orientation toward issues, one
which reappears in most writings and studies - so
much more persuasive and convincing than Slater's
version or that of less detailed arguments (77). It
should also be made clear that Jay interjects many
notes, details and important modifications into his
exposition. The argument is certainly not one-sided
or insensitive.

Yet there is also something in Jay's style and
language - as Jacoby perceptively remarks with regard to other issues the book raises - which tends
to work in the opposite direction, and often suggests a far more certain and dogmatic position than
the one in fact argued (78). As for the issue at
hand, it is difficult when closing these 300 pages
of dense, closely argued text, together with 60-70
pages of notes and bibliography, not to be struck by
the remarkable unity and coherence the text conveys
of an institution with so long and so varied a
history. On closer reading, however, it is difficult
to find out exactly on what evidence this "unity in
diversity" rests, if not Jay's own conception of the
history of the Institute of Social Research.

This is also the position advanced by Lubasz's
informed review of the book and its subject (79). He
partly retraces the powerful impression of overall
unity and coherence - and justifies Jay's application of the term "Frankfurt School" - to his understandable desire to bring forth the common features
and overall consistency of the work produced by the
members of the institute. He also partly attributes
it to Jay's curious disregard for the early years of
the institute, between 1923 to 1933, where much less
philosophical yet original research was carried out
or begun. He also argues that this apparent continuity has only been bought at the price of an inor-
dinate emphasis upon the role and research orienta-

tions of Horkheimer, and to a lesser extent Adorno.
What this does mean is that many of the lesser-known
figures of the institute (Neuman, Kirchheimer, Lowenthal, Grossman, and others) and the differences
amongst the institute's members are left in the
shadows.

It is well to keep all these points in mind, as
well as Jay's explicit position, when considering
Marcuse's relation to the somewhat mythical "Frankfurt School" (80). It would be difficult to deny
that Marcuse was not influenced by his eight years
at 429 West 117th Street in New York City. Marcuse
was by all accounts a major figure in the institute,
participated actively in discussions and seminars,
and has on several occasions acknowledged the decisive role of both Horkheimer and the institute in
his work and the development of positions on specific issues. The fate of Germany under Nazi rule, the
shared exile in a very different cultural and intellectual environment and the continued publication of
the institute's journal in German until 1940 can
only have re-enforced the bonds fostered by daily
interaction and similar academic pursuits (81). Yet
it is essential not to be swayed entirely by the
"Frankfurt School" perspective. As Jay himself
points out, Marcuse's position on a number of issues
differed sharply from that of Horkheimer and Adorno,
and these issues, as we will see, are central ones -
the role of labour within marxian theory, the question of the identity of the subject-object, the
treatment of recent philosophers, the position of
economics within marxist theory and the practical
implications of "critical theory" are all points
where differences played a crucial role for later
developments (82). Marcuse furthermore showed a far
greater willingness than other members of the institute (certainly Horheimer and Adorno) to adapt himself to the changed circumstances - <u>Reason and Revo-
lution</u> was the first major exposition of "critical
theory" in English, and Marcuse, unlike others,
never returned to Germany or to the Institute when
the latter was re-instated in Frankfurt.

These divergences, which I hope to show are not
accidental, also throw a different light upon the
wider thesis implied by the phrase "Marcuse is a
member of the Frankfurt School". The shared positions and interests that existed between Marcuse and
other members of the Institute for Social Research
in the years 1933-1941 tend to disappear progressively during the years. While it is not difficult to
find parallels, common concerns and, on occasions,

similar views on specific subjects, the "Frankfurt
School" approach is a poor predictor of Marcuse's
later works, especially because the common vocabulary often stands for quite different substantial
positions. It furthermore tends to lead away from
rather than highlight the importance of both an
overall structure in Marcuse's work (one very different from that of either Horkheimer or Adorno) and
of Marcuse's relation to marxism. In a similar vein,
it should also be stressed that the obvious similarities between Marcuse's earlier works and those of
the later "Frankfurt School member" Habermas should
not conceal the fundamental shift in orientation
these ideas have received in the latter's work (83).

1.6 The Approach Further Specified

The approach adopted here differs in several respects from the orientations of the secondary literature as outlined above. First of all, and most
importantly, it does not assume that an adequate
grasp of Marcuse's works can be gained by focusing
on one major influence or even a set of influences
as the decisive explanatory tool. On the contrary,
it is precisely the variety of opposing, shifting
and counterbalancing impulses running through Marcuse's fifty years of academic production which
makes his work so fascinating. Furthermore, it
should be noted that Marcuse seldom adopts a given
notion, philosophical category or thesis from this
or the other source without substantially changing
its meaning to suit his current project. We shall
consider Marcuse's particular method of text interpretation more closely in the following chapters,
but the importance of that constant reshaping of
ides and concepts cannot be overstressed. It makes
for much of the difficulty in understanding Marcuse,
but also for a great deal of originality. This André
Nicholas has captured nicely with his formula "the
Marcusian heresies are the truth of Marcuse" (84).
This in turn entails that any interpretation capturing Marcuse's central ideas from the outside - by
postulating a dominating external influence such as
Heidegger, Hegel, or the "Frankfurt School", by
mechanically explaining the works of Marcuse in
relation to the intellectual (85) or socio-political
context (86) or by attributing to Marcuse a common-
sense, unreflected and unstructured approach (87) -
must fail to grasp not only the complexity of Marcuse's thought, but also the structure and richness
of many of his interpretations of culture and ideo-

logy. The approach adopted here, to the contrary, attempts to reconstruct Marcuse's arguments from the inside, building as far as possible on the concepts that Marcuse himself provides, in order to uncover both the assumptions upon which his analyses rest and the nature of the conclusions he derives.

There is a second point at which this approach departs from most of the relevant literature. The guiding assumption, and one which further research and new finding showed to be sound, is that not only the individual works but the totality of his work should be approached in this way. In other words, only by considering the whole of Marcuse's academic production and paying close attention to early assumptions, shifts in thinking and new developments is it possible to obtain a picture complete enough to fully grasp the role and significance of Marcuse's individual works.

There are two different, if related contentions at play here. The first, one which in varying degrees is shared by most of the literature, is that there is essentially only one Marcuse. It is felt that the author of Reason and Revolution is substantially the same as the author of Eros and Civilization or of Soviet Marxism. Let me immediately qualify this by pointing out that this should not be understood in the sense that there are no phases or periods in Marcuse's career. There clearly are. There are many views on this question, but my own position is that five such periods should be distinguished. The first runs from 1928 to roughly 1932 ("Heideggerian period"); the second from 1932 to 1941 ("Marx and the Frankfurt School"); the third from 1941 to 1959 ("The post-war years") the fourth goes from 1959 to roughly 1966 ("the period of One Dimensional Man"); the last from 1966 to 1979 ("The later writings"). I shall return to these periods and headings but the important point here is that throughout and despite these various distinctive phases in Marcuse's career there is enough continuity to treat his writings as a single whole.

The other contention underlying this approach is that despite the shifts in interest or perspective brought by changing political situations or personal circumstances, Marcuse develops an essentially cumulative body of ideas and theories. The conclusions from one body of research are carried over into another, and re-emerge, sometimes substantially modified, into a third. An idea conceived in the course of a given study will be reshaped through successive articles or essays to the point where it

can become quite different from its original formulation, even if the intention remains the same; an
area of research, once explored and reflected upon,
will remain as a theme or a hidden motive in later
publications. Marcuse is naturally not alone in
this. But he tends to be singularly casual and
uninformative about where, when and why he derives a
particular favourite contention which he presents to
the reader as either a foregone conclusion or simply
evident; and he does this in such a way - as Marks
for instance points out - that it is difficult to
simply dismiss such statements as no more than spin-
offs of a lively imagination (88). This particular
cumulative character of Marcuse's research means
that only in earlier works will crucial assumptions
and perspectives be fully stated and developed. Yet
only in relation to the whole does it become possible to identify the global structure of an academic production stretching over five decades.

This leads to the third point at which the
present approach differs from the previous orientations to Marcuse. This research claims that the
sense of unity and inner coherence which for most
commentators exists in Marcuse, is one which can be
retraced to a specific project and one which in turn
is related to a specific reading of Marx. This
project is a distinctive and original theory of
freedom, elements of which can now be found in
Habermas' Knowledge and Human Interests, and to a
lesser extent in Carol C. Gould's Marx's Social Ontology (89). It is a theory that Marcuse first
develops in the Freiburg years, largely in opposition to Heidegger's own philosophical thinking, and
which was then carried over in the essays of the
thirties and Reason and Revolution, continued in
Eros and Civilization and Soviet Marxism, only mar-
ginally in One Dimensional Man, to reappear in An
Essay on Liberation and Counterrevolution and Revolt. It is this particular project which gives
force and unity to Marcuse's thought, and it is the
presence of this idea in virtually every single one
of his writings whch separates Marcuse not only from
the Left Hegelians and Heidegger, but also from
Horkheimer, Adorno and other later collaborators of
the Institute for Social Research, such as Habermas.

The argument, in short, is as follows: There
exists underlying unity given by a largely implicit
idea of freedom derived from an original interpretation of the young Marx. Many commentators have noted
such a sense of unity in Marcuse's otherwise very
diverse political and philosophical writings. Yet

the source of this unity has always be thought of as
being Marcuse's own works. As we saw, Hegel, Heidegger, the "Frankfurt School", and even Neo-Kantian
influences or Freud have variously been put forward
as the major directing force in his writings. Contrary to these approaches, this thesis takes Marcuse's 1932 essay on Marx's Economic and Philosophical Manuscripts of 1844 as the turning point of his
philosophical and political career. It argues that,
under the impact of the newly rediscovered manuscripts, and based upon an at the time radical re-
interpretation of Marx's entire legacy, Marcuse here
effects an original synthesis of the early influences upon his thought: the core of this synthesis is
a utopian vision of the good society as one of co-
operation, mutual understanding and all round individual development. This "co-operative society" is
defined by the extent to which each of its members
can freely impart upon the environment the mark of
his/her whole self, as well as the aspirations of
the collectivity, themselves defined through joint,
full and equal planning decisions whose primary goal
is the best possible satisfaction of each individual's needs and powers. The thesis claims that it
is this idea, together with the wider theory in
which it is inserted, which gives direction and
vigour to virtually all of Marcuse's later writings.
It further contends that it is this idea of freedom
which guides Marcuse's sensitive re-interpretation
of the marxist dialectical method. It also claims
that it is only in the light of this idea of freedom
that it is possible to understand the comprehensive
character of Marcuse's critique of the lack of freedom in modern societies, at the level of the market,
at the level of individual life and at the level of
society as a whole.

1.7 Methodology and General Outline of the Study
The overall methodological perspective for both this
method of research and the method of exposition
described below is that of an "immanent critique".
Its general aim is to bring to light the implicit or
rarely stated premises in each work and to follow
them through in later writings, so that changes and
developments in the underlying body of assumptions
become evident. The overall unity - or lack of such
- of a given body of texts becomes also thereby
immediately apparent.
        The perspective of an "immanent critique" im-
plies also that full justice be done to the texts.

INTRODUCTION

Its aim is to reconstruct the internal structure of
a given text from the author's own perspective, as
it can be derived from a close text analysis, the
stated intentions from the specific historical or
academic context, or again from the thrust of the
author's entire academic production. Such an "immanent critique" aims in other words to <u>understand</u> the
given author in the situation in which he wrote and
in relation to his stated or most plausible aims,
not to <u>explain</u> his ideas or intentions, be it with
reference to religious background, class position or
early childhood. Explanations are brought to bear
upon the analysis, but only insofar that they serve
to highlight the most plausible relations between
various texts or the impact of outside social or
historical factors. Other forms of explanation are
considered of no interest, as it is ultimately the
intrinsic validity/non validity of ideas or insights
which constitute the object of this form for critique (90).

<u>The method of research</u> is as follows. A common
procedure was applied to virtually all important
texts. It consists in:

1) Identification and clarification of the main
assumptions in the text.

2) Determination of the logical structures of
the argument(s).

3) Analysis of the historical context and assessment of its importance for the text.

4) Reconstruction of the entire set of assumptions, implications and conclusions structuring
the text.

5) Check and further clarification of the resulting body of statements with earlier assumptions or conclusions on similar issues, paying
due attention to the analyses of 2) and 3).

This last point follows from the assumption of continuity in Marcuse's writing. The texts were examined in strict chronological order. The results from
the analysis of one text were entered into the
analysis of the next text in two ways. First they
served as general background for the elucidation of
the main argument and/or perspective of the text in
question. This often provided important clues, by
contrast or by analogy, to the ongoing analysis

itself. Second they helped to clarify or re-arrange
the resulting set of statements, so as to make
comparisons immediate and evident. The final set of
statements consisted in each case of assumptions of
implications explicitly stated in the text or logically necessary for a full comprehension of the
given arguments; in the latter case this was so only
insofar that they were stated unambiguously elsewhere in the body of texts as a whole, could be
assumed as evident for the given readership, or were
otherwise plain from the overall context of the
given text. Given the imperatives of clarity and
conciseness the terminology adopted is otherwise
everywhere that of the texts themselves.

The following general rules were furthermore
guiding for the research, as most consistent with
the overall methodology. Firstly, each individual
text is in principle treated as an independent
whole, to be understood within itself or with reference to the immediate socio-historical context.
Secondly, Marcuse qua author is first of all defined
by the totality of his own writings, and all other
information is accordingly treated as secondary to
that. These two ground rules imply that the pre-
eminence will be given to his own texts, and that
long citations will as a rule be preferred. Thirdly,
Marcuse's various interviews and public statements
will constitute a privileged, but not determining
source of further information. Fourthly, biographical material will only be used insofar that it is
deemed reliable, uncontroversial and useful to illuminate the texts themselves. Fifthly, the secondary
literature reviewed above will enter insofar that it
brings new facets to light in the texts themselves
or has otherwise been useful for present research.

The method of exposition will consists in a
presentation of each major development or facet of
Marcuse's conception of freedom, through a series of
analyses, interpretations or commentaries on the
texts themselves, together with the necessary context. These analyses will be grouped in the following seven chapters and conclusions, as well as in 9
tables of assumptions and implications. The tables
can be consulted separately; they aim to present the
reader with an easily accessible summary of Marcuse's major assumptions, in a logical sequence and
formalised. The chapters will often be structured
differently, depending upon the function of that
chapter in the work as a whole. The need to follow a
given text very closely may imply that the chapter
leads up to rather than follow from the correspon-

ding table; again, the focus of attention will often be upon broad issues cutting across the sequence indicated in the table. The tables and the chapters are nevertheless conceived as an integrated whole, and should serve to complement each other in providing as clear a picture as possible of Marcuse's overall conception of freedom.

The plan of the thesis is as follows. Chapter 2 will examine in detail the premisses and internal articulation of Marcuse's first essay, together with a brief review of the developments in the period 1928-32. The aim of the analysis is to bring to the fore the guiding ambition of that first essay, namely a grand theory of human liberation resting upon marxist perspective. This theory is outlined in table 2.

Chapter 3 will focus upon the profound transformation that this first theory undergoes under the impact of the newly rediscovered Economic and Philosophical Manuscripts of 1844. The emphasis will be upon the singular character of that interpretation and the broad conclusions Marcuse derives from it. These will be presented in table 3.

Chapter 4 will bring together the threads of the previous analysis and develop the central idea emerging from that interpretation, namely the idea of the "co-operative society". Its salient features will be listed in table 4. There is also a discussion of liberal and marxist notions of freedom.

Chapter 5 will examine the continuity and development of this idea of a free society in the writings of the period 1932 to 1941. The conclusions will appear in table 5.

Chapter 6 will be devoted to a discussion and assessment of the developments which take place in the post-war period with respect to this idea of the "co-operative society". It will be shown that it is everywhere present in Marcuse's texts, but for the period of One Dimensional Man (1959 to 1965). The modified picture of the "co-operative society" is summarised in table 6. It is organised so as to make possible easy comparisons with tables 4 and 5.

Chapter 7 will focus upon the wider theory of liberation surrounding the idea of the "co-operative society", as it stood in the years 1941 to 1972, with particular attention to the role of a re-interpreted marxist dialectic within this theory. The main features of the theory are summarised in table 7.

Chapter 8 will then be concerned with the role that this global theory of liberation and the idea

of the " co-operative society" play for Marcuse's
critique of contemporary civilisation. In particular
it will be shown that this body of work is best
understood as comprehensive critique of the lack of
genuine freedom in contemporary capitalistic or
state capitalistic societies. The major propositons
underlying that critique are listed in table 8. It
also allows a discussion of Marcuse's conception in
relation to other notions of freedom, such as liberal political freedoms or Sartre's ontological freedom.

Chapter 9 forms the conclusion of this research. An overall assesment will be given there.

NOTES

1. On the latter point see Ruggerio, G. de:
The History of European Liberalism, USA, Boston:
Beacon Press, 1959, first published 1932, passim.
2. See variously Murray Edelman, The Symbolic
Uses of Politics, USA: University of Illinois Press,
1964, for a virulent denunciation of symbolic mani-
pulation; Cornford, J. (ed.), The Failure of the
State, London: Croom Helm, 1975, for a series of
essays attacking the record of a number of European
states; Jordan B., Freedom and the Welfare State,
London: Routledge and Kegan Paul, 1976, for a perceptive account of the changes new politics and
outlooks have effected at the level of individual
liberty and responsibility.
3. See the brief discussion of the classical
political theorists in MacFarlane, L.J., Modern Political Theory, London: Merlin Press, 1970. See also
Mészároz, I., Marx's Theory of Alienation, for a
vivid account of Marx's own vision. With respect to
the development of a "positive" concept of freedom
within the liberal tradition itself, see Nicholls,
D., "Positive Liberty, 1880-1914" in the American
Political Science Review, vol. 56, 1962. See also
Freeden, M., The New Liberalism, England, Oxford:
Clarendon Press, 1978, for the interplay of political and philosophical impulses within that tradition
in the second half of the nineteenth century in
England, as well as Jordan, B., Freedom and the Welfare State, op. cit. See Sartre's extraordinary
analysis of Being and Nothingness, London: Methuen,
1958. (First published as L'Etre et Le Neant, 1943),
Chapter four.
4. See Cranston, M., Freedom, A new Analysis,
London: Longmans, 1953, Pennock, J.R., "Hobbes Con-
fusing 'clarity': the case of 'Liberty'" in Brown,

K. (Ed.) Hobbes Studies, Oxford: Basil Blackwell, 1965; Werham, A.G., "Liberty and Obligation in Hobbes" in Brown, K. (Ed.) Hobbes Studies, Oxford: Basil Blackwell, 1965.
   5.   Benn, S.I. and Peters, R.s., Social Principles and the Democratic State, London: Allen & Unwin, 1959; Dahl, R.A., "Madisonian Democracy" in his Preface to Democratic Theory, Chicago and London: Oxford University Press, 1966, first published by the Canadian Broadcasting Corporation, 1965.
   6.   See Oppenheim, F.E., Dimension of Freedom, New York, St. Martin's Press, London: Macmillan, 1961, for an excellent instance of such approach.
   7.   See P. Lind, The Idea of Freedom, Unpublished Cand. Scient. Pol. Thesis, Aarhus, 1978, Chapter 3.
   8.   An interesting account of such problems can be found in Lucas, J.R., Democracy and Participation, London: Penguin Press, 1976.
   9.   See in this context also the recent literature on participation, for instance Milbrath, L.W., Political Participation, USA, Rand McNally & Co., 1965; Verba, S. and Nye, N., Participation in America, New York & London: Harper & Row, 1972; Carol Pateman, Participation and Democratic Theory, England: Cambridge University Press, 1970; Cook, T.E. & Morgen, P., Participatory Democracy, USA - San Francisco: Cranfield Press, 1971.
   10.   Berlin, I., "Two concepts of Liberty" in his Four Essays on Liberty, London: Oxford University Press, 1968. Various commentaries and criticisms can be found in Cohen, M., "Berlin and the Liberal Tradition", Philosophical Quarterly, vol. 10, No. 40, 1960.
   11.   See for instance Berlin, I., "Two Concepts of Liberty", in his Four Essays on Liberty, op. cit., and Berofski, B., Free Will and Determinism N.Y. & London: Harper & Row, 1966 on the first; Bay, C., The Structure of Freedom, USA - California: Stanford University Press, 1958 and Dahrendorf, R., The New Liberty, London: Routledge and Kegan Paul, 1975 on the second; Barber, B.H., The Death of Communal Liberty, USA - Princetown, New Jersey: Princetown University Press, 1974 on the third; Dahl, A Preface to Democratic Theory, op. cit., and Kaplan, M.A., On Freedom and Human Dignity (The Importance of the Sacred in Politics) USA, New Jersey, Morristown: General Learning Press, 1973 on the fourth.
   12.   See Lind, P., The Idea of Freedom, op. cit., Chapter 2, also Cranston, Freedom, A New Ana-

lysis, op. cit., part 1.
13. See Lind, P., The Idea of Freedom, op.
cit., Chapter 2 and Peters "Freedom and the development of the free man", op. cit., passim.
14. See MacCallum's not uninteresting linguistic jugglings in his "Negative and Positive Freedom"
in The Philosophical Review, 76, 1967, also in Las-
lett & Runciman (Eds.) Philosophy, Politics and Society, fourth series, Oxford: Blackwell, 1972.
15. See Berlin, Four Essays on Liberty, op.
cit., Introduction, for an appealing if hopelessly
ambiguous assertion to that effect. See also Bernal,
J.D., The Freedom of Necessity, London: Routledge
and Kegan Paul, 1949, for a convincing discussion of
Mill's criterion of harm to others, and its implications for indiscriminate entrepreneurial freedom.
See also Caudwell, C., The Concept of Freedom, London: Lawrence and Wishart, 1977 (originally published in "Studies in a Dying Culture", London: John
Lane, The Bodley Head, 1938).
16. See Berofsky, Free Will and Determinism,
op. cit., and especially Edwards, P, "Hard and Soft
Determinism" in Hook, S., Determinism and Freedom
in the Age of Modern Science, USA - New York: The
Macmillan Company, 1958, and MacIntyre, A., "Determinism", Mind, LXVL No. 26, January 1957, reprinted
in Berofsky, B. (Ed)., Free Will and Determinism,
New York and London: Harper and Row, 1966.
17. Garaudy, La Liberté, Paris: Editions so-
ciales, 1955; Raya Dunayevskaya, Marxism and Freedom, London: Pluto Press, 1971.
18. MacLellan's various books on Marx all seem
to address themselves to the issue with some uneasi-
ness, see Karl Marx, his Life and Thought, London:
MacMillan Press, 1973 and also The Thought of Karl
Marx, London: MacMillan Press, 1971. Mészáros's attempt to answer the question once and for all in his
Marx's Theory of Alienation, op. cit., is certainly
not easy to follow, although he brings in some good
material; O'Rourke, J.J., The Problem of Freedom in
Marxist Thought: An Analysis of the Treatment of-
Human Freedom by Marx, Engels, Lenin and Contemporary Soviet Philosophy, Dordrecht: Holland, Boston -
USA: D. Reidel Publising Company, 1974, constitutes
on the other hand a fairly clear account, but at the
price of some gross over-simplifications; fairly
useful material can also be found in Fetscher, I.,
"Marx's concretization of the concept of freedom" in
Fromm, (ed.), Socialist Humanism, New York: Anchor
Books, Doubleday and Co., 1965.
19. See for instance ibid.

20. See Engels' still authoritative <u>Anti-Dühring</u>, Peking: Foreing Language Press, 1976, pp. 136-150, for a particularly simplistic, although not entirely misplaced discussion of this question.

21. <u>Being and Nothingness</u>, op. cit., passim.

22. See Lucas, <u>Democracy and Participation</u>, op. cit., and Berlin "Two Concepts of Liberty, op. cit., as good instances of such a complacency.

23. Marcuse, <u>One Dimensional Man: Studies in the Ideology of Advanced Indusrial Society</u>, Boston: Beacon Press, 1964; paperbound edition, 1966, p.21, emphasis in the text. The edition used here is Abacus, 1972.

24. Marcuse has only recently re-affirmed his marxism in no uncertain terms; see his 1978 interview with Magee in "Herbert Marcuse on the Need for an Open Marxist Mind", <u>the Listener</u>, vol. 99, No. 2546, 9th February, 1978, pp. 169-171. Reprinted in B. Magee (editor), <u>Men of Ideas</u>, London, BBC 1978, pp. 66-67.

25. See Perry Anderson, <u>Considerations on Western Marxism</u>, London: New Left Books, 1976, and New Left Review, <u>Western Marxism: A Critical Reader</u>, London: New Left Books, 1977. See also Howard, D. and Klare, K. (Eds.), <u>The Unknown Tradition: European Marxism</u>, New York & London, Basic, 1972.

26. Herbert Marcuse, <u>Reason and Revolution: Hegel and the Rise of Social Theory</u>, New York: Oxford University Press, 1941. The edition used here is Routledge & Kegan Paul, 1973; <u>Eros and Civilization, A Philosophical Inquiry into Freud</u>, Boston: Beacon Press, 1955 - The edition used here is Abacus, 1973; <u>Soviet Marxism: A Critical Analysis</u>, New York: Columbia University Press, 1966 - The edition used here is Pelican, 1971.

27. See among others Cotten, J.P., "Comment Lire Marcuse?", in <u>La Nef</u>, Paris: Vol. 26, No. 36, January-March 1969. pp. 139-174.

28. Lipshires, S., <u>Herbert Marcuse: From Marx to Freud and Beyond</u>, Cambridge Massachusetts: Schenk-man Publishing company, Inc., 1974, p. 11.

29. MacIntyre, A., <u>Marcuse</u>, London: Fontana 1970. p. 17.

30. Ibid., p. 17.

31. Cotten, op. cit., p. 150.

32. Jay, M., <u>The Dialectical Imagination</u>, London: Heinemann Education Books, 1973. p.4.

33. Perry Anderson, <u>Considerations on Western Marxism</u>, op. cit..

34. Trent Schroyer, <u>The Critique of Domination: The Origin and Development of Critical Theory</u>,

New York: Geo Braziller, 1973.
35. Sidney Lipshires, op. cit.
36. Robinson, P.A., The Sexual Radicals, London: Temple Smith, 1970. Originally published as
"The Freudian Left", USA, 1969.
37. MacIntyre, Marcuse, op. cit.
38. Slater, P., Origin and Significance of
the Frankfurt School - A Marxist Perspective, London: Routledge and Kegan Paul, 1977.
39. Arato, A. and Gebhardt, E., The Essential
Frankfurt School Reader, Oxford: Blackwell, 1978.
See in particular the second introductory essay by
Arato and Gebhardt, pp. 164-185; Vincent Geoghegan:
Reason and Eros: The Social Theory of Herbert Marcuse
London: Pluto Press, 1981; Barry Katz: Herbert Marcuse - Art of Liberation, London:Verso, 1982.
40. See Althusser, Pour Marx, Paris: Maspéro,
1965, and especially the essay on "Marxism et huma-
nisme", pp. 225-258. See Marcuse, Herbert, Counter-
revolution and Revolt, first published USA, Boston:
Beacon Press, 1972; the edition used here is Allen
Lane, The Penguin Press, 1972, p. 64.
41. Marx, K. and Engels, F., The German Ideo-
logy, edited by C. J. Arthur, London: Lawrence and
Wishart, 1970; Marx and Engels, The Holy Family,
Moscow: Progress Publishers, 1956.
42. See MacLellan, The Young Hegelians and
Karl Marx, London: MacMillan Press ltd., 1969; a
sympathetic portrait of Stirner can also be found in
Woodstock, G., Anarchism, London: Penguin, 1975,
first published USA: World Publishing Co., 1962; on
Feuerbach, see Arvon, H., Feuerbach, sa Vie, son
Oeuvre avec un Exposé de sa Philosophie, Paris:
Presses Universitaires de France 1964, and Wartofsky, M.W., Feuerbach, Cambridge: Cambridge University Press, 1977.
43. On these points see Touchard, J., Histoire
des Idés Politiques, Paris: Presses Universitaires
de France, 1969
44. In fairness I should mention that I have
come across one reference to religious alienation by
Marcuse in "A conversation with Herbert Marcuse", by
S. Keen and J. Raser, Confrontation, No. 6, Summer
19/1, p. 14. In a reply to a biblical quotation,
Marcuse should have answered as follows: "My allergy
to the Scriptures is not such that I must say a
priori that every single thing in the Scriptures is
reactionary and repressive".
45. MacIntyre, Marcuse, op. cit., pp- 21-22.
46. See Morton Schoolman, "Introduction to
Marcuse's 'On the Problem of the Dialectic'", In

Telos, No. 27, Spring 1976, pp. 3-39, for an excellent discussion of this question.
    47.   Ibid., pp- 23-24, and in particular p.
32.
    48.   Martin Nicholaus, "Foreword" to Marx, K.,
Grundrisse, London: Penguin, in association with New
Left Review, 1973.
    49.   Lenin, Collected Works, XXXVIII, p. 180,
cited from Nicholaus, Ibid., p. 60.
    50.   MacIntyre, op. cit., pp. 37-38, Marcuse,
Reason and Revolution, op. cit., pp. 317-318.
    51.   MacIntyre, Ibid.; citation runs as fol-
lows: "Capitalism begets, with the inexorability of
a law of nature, its own negation". MacIntyre appears to be unaware that the interpretation of
Marx's varied and contradictory statements on the
question of voluntarism versus economic determinism
is at the heart of a huge controversy within the
marxist camp for at least the last half a century.
See for instance Colletti "Introduction", in Karl
Marx, Early Writings, London: Penguin, 1975, as well
as Anderson, Considerations on Western Marxism, op.
cit. and Howard, D., "The Historical Context", in
The Unknown Tradition: European Marxism, op. cit.
    52.   In addition to Marx and Engel's Selected
Works, in 3 volumes, Moscow, Progress Publishers,
1969, passim, see MacLellan, The Life and Thought
of Karl Marx, op. cit., possibly Wilson, E., To the
Finland Station, London: MacMillan, 1972, chapters
10, 12 and 15, and most certainly Berlin's Karl
Marx, Oxford, London and New York: Oxford University
Press, fourth edition, 1978, which draws forth very
vividly precisely this dimension of Marx.
    53.   MacIntyre, Marcuse, op. cit., pp. 59-60.
    54.   Karl Marx, "Critique of the Gotha Pro-
gramme", in Selected Works, op. cit., vo. 3, p. 19.
    55.   See the whole of the "Critique of the
Gotha Programme" for context.
    56.   "Critique of the Gotha Programme", ibid.,
pp. 20-21.
    57.   The record of the French Communist Party
as regards its attraction upon intellectuals in the
course of its 60 odd years of existence is truly
remarkable. It has acted as a pole of attraction,
recruited within its ranks or regrouped around it a
whole array of intellectual figures - among which
Aragon, Merleau-Ponty, Sartre, Garaudy, Romain Ro-
land, Andre Gide are but a few. It should be unnecessary to add that the party's relationship to
"its" intellectuals has traditionally been tense,
complex and ambivalent. See Fauvet, J., Histoire

du Parti Communiste Francais, Paris: Fayard, 1965,
and Kriegel, A., Le Parti communiste français, Paris, 1968.
58. Any such classification must necessarily be
tentative and somewhat arbitrary. It would nevertheless seem reasonable to include under that section
the large bulk of the authors represented in Fromm's
Socialist Humanism, op. cit., not excluding Fromm
himself, at leat since his Fear of Freedom, London:
Routledge Paperback, 1960 (first published as Escape
from Freedom, USA, 1941). If we consider Perry Anderson's list, in his Considerations on Western Marxism, op. cit., pp. 25-26, Sartre, Della Volpe and
Goldmann would appear very much on the borderline.
As for the "Frankfurt School" itself, it would again
seem reasonable to add to Fromm, Benjamin, the late
Horkheimer and the late Adorno, as well as, and more
certainly, Habermas, whose major work Knowledge and
Human Interests, London: Heinemann, 1972, although
clearly written with a different intent, definitely
falls under the heading. The earlier works by Horkheimer, Adorno and virtually the whole of Marcuse's
own writings cannot in my view be ranged in this
broad category.
59. A similar perspective is already developed
by Korsch, K., Marxism and Philosophy, London: New
Left Books, 1970. See furthermore Coletti, "Introduction to the Early Writings", op. cit., and
Breines, p., "Praxis and its Theorists: The impact
of Lukács and Korsch in the 1920's", in Telos, No.
11, Spring 1972, pp. 67-103.
60. See on this point Therborn's well balanced
account in "Science and politics", the little essay
which serves to introduce his What does the Ruling
Class do when it Rules?, London: New Left Books,
1978.
61. See Piccone and Delfini, A., "Marcuse's
Heideggerian Marxism", in Telos, fall 1970, pp. 36-
46; Alfred Schmidt, "Existential-Ontologie und Historischer Materialismus bei Herbert Marcuse", in
Antworten auf Herbert Marcuse, edited by J. Habermas, Frankfurt, 1968,pp. 17-49; Michael Franklin,
"The irony of the Beautiful Soul of Herbert Marcuse", in Telos, No. 6, fall 1970, pp. 3-35; Morton
Schoolman "Introduction to Marcuse's "On the Problem
of the Dialectic", op. cit., and Habermas "Zum Geleit" in Habermas, j., Antworten auf Herbert Marcuse, Frankfurt am Main: Suhrkamp, 1968.
62. Various introductions to Heidegger's difficult and demanding philosophical work can now be
found in English. See in particular Biemel, W.,

Martin Heidegger, An Illustrated Study, London: Routledge and Kegan Paul 1977, and Metha, J.L., *Martin
Heidegger: The Way and the Vision*, Honolulu: University Press of Hawaii, 1976. See also Heidegger's
Basic Writings, London: Routledge and Kegan Paul,
1972, edited and introduced by D.F. Krell, as well
as Heidegger's *Being and Time*, Oxford: Blackwell,
1978.

63, See for instance Rhodes, J.M., "Plesure
and Reason: Marcuse's Idea of Freedom" in *Interpretation*, Vol, 2, Winter 1971, pp. 93-98.

64. For a detailed, if superficial account of
Marcuse's relation to the American way of life see
Michel Ambacher, *Marcuse et la Civilisation américaine*, Paris: Aubier Montaigne, 1969; while the
detailed argumentation is largely unconvincing the
central arument itself appears sound enough - much
of what Marcuse has to say applies primarily to the
States and only indirectly to other Western countries. This point, which may seem trivial, is too
seldom mentioned by critics and commentators of
Marcuse, who all appear to accept indiscriminately
Marcuse's sweeping generalisations concerning "advanced industrial societies".

65. Heidegger, M., *Being and Time*, op. cit.

66. Herbert Marcuse, "Contributions to a Phenomenology of Historical Materialism" in *Telos*, No.
4, Fall 1969, pp. 3-4.

67. See Martin Jay, *The Dialectical Imagination*, pp. 28-30 for a more detailed account of this
period of his life.

68. Frankfurt am Main: V. Klostermann Verlag,
1932. Also in French: *L'Ontologie de Hegel et la
Théorie de l'Historicité*, Paris: Editions de Minuit,
1972.

69. See Alfred Schmidt, op. cit., and Habermas, "Zum Geleit" op. cit., and Lucien Goldmann, "La
pensé de Herbert Marcuse", in *La Nef*, Paris: Vol.
26, No. 36, January-March 1969, pp. 7-34.

70. Piccone and Delfini, "Marcuse's Heideggerian Marxism", op. cit.: Franklin, m., "The Irony of
the Beautiful Soul of Herbert Marcuse", op. cit. and
Rhodes, J.M., "Pleasure and Reason", op. cit., passim.

71. Morton Schoolman, "Introduction to Marcuse's "On the Problem of the Dialectic", op. cit.,
passim.

72. Arato and Gebhart, *The Essential Frankfurt
School Reader*, op. cit.; Connerton, (Ed.) *Critical
Scciology*, London: Penguin, 1976; Hamilton, P.,
Knowledge and Social Structure, London: Routledge

and Kegan Paul, 1974; Jacoby, R., "Towards a Critique of Automatic Marxism: The Politics of Philosophy from Lukács to the Frankfurt School, in _Telos_,
No. 10, Winter 1971, pp. 119-146, and "The Politics
of the Crisis Theory: Toward a Critique of Automatic
Marxism II", in _Telos_, No. 10, Winter 1971, pp. 3-
52; Martin Jay, _The Dialectical Imagination_, op.
cit.; Kallegerg, R., _Horkheimer, Marcuse, Adorno,
Habermas, Kritisk teori_, Oslo: Gyldendal Norsk For-
lag, 1970; Lichtheim, G., "From Marx to Hegel: Reflections on Georg Lukács, T.W. Adorno, and Herbert
marcuse, in _Tri Quarterly_; Vol. 12, Spring 1968, pp.
5-42; Slater, P., _Origin and Significance of the
Frankfurt School_, op. cit., Gustav Therborn "The
Frankfurt School", in _New Left Review_, Vol. 63,
1970, pp. 65-96. Also in _Western Marxism_, New Left
Books, 1977.

     73.   Slater, _Origin and Significance of the
Frankfurt School_, op. cit., p. XIII.
     74.   Ibid., passim.
     75.   Martin Jay, _The Dialectical Imagination_,
op. cit.
     76.   See the review of Jacoby, R., "Marxism and
the Critical School: A Marxist Perspective: Phil
Slater", (Review), In _Telos_, No. 31, Spring 1977,
pp. 198-202; Kellner, D., The Frankfurt School Revi-
sited: A Critique of Martin Jay's 'The Dialectical
Imagination'", in _New German Critique_, Vol. IV,
1975, pp. 131-152; Lubasz, H., "The Dialectical
Imagination. A History of the Frankfurt School and
the Institute of Social Research, 1923-1950, by
Martin Jay", (Review), in _History and Theory_, Vol.
XIV, No. 2, 1975, pp. 200-212; Piccone, P., "Martin
Jay - 'The Dialectical Imagination: A History of the
Frankfurt School and the Institute of Social Research, 1923-1950", (Review), in _Telos_, No. 16,
Summer 1973, pp. 146-50.
     77.   It is certainly Jay's book which more than
any other has contributed to give force and credibi-
lity to the idea of a distinctive "Frankfurt
School", and this not so much by virtue of a sustained academic argument than by the impact of such
a rich, detailed, minutiose and yet comprehensive
picture of major and minor figures within the Institute as they relate to people, impulses and situations during nearly three decades. If the resulting
book is invaluable as introductory reading as well
as a tool for further research, it is also somewhat
overwhelming. It becomes difficult to disentangle
what constitutes Jay's specific position and interpretations from the wealth of details and data he

provides. This is particularly true of the main
thesis of the book, namely the thesis implied by the
use of the term "Frankfurt School".

78. Jacoby, "Marxism and the Critical School",
op. cit., p. 232-233.

79. Lubasz, "The Dialectical Imagination", op.
cit., passim.

80. "I discovered that the expertise I lacked
in specific disciplines was compensated for by the
very comprehensiveness of my approach. For I came to
understand that there was an essential coherence in
the Frankfurt School's thought, a coherence that
affected almost all of its works in different areas.
I soon learned that Erich Fromm's discussion of the
sado-masochist character and Leo Loewenthal's treatment of the Norwegian novelist Knut Hamsun illumi-
nated one another, that Theodor W. Adorno's critique
of Stravinsky and Max Horkheimer's repudiation of
Schiller's philosophical anthropology were intimately related, that Herbert Marcuse's concept of one-
dimensional society was predicated on Friedrich
Pollock's model of state capitalism, and so on. I
discovered that even when conflicts over issues did
develop, as they did, for example, between Fromm and
Horkheimer or Pollock and Newman, they were articulated with a common vocabulary and against a background of more or less shared assumptions. An overview of the Institute's development, despite the
superficiality it may entail on certain questions,
thus appeared a justifiable exercise". Jay. op.
cit., p. XVI.

81. See on this point Jay, The Dialectic Imagination, op. cit., p. 143, and Franz l. Neumann,
"The intelligentsia in exile" for some perceptive
remarks on this question in Paul Connerton, Critical Sociology, op. cit.

82. See Jay, The Dialectical Imagination, op.
cit., pp. 71-80. It is an approach which is very
different from that of either Horkheimer or Adorno.
This is well perceived by J.P. Thomas, "Dialectic
and/or Totality, Review of Martin Jay 'The Dialectical Imagination'. A History of the Frankfurt
School and the Institute for Social Research, 1923-
50", in Radical Philosophy, No. 22, Summer 1979,
whose formulation conveys some of the essential
differences. For him "there never was any real theoretical homogenity between Marcuse on the one hand
and Adorno and Horkheimer on the other. They represent two distinct sets of perspectives and problematics which need to be reconstructed independently of
one another. I am not thinking here of the customary

distinction made between Marcuse, always preoccupied
with discovering the new paths of Revolution, and
Adorno, the hermetic, difficult, aristocratic thinker finally repelled by the character of the German
New Left. I have in mind the deeper distinction
between two different readings of Lukács which lead
back to two readings of Marx, and hence of Hegel.
Whereas Adorno and Horkheimer develop, as we have
seen, a logic of non-identity installed in the moment of 'scission', of non-reconciliation, taking
refuge in a sort of polemical, provisional Kantia-
nism which they are ultimately unable to escape,
Marcuse draws essentially from Hegel a logic of
transcendence of contradictions, and hence an increasingly synthetic, systematic mode of thought
which culminates in the fragile monument of Freudo-
Marxism, Eros and Civilizaton".
        83. Particularly striking are the parallels
between Marcuse's overall reading of Marx and the
interpretation given by Habermas in the first part
of his Knowledge and Human Interests, op. cit., pp.
7-63.
        84. André Nicholas, Herbert Marcuse ou la
quête d'un univers transprométhéen, Paris: Editions
Seghers, 1970, p. 13.
        85. As for instance is done in Franklin's "The
Irony of the Beautiful Soul of Herbert Marcuse", op.
cit.
        86. What appears to be the case for Shapiro's
otherwise perceptive approach to Marcuse's work, see
Shapiro, J. J., "The Dialectic of Theory and Practice in the Age of Technological Rationality: Herbert Marcuse and Jürgen Habermas", in The Unknown
Dimension - European Marxism since Lenin, Basic
Books, Inc., 1972, pp. 276-303.
        87. Marks, R.W., The Meaning of Marcuse, New
York: Ballantine Books, 1970, p. 56. It would be too
long to comment further on this point now. Here are
some suggestions which may perhaps be food for
thought; it is because the theme is echoed in related literature (for instance, market freedom and
marxist views on the question); because the sheer
arrogance suggests that more serious research may
underlie such statements (Eros and Civilization
builds on much of Fromm's early works); because
these statements are intermingled with what are
evidently detailed, well illustrated or well thought
out considerations on the same subject (Marcuse on
art in later writings).
        89. Carol C. Gould, Marx's Social Ontology:
Individuality and Community in Marx's theory of So-

cial Reality, Cambridge, Mass. and London: MIT,
1968.

90.   The parallels with the hermeneutic tradition are not fortuitous. See for instance Dilthey,
W., Selected Writings, edited by P. Rickman, Cambridge: University Press, 1976, pp. 247-263; see
also the essays by Gadamer and Ricoeur in Connerton
(eds.), Critical Sociology, op. cit., pp. 117-133
and pp. 194-203; for an excellent introduction to
Dilthey, see Habermas, Knowledge and Human Interests, op. cit., pp. 140-186.

Chapter Two

MARX, MARXISM AND HEIDEGGER. MARCUSE'S FIRST THEORY
OF HUMAN LIBERATION

2.1 The Context of Marcuse's First Publications

The first years of Marcuse's academic career, beginning with his first publication in July 1928 to late
1932, were mostly spent in Freiburg. He moved there
from Berlin in 1929, and began to work on his "Habi-
litationsschrift" under the supervision of Heidegger. The thesis was published in 1932 and in the
intervening years Marcuse published several articles
and book reviews. Among the books he reviewed are a
biography of Karl Marx by Karl Vorländer, a thesis
on the young Hegel's approach to Kant, a book on
Noack dealing with the historical character of philosophy itself and a work by Hans Freyer on sociology as a science of the real (1). Sociology is also
the subject of two long articles, in one of which
Marcuse challenges the new discipline's claim to
truth in a critical, but not entirely negative,
discussion of Mannheim's newly published Ideologie und Utopia (2). A more comprehensive critique of
sociology is developed in an article from 1931 focusing on sociology's systematic neglect of the all-
important individual existence, its futile and ultimately destructive attempt to force a specific historical situation into a frozen objectivity and the
sharp rupture it establishes between man and his
world (3). An earlier article develops an altogether
different approach to knowledge, namely that of a
philosophy which is concrete and rooted in the existence of the individual and his society (4). Similar
themes reappear in a largely positive review of Dilthey's "philosophy of life" where his concept of
historicity as a point of departure for all investigations of social reality is discussed at length
(5). That article, interestingly enough, is introduced by a short commendatory review of Korsch's
Marxism and Philosophy. A long two-part essay, published in 1930 and 1931, deals with the present

state of the dialectic in marxism and contemporary
philosophy (6). There is also a highly critical
review of the work of Max Adler, the Austrian marxist who most vigorously argued for a scientific
marxism founded upon a well understood Kantian epistemology (7).

These early writings are important for a variety of reasons. Firstly they show Marcuse taking up a
variety of issues, political or scientific, trying
out ideas and new approaches in relation to the
subject at hand, and developing a set of positions
of his own in relation to classical and newer philosophical or scientific currents. Secondly, it is in
the essays of the period that we must look for the
influence of Heidegger, which, according to some
commentators, has marked his work in part or as a
whole. No period in his career can more fittingly be
described as "Heideggerian marxism", if the label is
at all applicable to any of his writings. Thirdly,
and this will be my contention throughout this chapter, it is in this period that Marcuse first develops a comprehensive theory of liberation, a theory
which will later be profoundly transformed under the
impact of his reading of the young Marx, and which
will thereafter constitute the overall structure for
his entire academic production.

These issues are never more clearly brought to
the fore than in the very first work of this period,
preceding even his return to Freiburg, when he ex-
poses a number of his basic positions in a long
review of Heidegger's newly published Being and
Time. This article, entitled the "Contributions to a
Phenomenology of Historical Materialism", deserves
to be singled out for a number of reasons. Not only
is it the first published work of Marcuse, but it is
characterised by a powerful and original treatment
of Marx, Heidegger and the marxist tradition since
Marx's death (8). It is an ambitious attempt to
reconcile these various influences, together with
reflections on Dilhey, Hegel and others, within a
single overall framework. The combination of a declared marxist standpoint with an imaginative critique of Heidegger has meant that it is often regarded as the earliest attempt to effect a synthesis of
Marx and Heidegger, long before that of Sartre or
Merleau-Ponty. It is this article which more often
than not is cited as the authoritative source for
the "Heideggerian marxism" thesis or other characte-
risations of Marcuse as a "Neo-Kantian." Some interesting parallels with One Dimensional Man have also
recently been brought to the fore (9).

The "Contributions...", partly because of the
multiple aims Marcuse nevertheless seeks to achieve,
partly because of the difficulties of his style of
presentation, is a piece which is neither easily
read, nor easily assimilated. It is therefore essential to have clearly in mind what was the guiding
thread of the argument. To pick up and follow that
thread requires in turn some feeling for the political and philosophical context in which Marcuse was
moving at the time.

The philosophical context will be merely touched upon. The half a century following Hegel's death
in 1831 was marked by the collapse of the progressive Neo-Hegelianism of the 1840s, in which Marx and
Engels had been formed, and by the advances of
positivism and Neo-Kantianism. Positivist thought,
characterised by nominalist and phenomenalist positions, a profound empiricism and the exclusive reliance upon method derived from the physical sciences, was to gain much from the patent success of
these sciences on a variety of fronts; it had been
introduced in the social sciences by Comte and Saint
Simon, received a powerful impetus in various forms
of darwinism and had become a pervasive trait of
both university research and much marxist thinking -
not only Bernstein, but Plekhanov, Kautsky and even
Lenin (9a). Neo-Kantian schools played likewise and
concurrently a dominant role, especially that of
Marburg, oriented toward logic and the philosophy of
sciences, and that of Heidelberg, oriented toward
the historical sciences.

This background helps to explain the novelty
and importance of Heidegger's philosophy at the
time. Heidegger, who in some respect can be described as Neo-Kantian, nevertheless differs sharply
from these dominant philosophical currents in a
number of ways. The general area for Heidegger's
enquiries is that of metaphysics, an area of philosophy which had largely fallen into obscurity since
Hegel's death. His major interest rested with the
elucidation of the fundamental ontological (concerning the nature of what is) features which are common
to all that is human, and which can help to better
understand both the fundamental attitudes underlying
other disciplines within or outside of philosophy,
as well as man's general relation to the world.
Heidegger's ontological search aimed to investigate
and provide answers to the nature of philosophical
thought itself (10). Heidegger's explicit aim, to
have constituted the second part of the never-com-
pleted <u>Being and Time</u>, was to proceed to a "destruc-

tion" of Western metaphysics through the systematic application of a novel understanding of the classical Greek philosophical heritage (11).

It is these classical texts of Greek antiquity, as well as language and common day-to-day experiences, which Heidegger submits to a novel form of analysis, a phenomenological analysis only nominally reminiscent of Husserl's own scientific approach. In essence it consists in letting the appearance of things (i.e. the phenomena) come fully into view by suspending all judgement and all expectation, until it rests entirely upon itself, and is experienced as nothing but this full appearance. A hammer, a desk, a well-known word or a fragment of text can thus be made to appear in a new and fresh light. Only then can the analysis proceed to explore new facets of this appearance, or discover more fundamental appearances and structures behind it. This new phenomenological approach is meant to go beyond the traditional problems of philosophy, and uncover man's hidden relation to the natural world, which has been lost in the modern streamlining of thought into instrumental, technical and narrow scientific preoccupations. It leads first of all back to the ancient Greek masters, but also takes up the threads from Hegel, Kierkegaard, Nietzsche, Dilthey, and even perhaps Lukács. The philosophy that Heidegger elaborates becomes a strange admixture of marked existentialism, not a little Hegelianism, historicism, anti-positivism and a measure of romanticism fiercely apposed to the modern notions of rentability, effectivity and predictability.

Yet there is an element in Heidegger's whole approach to philosophy which is at least, if not more important in explaining the enthusiasm with which many people from Marcuse's generation were prepared to embrace this new brand of philosophy. Heidegger's reputation rests today on what was published of Being and Time, and some of his later writings; what preceded is by all accounts minor pieces. Heidegger was nevertheless enjoying, long before the publication of what was to become his masterpiece, an extraordinary reputation in academic and non academic circles alike, as a distinctive interpreter of the classical texts of philosophy and as an original thinker of his own. This rested primarily upon his very great gifts as a teacher and a philosopher. He had an almost uncanny ability to restore to the works of Greek philosophers a vitality and a freshness of their own; he was able to engage the full attention of his audience into a

long series of unsolved questions, unusual intellectual puzzles and exciting arguments in turn leading
to new questions. His whole manner of teaching was
in sharp contrast to what then prevailed in German
universities; instead of the traditional authoritative interpretation of a given problem or authors,
he offered questions, suggestions, new ideas; his
manner was extraordinarily open-ended, provocative,
demanding (11). Proceeding in such a fashion, Heidegger was able to lead his students, other interested auditors and later his readers, through a laby-
rinth of difficult analyses, expressed in a language
constructed for the purpose, to his famous discussions of "Being and Temporality", "Being and Curio-
sity", and "Being toward Death", "Anxiety", "Idle
Talk" and still more (12).

The passionate, open-ended and didactic quality
of Heidegger's thought cannot be overstressed, and
it has important implications for Marcuse's relation
to his first mentor. Heidegger was first of all a
teacher of philosophy, and an extraordinarily gifted
one. Virtually all his publications derive from
lecture notes. He was passionately engaged in his
task, and it is impossible to distinguish the scholar from the teacher, no more than the man from the
philosopher. The questioning quality of his thought,
its engagement, its willingness to go beyond established norms and customs is first of all what attracted the Young Marcuse. The search for fundamental questions will lead Marcuse back to Hegel and
Dilthey for a better understanding of historicity
and the dialectic; it will also, and that will
remain his major goal, lead him to a reconsideration
of the marxist heritage, in the light of the new
circumstances of the 20th century. What matters in
this context is naturally also Marcuse's own
position in relation to the situation of late Weimar
Germany.

Marcuse only joined the German Social Democratic Party for a short period (1917-19) and never
became actively involved in politics after that
time. We have no reason to doubt his word when he
says that he left the party because of his radical
views. We cannot here retrace the history of that
party, but it is worth remembering that it was the
leading marxist party in Germany, the largest party
in Reichstag until 1932 and remained the most prestigious socialist party in Europe by virtue of a
truly impressive mass following and a remarkable
mass organization (13). Characteristic of the SPD
was the curious combination of a forceful, even

dogmatic, marxist rhetoric with an increasingly
reformist incrementalism and willingness to compro-
mise with the existing powers - a willingness that
went to the point of actively helping suppress the
Spartakist-led uprisings of the early twenties. The
marxism of the SPD and that of the Second International, of which it was the uncontested leading
member, had also during the years almost taken the
form of an empty ritual, with simplistic formulae
and without the continuous reassessments characteristic of Marx's own work. The new credo had
become more and more irrelevant to both the actual
decisions taken by the leadership and to the ordinary lives of the well-disciplined members.
    This helps to explain why Marcuse in the "Con-
tributions..." sets out to re-examine the nature of
"the Marxist predicament" (the fundamental problematic) with particular attention to later developments
in German philosophy (Heidegger's Being and Time
being the main focus of these developments) and in
more recent marxist analyses (Lukács, Lenin, and
Karl Liebknecht) (14). This task was necessary if
marxism was ever to emerge from the static and
mechanistic interpretation of the Second International. This task was urgently needed to revitalize a
marxist camp which so clearly failed to bring the
revolutionary change that all expected. It is this
broad project, rather than simply the critique of
Heidegger, which directs the analysis of the "Contributions to a Phenomenology of Historical Materialism".

2.2. The Question of Radical Action

Seen in this light, the general thrust of a number
of observations (and of some of his less predictable
assumptions, at least in the Marx-Heidegger reading
of them) takes on a new significance. It is no
accident that Marcuse starts by affirming "the inse-
parable unity of theory and praxis" in marxism and
that he rejects any attempt to anchor "the theory of
the proletarian revolution" in some point over or
beyond marxism, whether it be Kantian philosophy or
the methodology of the natural sciences. His vehe-
ment opposition to the marked scientism of the 2nd
International goes as far as stating that for marxism at least, "its truths are not cognitive but
actual" (15). Marxism as first and foremost a guide
for action, conscious revolutionary action.
    Marcuse nevertheless asserts that Marxism is a
"science to the extent that the revolutionary acti-

vity which it seeks to bring about and direct requires the comprehension of its historical necessity
and the validity of its own nature" (15). This is
where philosophy can come into its own and play a
significant role. What philosophy can bring to marxism is a new form of rigorous knowledge. It is
Marcuse's thesis in this article that where such
knowledge is necessary, is in gaining a better grasp
of the historical situation which historical materialism attempts to determine. The central question
is therefore:

> "Does the theoretical basis whence Marxism
> arises, i.e. the necessity for the historical
> activity that it recognizes and proclaims, come
> from a full grasp of the phenomenon of histo-
> ricity?"

In other words, does "Historical Materialism"
properly derive from "historicity" all the knowledge
available concerning "the character, structure and
restlessness" of actual events? (16).
Some of the answer is to be found in Heidegger's recently published work. But only some. A
substantial section of the article is further devoted to a re-examination of the dialectic. Marcuse
also then briefly sketches out an interpretation of
marxism very different from that of the major
strains within the 2nd International. He defines the
Marxist predicament (foundation, starting point) as
follows:

> "The central point of the Marxist predicament
> is the historical possibility of <u>radical action</u>
> which is to bring about a <u>necessarily new rea-
> lity</u> that makes possible the <u>total</u> man. Its
> agent here is the <u>historically conscious</u> man;
> his only domain is history, which is the funda-
> mental category of human existence. This radi-
> cal action turns out to be revolutionary, his-
> torical activity, and the 'class' becomes its
> historical unity" (17).

Nothing could be further removed from the reformist
incrementalism which had increasingly come to characterize the 2nd International's progression toward
the socialist paradise. Marcuse puts "radical action" squarely at the center of his argument. It
becomes the point of departure and leading thread
for the whole analysis. The assumptions and logical
implications underlying or following from this ana-

lysis are set out in table 2, where the reader can
find a compressed summary of the argument presented
here. In order to show how this theory of liberation
appears as an underlying structure of what is explicitly presented as a review of Being and Time, a
structure which finally guides the whole text, it
will be derived as faithfully as possible from the
text itself, and, whenever possible, in the order
given by that text. We shall in turn consider the
modalities and determinants of "radical action",
thereunder the main features of the "historical
movement", i.e. the fundamental structures of Marcuse's conception of the dialectic; we will then
turn to the contribution that Heidegger's philosophy
can make to this dialectic, and thereafter turn to
the central elements of the theory of liberation
itself.

Radical action must be rooted in man's daily
existence, must be grasped as "existential", i.e.
as "an essential attitude of, and deriving from,
human existence" (18). It is an action which must
arise out of ordinary concerns of people in general,
and not out of metaphysical speculations or other
abstractions. Marcuse stresses the importance of the
purely "existential", i.e. as "an essential attitude
of, and deriving from, human existence" (18). It is
an action which must arise out of ordinary concerns
of people in general, and not out of metaphysical
speculations or other abstractions. Marcuse stresses
the importance of the purely "practical" aspect of
well understood marxist theory. Equally important is
its all embracing character, in that it should touch
upon all aspects of daily existence and not merely
the economic side of any such existence. For both of
these reasons it is not sufficient to create some
utopian community, get Social-Democratic candidates
into Parliament, control municipalities or facto-
ries, or even let the working-class take over the
means of production. The goal is much more radical
and the break with the past must touch upon all
sides of human existence. Mere reforms or power-
sharing will not do. "Only radical action changes
both the circumstances and human existence"(19)

Furthermore, radical action is only possible if
it appears as "essentially necessary" both for the
agent and the environment in which it occurs. "Every
action lacking this specific character of necessity,
is not radical, and need not happen" (20). This
necessary character of genuine radical action is
crucial. It implies that it is not something which
can be imposed upon the agent from outside, not

given to him from outside (i.e. the Leninist model),
but must emerge from within himself, must present
itself as an inner need, a compulsive need, rooted
in the agent's whole existence. "The radical action
is in itself part of the agent's own existence. Only
as such is radical action truly necessary. The activity is not external, but part of its very being"
(21).

The impulse for radical action is a dual one.
The most crucial aspect is the reality and force of
the misery and unhappiness in present day societies,
whatever the advances made in relation to natural
disasters or constraints. This is a theme that Marcuse explores further in his essay "On Concrete
Philosophy" (22). The other aspect is the realization of the historical character of this misery and
unhappiness, whether personal or collective, and the
implications this entails for radical action. When
radical action is fully comprehended as necessary -
when the true potentialities for revolution have
become evident for the agent - then this possibility
"substitutes a necessity for the suffering and for
the intolerable" (23). These two conditions can be
summarized as follows: "radical action must come
about (from the agent's standpoint) as a concrete
necessity of concrete human existence" (24) (implication 6).

Radical action can only be based upon full and
adequate knowledge of the total situations: "only in
knowledge can one become certain of necessity" (25).
This knowledge is first of all to be provided by the
theory of the "proletarian revolution", which best
combines a comprehensive theoretical framework with
a fundamental orientation toward political action.
Yet other forms of knowledge may also contribute to
men's awareness of the limitations of their present
existence and of the need to act upon this knowledge. For Marcuse in 1928, "all genuine knowledge is
'practical'", that is, it helps to understand and
act upon the world. Genuine knowledge "leads human
beings 'to truth'. In the realization of this meaning lies the mission of science" (26). It remains
that historical knowledge is the form of knowledge
which is primordial for radical action. An adequate
grasp of the situation necessitates, for all, a
comprehension of "historicity". In Marcuse's words
"all determinations of radical action are part of
the basic determination of historicity" (27). His
account of "historicity" is complex, not less because well-known Heideggerian themes are interwoven

Table 2

Assumptions and logical implications of Marcuse's theory of
human liberation in his "Contributions....":

ASS 1   Society is the totality of human activities as they
        stand at a particular point in history.

ASS 2   The overall setting for these activities is given by:
           a) The basic physical structures in which the given
        society is situated.
           b) The available material and immaterial resources.
           c) The dominant mode of production in the society
        (antique, feudal, capitalistic, asicatic, etc...).

Implication 1: Hence society is at any time determined partly
        by the historical heritage inherited from past genera-
        tions and by the human activities of the present gene-
        ration. Society is in that sense historical per se, and
        constantly evolving. (ASS 1,2).

ASS 3   The "actual historical movement" refers to the general
        direction of social evolution at any given time.

ASS 4   The constantly reshaped physical structures and resour-
        ces of society, as well as, under given conditions, the
        mode of production of society can be affected by human
        agency.

Implication 2: Hence society as a whole, within very broad
        limits, can be changed by those who carry out the human
        activities constituting society. Within these very
        broad limits, men in society and they alone determine
        what society is to be. (ASS. 1,2 & 4).

ASS 5   a) No one set of these activities determines all the
        others.
           b) All different kinds of activities influence all
        others.

Implication 3: Hence a radical change in society can only
        take place as a total change, not an incremental one.
        (ASS 1,2,3,4 Imp. 1,2).

ASS 6   Existential (basic human) needs are the need not to be
        exploited, unequal and subordinated, and to be social,
        mutually understanding, trusting and honest. They in-
        clude the need to sense and express spontaneity, real
        individuality and true vitality.

ASS 7 All existential needs should be fulfilled (as much as
       the given overall setting at any one time makes it
       possible).

ASS 8 Human beings wish to fulfill all their existential
       needs.

ASS 9 Greater freedom is conferred by a greater ability to
       fulfill existential needs; complete freedom is living
       within a society which facilitates the fulfillment of
       all existential needs to the full.

ASS 10 Existing societies are class societies and therefore
       dominated by forces other than the common and mutual
       concern for the best possible satisfaction of all exis-
       tential needs. These forces are the direct coercive
       power of the ruling class(es), competing class inte-
       rests, impersonal market forces, the power of ideas and
       traditions going counter such a concern, etc.,...The
       division of labour is at the origin of these processes.

Implication 4: Hence in the existing class society needs can
       only be fulfilled very inadequately.

Implication 5: Most individuals, if made aware that existing
       class societies frustrate any adequate fulfillment of
       their existential needs, will want to engage or support
       radical collective action to change society (ASS 1, 4,
       5, 6, 7, 8, 9 & 10 & Imp. 1, 2, 3, 4).

ASS 11 "Reification"/"estrangement"/"objectification" refers
       to the processes whereby the individual member of an
       advanced class society is led to perceive the world
       primarily as a world of objects and things dissociated
       from his own activities and aspirations, and from those
       of most other human beings. Thus,
            a) The objects he encounters in his daily life are
       all seen as "commodities" robbed of any human content.
            b) The institutions of society are perceived as
       alien and beyond his power and that of his fellow men.
            c) The activities he must perform are unrelated and
       irrelevant to his own needs and wants.
       These processes have their historical origins in:
            a) an extensive division of labour,
            b) a vastly extended market system based upon the
       large scale production of standard objects,
            c) the ensuing impossibility to establish an imme-
       diate, meaningful relation between human activities and
       social objects.

ASS 12 Post first world war capitalism (late capitalism, advanced capitalism) is characterised, to an unprecedented degree, by the pervasive character of the processes of "reification".

ASS 13 Advanced capitalism fulfills all the necessary conditions for a successful transition to socialism, and has long done so. That a socialist revolution has not yet taken place is due to:
a) the unprecedented and pervasive power of the processes of "reification".
b) lack of will and commitment and/or insufficient awareness on the part of potential revolutionaries.

Implication 6: A revolution leading to a socialistic society will take place in an advanced capitalist society when the individuals in these societies:
a) become fully aware of their own existential needs, and realise that the existing capitalist societies make a more adequate fulfillment of these needs impossible (ASS 8, Imp. 3,4 & 5).
b) fully realise the historical character of society and that the power to change society rests with those carrying out the human activities constituting society. (ASS 13, Imp. 1,2).
c) feel compelled to engage in such a radical collective action (ASS 13).

ASS 14 The "authentic historical movement" refers to an evolution of society where the existential needs of its members determine equally the direction of its evolution/radical change.

ASS 15 Heidegger's phenomenological analyses show that the existential subject is born into a world shaped by and shared by others, necessarily perceived as the impersonal "they". He cannot therefore but become the impersonal "man" for whom all existential possibilities and decisions are given. His values, attitudes, daily actions and even the direction of his life are prescribed by the multiple pressures of the "they" of others. The public "world" constituted by the others will prevent any spontaneity, real individuality or true vitality to emerge in the necessarily "average" existential subject.

ASS 16 The "meaning world" formed by others as "they" will differ widely for the bourgeois, peasant or worker of late capitalism. The extensive and pervasive "reification" of late capitalism will nevertheless entail that for all classes the world of "commodities" and the

impersonal relations on the "they" mode are the dominant features of most people's existence.

ASS 17 With the full realisation of the historical character
of his existence, the average existential subject
is able to break through the walls of "reification" and
impersonalisation. Every individual has within him a
particular form for self-concern, which Heidegger describes as "concern". Under given conditions this leads
the individual to take a full view of his life, accept
what his historical existence has made him to be, and
on this basis make a whole-hearted and resolute choice
for a destiny of his own, which will have the character
of necessity and for which he is ready to die.

ASS 18 The following conditions are necessary for "care" to
become operative:
     a) adequate knowledge of the past is available.
     b) this knowledge must be certain and action orien-
tated.
     c) this knowledge must be directly related to one's
own existence.

Implication 7: For a radical change of existence to be possible, a radical change in society is necessary. (ASS
1,4,5,7 & Imp. 1,2,3).

Implication 8 If a large number of individuals in a society
are to wholeheartedly support and engage in a collective radical action, this action must lead to a greater
freedom. It must therefore be an action conducive to an
"authentic historical movement", which may or may not
be in opposition to the "actual historical movement".
The processes described by Heidegger in relation to
"care" will ensure that in late capitalism the "authentic historical movement" and only such a movement will
inspire sufficient commitment for the individuals concerned to break through "reification" and impersonalisation. (ASS 1,3,4,5,8,9, 11-12,13,14,17 & Imp.
2,3,5,6,7).

ASS 19 Historical materialism is able to provide a knowledge
of the past which is adequate, certain and action-
orientated. Heidegger's phenomenological analyses sup-
plement this knowledge by showing:
     a) the fundamentally historical character of human
existence,
     b) the crucial role of action in determining exis-
tence and
     c) the multiplicity of concrete and necessary rela-
tions that exist between society and the individual

existence within such a society."

Implication 9: Hence for those who wish to change society in any radical way the most promising strategy is to spread the awareness of the unnecessary, unfulfilled existential needs by increasing the knowledge of the preceding propositions (and of the body of theories and practices supporting them). (ASS 1,4,5,13,15,16,17,18 & Imp. 1,2,5,6,8).

into a transformed, yet basically marxist framework.
    The heart of the problem for Marcuse is the question of "historical movement". It is a question to which Marcuse devotes more than half of his "Habilitationsschrift", Hegel's Ontology and the Theory of Historicity (28). The account which Marcuse gives in this first article is already highly complex. We shall only indicate its main features. First, this "historical movement" is not to be explained as "somehow added on to the originally static society" (29). Society is historical and dynamic by its very nature. The key to this movement can ultimately be retracted to the fact that man is constantly acting upon environment to attain his goals. Secondly, it is essential to realise that "originally historical man does not appear as an isolated individual, but as man among men in a social world, 'dependent' and as 'part of a larger whole'" (30). This perspective should make it clear, that Man is always "man-in-society". Thirdly, men in society have to move in the direction broadly indicated by the need to reproduce that society - "Reproduction gives drive and direction to social strength (effectivity in relation to its goal "Wirk-samkeit") in continuous self renovation" (31). Fourthly, this "reproduction" includes the world of idea and language, the "ideations" ("idealtes") which are interwoven in and dependent upon "material realities"; in other words "...laws, morality, art, science, etc....arise from, and are rooted in, the concrete character (Sein) of a concrete society" (32). Fifthly, while modern men only exist and act in society, it is men and not society who make this "historical movement". Marcuse cites Marx in The German Ideology and The Holy Family - from which much of the above is derived, albeit with a characteristic Marcusian slant. "It is surely not 'history' that uses men as its means - means in order to realise its goals - as if it was a separate entity. Rather, history is nothing but the expression of man following his goals" (33). This point is crucial.

This is so because for Marcuse neither history, nor the "historical movement" develops automatically and unilaterally. Man, consciously or not, cannot but change his natural and social environment because he is continually interacting with it; yet each generation is always faced with a broad historical choice. This choice, to which he returns at several points in the essay, is whether or not to develop to its maximum the array of potentialities that earlier generations have made possible. He maintains that historical change on a large scale always takes place, as man, whether he plans it or not, cannot but change the natural and social environment with which he is continually interacting. Yet each generation had always the choice to build upon, transform or broaden the inherited potentialities; new social forms and, at the limit, an entirely new society, are always on the agenda; and it is men, and men alone, who can decide to act upon it. (ass. 1, 3, 4, and implication 1 and 2).

Marcuse further outlines the importance of the division of labour, the spread of the capitalist world order and the subsequent central role of the last and universal class, the proletariat (assumption 10). Marcuse does not discuss why the proletariat is to be the backbone of the revolution, nor how other classes or indivuduals will relate to that process. He simply states that "the universal class is forced to undertake this action" (34) and otherwise refers to Marx's statement in The Holy Family: "It does not matter what the proletariat imagines to be its goal. What is important is what it really is, and what it will be forced to do according to its historical being. Its goal and its historical action is irrevocably predetermined in its own life situation" (35).

Why the proletariat has hitherto failed to carry out the marxist revolution, despite the remarkable advances of socialism in Germany, can have many explanations even within a broad marxist framework. Yet for Marcuse the core of the problem is first of all a question of knowledge.

If historical materialism offers the most rigorous and adequate knowledge, as the "practical" knowledge per excellence, it is not the only form of knowledge. Marcuse is quite explicit on this point. All science is not necessarily dialectical and/or related to the struggle for a better world. There exist sciences which are non-dialectic. "Mathematical physics" is such a science, and from the context it is clear that natural sciences in Marcuse's understanding are truly sciences in their own right. These sciences, which lie outside Marcuse's own span of interest, are however regarded as "fundamentally" different from social sciences and in particular the master science, history" (36).

Furthermore, and this is crucial, even philoso- phical, literary or sociological knowledge which ignores or even opposes historical materialism as the most adequate approach to the social world can contribute to truth and to further the advances of genuine revolutionary knowledge. Marcuse thus as- serts that "a fundamental distinction must be drawn between the immanent meaning of an ideology and its historical sense (location)" (37). What is more, such knowledge which exists outside historical mate- rialism cannot be drawn with the help of a dialecti- cal, economic or political analysis. It must be gathered from within the ideology itself. In other words, the ideas of a given philosopher - such as Kierkegaard, or Nietzsche, neither of which can be accused of even moderate socialist leanings - can be used for a better understanding of man's historical situation. There is no point in analysing the class position of these philosophers. This may be useful in a different context, just as it may be useful to place Hegel or Saint Simon as particularly articu- late representatives of a progressive bourgeoisie. But this method, adequate to assess the historical meaning of a given ideology, is useless to get at its immanent meaning, i.e. the truth value it may contain over and above the expression of certain class or group interests. Marcuse insists that this latter "immanent" meaning requires that the ideology be grasped "as a close and independent entity" (38). Only in accepting the stated premises and following them throughout the given arguments to their logical conclusions, will the full value of a given text or philosophy come to light. Only at that stage is a critical assessment not only useful, but necessary. The nature and the perspective of Marcuse's own critique of Heidegger is hereby defined.

What Heidegger can provide, regardless of the overall political thrust of his philosophy - eli- tist, highly individualistic and reactionary in some respects - is a better grasp of the phenomenon of "historicity", which Marcuse has defined as so cen- tral for revolutionary marxist theory.

It should be stressed before we move to this part of Marcuse's account that this is so only in the context of a definite reading of the development of capitalism. Marcuse in the text makes clear that

the last stages of this historical phase have now
long been reached. The situation is potentially pre-
revolutionary because the general societal conditions for a different society have long prevailed.
So have the specific conditions for a revolution in
Germany, even if the opportunities have all been
missed - "recent history is full of such bungled
revolutionary situations" (39). The explanation for
the failure of the revolution to materialize is not
the lack of moral fibre, or will (Bernstein) of the
proletariat, nor is it the betrayal of the Social-
Democratic Party. It is so to an extent, but this is
not central. The core of the problem is an inadequate perception of history and the force of the
"historical movement" as described above. This becomes all important. "Only what must be done necessarily can be done radically, and only in knowledge
can one become certain of necessity. In this historical situation, the class is the determining historical unity, and the recognition of the specific
socio-historical necessity is the achievement of
'class consciousness'" (40). It is in relation to
this particular type of knowledge that Heidegger's
insights prove invaluable.

2.3 Heidegger and the Path Toward Authentic Existence

Heidegger's work is often fascinating, and many of
his positions original. While the idealist tradition
took the mind as a point of departure and the materialist one the objective world (as it can be ex-
plained by natural sciences), for Heidegger the
whole existence, the simple "being in the world",
constitutes the correct starting point. Existence is
given and the world is given, and this world is to
be understood in terms of meaning, rather than natural laws. Encounter with the world is simply a
matter of practical and necessary concern. From this
basis in the totality of human existence Heidegger
reaches a number of conclusions (41).
    Heidegger initially intended to discover the
meaning of being. But in fact his whole work is
centred around a privileged form of being, namely
human beings. These human beings are not conceived
as external to the world. For Heidegger, there is no
question of an essentially worldless, though already
constituted being, entering an externally constituted world which he can only at best imperfectly
grasp through the application of rigorous logic.
Heidegger opposes to the ever cogitating Cartesian

Ego, a being which is simply given, and whose existence and reality are unproblematical. This being
regards the world not as a gigantic question mark,
but as "stuff" whose significance is merely a practical one. How can he use this "stuff", how can he
orient himself in relation to it, what meaning does
it have in relation to his goals and desires? The
original relation of being to the world is one of
meaning, and it is by this relation that being
assigns meaning, time, place to people and things.
The further investigation of the "stuff" of the
world according to form and structure, in the complex causal systems we know from natural sciences,
is subsequent to and derived from the original relation to the world.

This conclusion has important implications. The
first of these is that we live in a shared world of
meaning. This we do because we live with others in a
historical world. Successive generations of human
beings have shaped the surrounding environment and
the meaning attached to its many aspects. We saw
that for the "being in the world" existence is inextricably interwoven with the world, so they are no
more than different aspects of one and same "indes-
tructible, concrete totality" (42). To this must now
be added that being is always living in and part of
a "shared-world" (mitwelt). Being is therefore
shaped, even in its very substance, by the "shared-
world" (i.e. others). The heideggerian being is
prisoner of the world, a world in which he is for
all practical purposes totally immersed.

For Heidegger, the average existential being
has all of his choices pre-given; he is properly
speaking "man" (Das Mann), "impersonal man", with no
individuality, bearer only of those values which the
world around him and in him has given.

This essential "forfeiture" to the world is
part of the very nature of being. Heidegger goes
further still and argues that there is a sort of
primal "dejectedness" which pervades being even
before being handed to existence. Being is always,
constitutionlly, to be forfeited to the world.

Yet, there is still a hope for existence because, despite all "dejectedness" and the ensuing,
if unavoidable "forfeiture" to an impersonal world,
there remains in the individual some understanding
of his very uniqueness. This famous, existentially
conceived "concern" (Sorge) for its own being makes
it possible to hope that being will reach, through a
tortuous path, "authentic existence".

Heidegger rejects both determinism and free

will as inadequate to resolve the puzzle of the "dejected" being. Being must accept this "dejection", accept the heritage of the past, "assume" it and work from there toward his very own destiny. "Freedom lies (thus) ... in the self-chosen fulfilment of necessity". In Heidegger's words "The determination with which existence returns to itself discloses the momentary factual possibilities of actual existence out of the heritage that existence accepts as dejected" (43).

For Marcuse this "authentic existence" is not a mere acceptance of the "dejectness" of existence. It is a return to the past by which being projects and opposes to the factual present the better of this past - his "essence" as concerned being. Marcuse thus affirms that "its possibilities can only be attained in opposition to factual existence 'qua' presence" (44). This idea of the Heideggerian "concern" as the "negation" of the present (i.e. the evils of capitalism) is crucial for his entire argument. Paradoxically it is here that Marcuse parts ways with Heidegger.

2.4 The First Theory of Liberation
Marcuse starts this process by affirming that Heidegger's work contains much truth about contemporary existence. It asks a fundamentally correct question, "What is authentic existence, and how is it at all possible?". The answer it gives leads, after an extensive detour, back to the plight and meaninglessness of daily existence. Heidegger is able to show that philosophical problems, questions of truth, science, understanding, reality, in fact express "existential struggle and plight, and the truths, lies or hypocrisies of being-in-the-world" (45). He is able to oppose the possibility of a "true and authentic existence" to the public forfeiture of everyday life, and to point toward the practical "concern" for one's existence as the key to well-understood freedom.

This is as far as Marcuse will go with Heidegger, and here the differences become unambiguous and explicit. Firstly, he rejects Heidegger's solution based on a solitary existence leading to self-discovery and self-recovery. The solution is action, and it is collective. Secondly, he reinterprets Heidegger's conception of history towards actual history instead of a philosophical category. Thirdly, in the same vein, he explicitly contrasts the "actual" of Heidegger with a very real present, Weimar Germany

in the late twenties. Fourthly, he opposes the un-
differentiated Heideggerian "meaning world", a picture in which sharply contrasting and essentially
different "meanings-worlds" co-exist uneasily. No
understanding is possible between the world of "the
modern bourgeois of advanced capitalism" and that of
the peasant or the proletarian (46).

This leads Marcuse straight into the "material
constitution of history". On that question he basically follows the Marxian scheme, but with a clear
emphasis on the role of the dialectic as the way to
grasp all the complexities of the given situation.
This account centres mainly around the idea of "historical Movement" described above. Marcuse now emphasizes that "the individual is not the historical
existential unit" (47). Society is. It is society
which ultimately constitutes the common framework
for all human activities and for all the other
systems of interactions in the private, economic,
cultural, or political spheres of individual lives.
Furthermore, society is seen as a totality whose
ideology is not simply rooted in but intertwined
with the economic base so as to form an almost
indissociable unity.

The "ideal objective domains" are nevertheless
founded in the "economy", and produced and reproduced with it. By "economy" Marcuse understands more
than simply wages and paid holidays. "Economy" here
is related to the Heideggerian concern, not as isolated self-discovery, but as a concern for existence. This concern is not (emphatically) the instinct
for survival, but the concern for "the maintenance,
shaping and perpetuation" of being, "including the
material and ideal entities which existentially
belong to him" (48). All those entities thus apprehended by being are "existential needs", and these,
together with the efforts they generate, constitute
the economy. The economy is what provides for material needs, but equally for emotional and intellectual ones as well. This is a theme which he develops
in the 1933 essay on the concept of labour, and it
appears to be the plausible interpretation in this
context. It is also a singularly modern formulation,
one which emphasizes motivations and benefits which
only recently, in Galbraith's work, for instance,
have received more than a casual consideration by
economists. Economy, in this comprehensive conception, is the primary terrain for long term social
changes. (Ass. 6).

Marcuse now returns to his original problem,
i.e. the necessity for "radical action". This neces-

sity ties in with the dynamic nature of history.
"Historical existence is dynamic in its very being
and can exist only in the historical movement. Concern for the living space necessarily implies the
use of resources (utilization of natural forces,
migration, search for food, maintenance and distribution of production, commerce, etc.). The whole
process whereby nature becomes history is part of
the primary character of existence and belongs to
the fundamental structure of historicity." (49).
Nature is engulfed in the "historical movement" and
in turn serves to give it a new impetus.

This historical movement is neither continuous
nor irresistible. The mode of production sets the
stage, or as Marcuse puts it, "the mode of production of society, which expresses its existential
needs, is the material basis from which its historical movement unfolds" (50). The impact of the "historical movement" will vary according to the attained level of the forces of production. This process is not automatic, but is mediated by the force
and degree of fulfilment of existential needs. The
division of labour makes it impossible for society
to organize around the satisfaction of existential
needs thus defined as its primary objective. These
develop all the same. The tension or the contradiction between the attained or demonstrably attainable
level of the forces of production and the satisfaction or lack of satisfaction of the developing existential needs is the fundamental lever for radical
action. If men become conscious of the degree to
which late capitalist society frustrates the fulfilment of their existential needs, not only in relation to what society at large could be like, but
also in the simplest things of their day-to-day
existence, they wil take up radical action. Such an
action will neither be an isolated act, nor a gesture of pure wil, but the logical continuation of a
vast historical movement toward a better existence
for all men in that society.

The "historical movement" can be arrested,
distorted, or cancelled by various ideological mechanisms. The first is a distortion of the attainable level of force of production which affirms the
present one as the only possible. The second, which
Marcuse attacks sharply, is the restriction of
"existential needs" to little more than "economic"
or purely material needs for bare survival. The
third is the restriction of the economic sphere to a
purely technical set of problems (and this in no way
denies the need for detailed economic analyses also

affirmed in that text). Any such approach entails
that the environment is taken for granted, both in
its social and "socialized" aspects (i.e. nature as
changed by man), and that the shared and socially
created world of men is turned "into a rigid world
which engulfs existence with the inescapability of a
natural law" (51).

Heidegger's analyses again can be of use to
complement the dialectic. The process of "reification", "objectification", "estrangement" has its own
momentum. What Heidegger so brilliantly describes is
nothing else but the multiple facts of the process
of "reification" when experienced by individuals.
Marcuse explicitly returns to this concept, that
Lukács developed a few years earlier, on the basis
of Marx's section on "commodity fetishism" in Capital. How the ever dynamic "historical movement" can
turn into its opposite, namely the appearance of
nature given, immutable and alien economic and social institutions, is indicated by the following
passage:

> "Everything is an endless sum of activities,
> one after the other, yet all inextricably in-
> terconnected and determined. All these activi-
> ties are divorced from the agent who is not
> part of them, but only deals with them, minds
> his own business, or - the final absurdity! -
> must undertake the activities in order to live.
> It is the 'metamorphosis of personal into mate-
> rial powers', which has left behind 'abstract
> individuals, deprived of all true vitality' so
> that 'man's own activity confronts him as an
> alien power'. This penetrates into the very
> foundation of capitalist society" (52).

As long as the world of meaning is essentially
reified, even if all other conditions are present,
the "historical" class will be unable to break
through and resolve the contradiction. What Heidegger provides is a scientific knowledge of the historical nature of the abstractions which rule the
lives of men, as well as a new understanding of the
fundamentally practical nature of the disciplines
purporting to investigate an objective and immutable
environment (53).

The key is the "concern" for existence, a concern which Marcuse reinterprets in terms of his
"existential needs" and the idea that the world is
to be "assumed" in its full temporality if man is
ever to be free. The Marcusian "historicity" gives

to this message an altogether different meaning. For
Marcuse, if men create the world they can re-create
it. The major condition at the present stage is a
clear and undeniable awareness of the human character of this world. He argues that "by recognizing
the historicity of the world, it (concerned existence) recognizes its own historicity which can create
a new world precisely through dejection into the
changing act", i.e. radical action (54). He insists
upon the fact that in his view, existence as such is
not frozen in the world as dejected mundane existence (In-der-Welt-sein) nor is worldliness in general,
as meaningfulness, even related to a particular
existence" (55). Contrary to Heidegger he asserts
that "existence is always concrete in a determined
historical situation (spatio-temporal context). As
such, it is always essentially determined by concretely demonstrable material data" (56). In other
words, the "dejectedness" of the Heideggerian man is
attributable to specific socio-historical conditions.
    "Concern" is no longer to lead to an individual
destiny. The knowledge of the past is no longer an
existentialist gesture against the meaninglessness
of an impossible world. "Concern" will lead to a
process of reflection over society, which, if adequate knowledge is available, will make the individual realise that his existence is inextricably
bound to the destinies of the whole society. Phenomenological insights will naturally round out into a
comprehension of the world as shaped by a complex
interplay of forces where capitalist requirements
are dominant, and unnecessarily so. In discovering
the "authentic historical existence" made possible
by this concern and this knowledge, the individual
will finally be led to the collective radical action
to change society.
    The first theory of liberation rests upon the
difficult synthesis of theoretical or descriptive
elements derived from very different intellectual
traditions, whose co-existence is precarious; in the
years that follow the tension will become more apparent, as Marcuse concurrently develops characteristic Heideggerian themes and elaborates a new fusion
of the dialectic with a revised phenomenological
approach. Yet even then the overall political orientation, which is almost entirely absent in Heidegger, remains pre-eminent in each of Marcuse's articles or essays throughout this period. The "Contribution..." will remain Marcuse's most explicit
and comprehensive political statement, however. The

marxism it displays, in the analysis of the current
political situation as well as in the interpretation
of the marxist heritage, places Marcuse clearly
apart from the dominant marxist currents within the
second international. The emphasis upon individual
commitment and the role of self-experienced knowledge sets it certainly clearly apart from any conception - or any practical politics - whereby a
socialist party is to decide for the supportive or
acquiescent members of the proletariat. It is equally sharply opposed to the Leninist emphasis upon an
elitist avant-garde of professional revolutionaries
showing the way. Perhaps the phrase "Heideggerian
Luxemburgism", if any such label is needed, would be
the most adequate one. At least Marcuse shares with
the latter a profound belief in the spontaneity of
the masses, albeit one which requires, besides socialist theory, the full knowledge of "historicity"
and the sense of the pervasive, all round and deep-
seated effects of capitalist social arrangements
(57).

2.5 The Evolution of Marcuse's Thought from 1928 to 1932

None of the publications which followed the "Contributions ..." showed the comprehensive character of
the latter, nor displayed the same breadth of interests. The stage was set with this very first essay,
and Marcuse in the years 1928 to 1932 takes up a
variety of more specific issues or subjects, together with the work on Hegel's Ontology, itself a
highly specialised philosophical product. The articles and book reviews of the period were briefly
described at the beginning of this chapter. They are
of more interest in this context than the "Habilita-
tionsschrift" itself, as they make it possible to
discern some broad lines of development in Marcuse's
academic production at Freiburg. In relation to the
1932 essay they show a movement away from the highly
visible Heideggerianism of that essay, a movement
reflecting similar developments in Hegel's Ontology,
towards more general philosophical issues and toward
writers such as Hegel or Dilthey, but also Kierkegaard, Lukács and the early German sociologists such
as Weber and Manheim. Yet, on the whole this period
is first of all characterised by a gradual retreat
from the immediate and burning political preoccupations of the first essay. Marcuse retains his political perspective and remains deeply critical of
Heidegger's emphasis on pure ontology and individual

salvation; he nevertheless takes up important Heideggerian themes such as the unity of individual existence or the methodological primacy of experience in genuine philosophical inquiry. The authors to which he devotes his research are also characteristically central sources for Heidegger's own philosophy. The phenomenological method also begins to play a role which is far beyond that of the 1928 essay.

The evolution in these essays points to further developments along the lines of a refined marxist phenomenology, well suited to traditional academic research, and to a socialist and humanist existentialism whose revolutionary overtones soon will fade.

Marcuse's actual political and intellectual development, however, is an altogether different one.

NOTER

1. See Herbert Marcuse, "Besprechung von Karl Vorländer: Karl Marx, sein Leben und sein Werk", Die Gesellschaft, Vol. VI, 1929, part II, pp. 186-199; "Besprechung von Heinz Heimsoeth: Die Errungenschaften des Deutschen Idealismus", Deutsche Literaturzeitung, Vol. 53 no. 43, 1932, pp. 2024-2029; "Besprechung von H. Noack: Geschichte und System der Philosphie", Philosophische Hefte, Vol. II, 1930, pp. 91-96; "Zur Auseinandersetzung mit Hans Freyers Soziologie als Wirklichkeitswissenschaft", Philosophische Hefte, Vol. III, nos. 1/2, 1931, pp. 83-91.
2. See Herbert Marcuse, "Zur Wahrheitsproblematik der soziologischen Methode", (On the Problem of Truth in the Sociological Method), Die Gesellschaft, Vol. VI, 1929, part II, pp. 356-369.
3. See Herbert Marcuse, "Zur Kritik der Soziologie", (Toward a Critique of Sociology), Die Gesellschaft, Vol. VIII, 1931, part II, pp. 270-280.
4. See Herbert Marcuse, "On Concrete Philosophy", op. cit.
5. See Herbert Marcuse, "Das Problem der geschichtlichen Wirklichkeit: Wilhelm Dilthey", (On the Problem of Historical Reality: Wilhelm Dilthey), Die Gesellschaft, Vol. VIII, 1931, part II, pp. 270-280.
6. See Herbert Marcuse, "On the Problem of the Dialectic", in Telos, No. 27, Spring 1915, pp. 12-39. Part I was translated by Morton Schoolman from "Zum Problem der Dialectic I", Die Gesellschaft, Vol. VI, 1929, pp. 356-369. Part II was translated by Duncan Smith from "Zum Problem der Dialectic II",

Die Gesellschaft, Vol. VIII, 1931, Part II, pp. 541-557.

7. "Transzendentaler Marxismus?", (Marxism Transcendental?), Die Gesellschaft, Vol. VII, 1930, part II, pp 304-326. Also published in French as "Marxisme Transcendental?" in Philosphie et Révolution, Paris: Denoël-Gonthier, 1969.

8. "Contributions to a Phenomenology of Historical Materialism", op.cit., For reasons indicated below in the main text the early works of Marcuse present special difficulties which make it necessary to refer to the German original. French translations exist for most of these works, and on occasion have been found to be superior to the English equivalent. For reasons of convenience, the English text, when available, will always be used as the main reference, unless otherwise indicated. The title will always be given in English, except for minor pieces. Each reference to major texts of that perod will be followed by two page numbers, the first referring to the English or French translation, the second referring to the German original.

9. Piccone and Delfini, "Marcuse's Heideggerian Marxism", op.cit., passim.

9a. On these points see Goldmann, Lucien, Lukács and Heidegger: Toward a new Philosophy, London: Routledge and Kegan, 1977; first published as Lukács et Heidegger, Paris: Denöel, 1973, Introduction. See also Bochenski, I.M., Contemporary European Philosophy, USA: University of California Press, 1974; and Colletti, "Introduction" to Karl Marx, Early Writings, op.cit.

10. Heidegger, Being and Time, op.cit., Introduction.

11. See Mehta, Martin Heidegger: The Way and the Vision, op.cit. pp 36 ff.

12. See Heidegger, Being and Time, op.cit., passim.

13. See for instance Jacques Droz, Histoire génerale du socialisme, Vol. II, Paris: Presses Universitaires de France, 1974. See also Cole, G.D.H. The History of Socialist Thought, Vol. IV, Parts I and II, London: MacMillan, 1961.

14. "Contributions...", op.cit., p. 5, p.41. For reasons of convenience, the Telos translation of Heideggerian terms as they appear in Marcuse's essay will be preferred. The reader familiar with more recent translations should translate "concern" into "care", "existence" into "Dasein" and "determination" into "resoluteness".

15. Ibid., p.3, p. 45.

16.   Ibid.,
17.   Ibid., p.5, p.47, my emphasis.
18.   Ibid., p.6, p.47, emphasis in the text.
19.   Ibid., p.6, pp. 47-48, emphasis in the
text.
20.   Ibid., p.7, p.48.
21.   Ibid.,
22.   "Über konkrete Philosophie", (On Concrete
Philosophy), Archiv für Sozialwissenschaft und So-
zialpolitik, vol. 62 (1929), pp. 11-126. Also published as "Sur la philosophie concrète in Philosophie et Révolution, Paris: Denoël-Gonthier 1969.
23.   "Contributions...", op. cit., p.8, p48.
24.   Ibid.,
25.   Ibid, p.11, p51.
26.   Ibid.,
27.   Ibid., p.7, p.48, emphasis in the text.
28.   op. cit. passim.
29.   "Contributions...", p.31, p.66.
30.   Ibid., p.8, p.49.
31.   Ibid.,
32.   Ibid., p.9, p.49.
33.   Ibid., p.9, p.50.
34.   Ibid., p.10, p.50.
35.   Ibid.,
36.   Ibid., p.23, p.60.
37.   Ibid., p.27, p.63.
38.   Ibid., p.11, p.51.
39.   Ibid., p.11, p.51.
40.   Ibid.; it should be noted that class consciousness becomes a problem of adequate knowledge,
We are far from Lenin's emphasis om the role of
"propaganda" and "agitation" in transmitting theory
and helping form praxis, and even further from any
question of organization and concrete achievements
as the way to make the working class realise itself
progressively, the so much sought for "unity of
theory and practice". Marcuse seems here to have an
almost mythical belief in the "transparency" and
impact of such knowledge within a society. The question of the "power" and impact of knowledge in his
thought during the Freiburg years and thereafter is
however more complex, as we shall see below.
41.   In addition to the works by or on Heidegger cited in chapter 1, section 4, see also the
short discussion in Bochenski, I.M., Contemporary
European Philosophy, Berkeley, Los Angeles, London:
University of Southern California Press, 1956.,
(First published as Europäische Philosophie der Gegenwart, Berne: Francke A.G. Verlag, second edition,
1951), pp. 154-173. While Bochenski in no sense can

be considered a Heidegger scholar, his relative
distance from the subject and the context in which
he is able to replace him allows him to bring up
interesting features of this extraordinary philosophical enterprise.

42. "Contributions...", p. 13, p.53.
43. Heidegger, Being and Time, op.cit. p.433.
44. "Contributions...", p. 15, p.54.
45. Ibid., p.16, p.55.
46. Ibid., p.18, p.56.
47. Ibid., p.27, p.63.
48. Ibid., p.29, p.65.
49. Ibid., p.31, p.66.
50. Ibid., p.30, p.65.
51. Ibid., p.32, p.67.
52. Ibid., p.6, p.47, emphasis in the text.
53. The connotations of the German "Wissen-
schaft" are far broader than the equivalent
"science" in English, and tend to include every
systematic academic discipline.
54. "Contributions...", p.33, p.61.
55. Ibid., p.22, p.62, emphasis in the text.
56. Ibid., p.22, pp.62-63.
57. On Rosa Luxemburg see Frölich, P., Rosa
Luxemburg, London: Pluto Press, 1972.

Chapter Three

THE SECOND ENCOUNTER WITH MARX: MARCUSE'S NEW THEORY
OF HUMAN LIBERATION

Between 1927 and 1932 appeared the first volumes of
the Marx-Engels Gesamtausgabe (MEGA), a German edition of the collected works of Marx and Engels,
which was never completed (1). Volume 3 of the first
section of this edition consisted of some of Marx's
early research papers written in 1844 during his
stay in Paris (2). Originally intended as background
material for a series of monographs on laws, ethics,
and politics, they were later rewritten for a book
on politics and economics which, for various reasons, was never published (3). These research papers
were published for the first time in 1932, sixty-
five years after Capital, under the title Economic
and Philosophical Manuscripts of 1844 (4). 1932 also
saw the appearance in Die Gesellschaft, the Social-
Democratic review edited by Rudolf Hilferding, of an
article entitled "Neue Quellen zur Grundlegung des
Historischen Materialismus" ("New Sources on the
Founding of Historical Materialism"), by Herbert
Marcuse; the article is now available in English
under the title "Foundation of Historical Materialism" (5). This article, scarcely noted by Marcuse's
critics and commentators, is Marcuse's first and
most explicit discussion of Marx's early works. It
also represents a crucial turning point in Marcuse's
academic career, probably more significant than his
acceptance as a collaborator of the "Frankfurt
School" the following year, or his exile to the USA.
The analyses Marcuse carries out in this essay imply
a profound transformation of an entire outlook and
constitute the point of departure for most of his
work in the 1930s and 1940s, including Reason and
Revolution.
     When reading this first essay on Marx's Econo-
mic and Philosophical Manuscripts of 1844, one is
immediately struck by the extraordinary claims that

Marcuse puts forward on the basis of the <u>Manus-cripts</u>. It is difficult today to imagine the role played for the whole marxist tradition by an ortho-doxy which disowned the philosophical origins of this tradition, stressed the "scientific" character of marxism and saw in Marx above all a gifted and prophetic economist (6). Marcuse introduces his essay by stating that the recent publication of the <u>Paris Manuscripts</u> "must become a crucial event in the history of Marxist studies. These manuscripts could put the discussion of the origin and original meaning of historical materialism, and the entire theory of 'scientific socialism', on a new footing" (7). What follows is a powerful and original recon-struction of the underlying structure of these frag-mented manuscripts, in which Marcuse quite convin-cingly shows Marx developing his own theory of so-cialist revolution by a dual critique of the English economists and of Hegel's entire philosophical per-spective. It is the latter in particular that holds Marcuse's attention, and it is this aspect of the manuscripts that is vigorously brought to the fore. To understand the perspective and method adopted by Marcuse in this essay, it is necessary to consider in more detail the character of Heidegger's philo-sophy. This essay marks an important decline in whatever <u>substantive</u> influence Heidegger may have had upon the young Marcuse. Yet it is perhaps in this essay that the <u>method</u> of Heidegger, probably the most lasting influence of the German philosopher upon Marcuse, is most clearly seen. To this "method" we shall now turn.

3.1 The Method of Marcuse

Marcuse seldom accounts for the method adopted with regard to his research on a given author or current of ideas. It would be a mistake to deduce from this that he regards methodological questions as unimpor-tant. In "Transcendental Marxism?", he declares that "the method of a scientific work is the part of it which gives us the most easy access to it, allows us to explain a system in terms of the fundamental attitude underlying it, and to understand a given philosophy as a corpus of philosophy" (8).

The reasons for this reticence against explicit methodological considerations in relation to his own work must be sought elsewhere. Part of the explana-tion has undoubtedly to do with his whole manner of presentation, a style which is both literary and academic, and presupposes much of his readers; Mac-

Intyre is probably right in retracing this whole manner to the tradition of German universities (9), yet this is not the whole story. Another explanation would be to relate this reticence to Marcuse's self-chosen position as a marxist philosopher committed to the idea of the revolution above all else. This in turn would go against placing undue emphasis upon methodological questions, as such questions cannot, nor more than a definitive epistemological or onto-logical stand, be allowed to form an anchor point over and beyond the socialist goal. This is a posi-tion that his later colleagues Horkheimer and Adorno most certainly would endorse (10). Marcuse never quite embraced his colleagues' overall rejection of systematic and discursive arguments, however; nor did he share their predilection for purely "nega-tive" critique, isolated insights and aphorisms. A more likely explanation would be to point to the nature of his research itself, which overwhelmingly is placed at the level of a meta-philosophy or a meta-sociology, i.e. a theory whose major function is to reflect upon the theories, insights and fin-dings of these disciplines, from the perspective of a broad theory of action aiming at a marxist revolu-tionary transformation of society, and which conse-quently cannot be bound by methodological procedures derived from these disciplines.

Each of these explanations contain probably something of the answer. Yet they fail to account for the positive, constructive and exploratory cha-racter of Marcuse's research; there is a pioneering quality to much of these writings. What is more, they do not account for the methodology which un-doubtedly structures Marcuse's better works. They patently rest upon the belief that the readers can be convinced by a systematic, well-argued and well-integrated perspective upon a given author or issue.

This is where it may be useful to return once more to Heidegger, to consider more closely the essential of his method of research. We have already considered the phenomenological approach used by Heidegger to progressively lead his readers from the usual appearance of phenomenon to another and more complete appearance, from which other appearances or facets in turn could be derived. Through these suc-cessive changes in the appearance, or meaning of a given fragment of text, a facet of the common lan-guage on some of our most habitual attitudes to objects around us, Heidegger aims to lead the liste-ner or the reader to a novel apprehension of his relation to the social and/or natural world of which he is a part.

The point of departure for these investigations of "Being" is more often than not Heidegger's powerful and original reconstruction of the classical texts of Plato, Aristotle or Parmenides. The new understanding of this classical Greek heritage is achieved through the bold and often startling reinterpretation of these texts, or fragments of texts, the unorthodox translation of key words or passages, and the introduction of a whole new vocabulary to convey the newly found insights. There is considerable philosophical acumen in these re-interpretations, and also a sense of the distinctiveness of Greek thought. But what guides these analyses - and what also appears to direct the application of a phenomenological method only nominally inherited from Husserl - is more than that. It is what Mehta describes as the "vision" of Heidegger, and others as the "ways" of his thought - namely an unusual power to evoke and project new and alien perspectives upon a given text, a given author or even banal and ordinary situations in daily life (11). Heidegger has great confidence in his ability to grasp the underlying dimension in a given text. The results are often startling, in that the ancient Greeks thereby acquire an altogether different stature, and can be seen to express thoughts and views which are quite alien not only to ordinary, commonsensical notions but also to much of traditional German philosophical teaching.

What is most striking in Heidegger's whole approach is precisely this determination, and ability, to project and hold a new perspective upon the given text or problem. A word, a passage, a common situation will often serve as the point of departure for an idea, an interpretation or a way of looking upon things which will then be developed on the basis of other facets of the given phenomenon, until a conclusion, mostly unexpected, will be reached, from which a whole new process may well be initiated. Heidegger will impose a single perspective upon a text, or fragment of text, and literally "push" it through the text itself, until his listener or reader is presented with a full or unusual picture of the given text or the habitual attitude under discussion. It is this ability, not only to cut through the accepted meanings of a phenomenon, as well as most of the usual philosophical or scientific procedures, but also to present a single, rigorous, coherent overall interpretation for a whole problematic which more than anything gives vigour and power to the Heideggerian approach.

I have already emphasised that Marcuse and Heidegger, even in the years 1928-1932, were on the whole concerned with very different problematics. From 1932 and onward, the marked Heideggerianism of Marcuse's diverse writings, mostly expressed in common themes and the reliance upon Heidegger's special terminology, will disappear altogether from Marcuse's writings. Certain traits will remain, such as the emphasis upon all aspects of the human experience, and the centrality of individual existence in even the most of all embracing theoretical considerations. Likewise, Marcuse wil share with Heidegger an outlook upon man as necessarily part and parcel of a world which is social and natural all at once.

However, it is with respect to a method of research and a way of approaching philosophical (or political) problems that Marcuse is first of all indebted to Heidegger. Already the character of Marcuse's evidence could be retraced to that early influence. There are no or few facts which are absolutely given, and no entirely reliable procedure to obtain the knowledge of the essentials of a given social, political or philosophical problem; the way in which knowledge can be established and communicated is therefore a combination of imaginative reasonings, personal reflections and unarguable, self-evident truths. More importantly, there is a common denominator in Heidegger's approach to philosophy and Marcuse's approach to Hegel, Marx or Freud, or even his treatment of positivism or technological rationality. There is the sense of an overall, directing, guiding perspective running throughout the treatment of the given problem. This is perhaps nowhere clearer than in Marcuse's interpretation of Hegel in Reason and Revolution. The power of that interpretation resides in the way in which detailed analyses are brought to bear upon a single ambitious reading of Hegel as the heir of the French Revolution of 1789, at some point the most progressive bourgeois thinker in Germany, and the major influence in the development of Marx's new social theory.

This is true of other major analyses of Marcuse. Underlying, directing and giving coherence to Marcuse's writings there is more often than not a definite perspective - which may or may not clearly emerge from the text itself. It is in the elaboration, construction and projection of this perspective that Marcuse is most indebted to Heidegger's powerful re-interpretations of the classical Greek texts. This he himself stated in his 1977 interview with Friedrich Olafson (12). In answer to a question about Heidegger's wider influence upon his work, he states that: "..There was, as I said, the mere fact that at least a certain type and kind of thinking I learned from him, and at least the fact - which again should be stressed in the age of structuralism - that after all the text has an authority of its own and even if you violate the text, you have to do justice to it. These are elements which I think continue to be valid to this very day." As Heidegger, Marcuse bases his own overall perspective upon a reading of the text itself. He uses a variety of texts, particular passages or sometimes mere sentences, a few words, a phrase, with which he reconstructs a larger system within the text itself. This interpretation is presented as a single whole or an entire projection with which to illuminate the text from inside. It is frequently directed against preconceived ideas, traditional wisdom and accepted notions. All these features can be seen in Marcuse's major works, be it Reason and Revolution, Eros and Civilisation or Soviet Marxism (13). Yet nowhere is it more true than in relation to Marcuse's interpretation of the Economic and Philosophical Manuscripts of 1844. Nowhere but in relation to these early manuscripts of Marx is the parallel with Heidegger's extraordinary interpretations of the texts of Plato or Heraclitus more evident. And nowhere can we gain such easy access to Marcuse's method. An insight into this method also helps illuminate the singular character of Marcuse's interpretation of Marx.

3.2 Marcuse and the 1844 Manuscripts

One thing should be stated from the outset: anyone unfamiliar with the complex exegeses, interpretations or essays relating to the Paris Manuscripts would not be impressed by these early research papers by Marx (14). Notwithstanding the careful editing and heavy footnote apparatus provided by the Russian publishers, it would be difficult at first to see much more in this work than a bundle of untidy research notes by a perceptive, but hopelessly disorganized scholar. There are comments and extracts from the English and French economists of the time, intermingled with detailed and evocative descriptions of the working conditions of the labouring classes, a long discussion of Hegel, several fairly obscure passages relating to then-current philoso-

phical or scientific debates, a section on the role
of money, and more. All this is mixed together in a
mumbo-jumbo of half-finished paragraphs, deleted
passages or words and incomplete arguments, none of
them very tidy or clear (15).

Yet this does not prevent Marcuse from decla-
ring that "... the <u>Economic and Philosophical Manu-</u>
<u>scripts</u> reveal, in a way clearer than any later
texts, the original meaning of the fundamental Marxian categories, and it could perhaps become necessary, not to revise, by reference to its origins,
the current interpretation of marxism in its fully
elaborated form, but, on the contrary, to recapture
the initial overall shape of this critique in the
light of later formulations" (16). The mildly cautious formulation should not mislead anyone. Marcuse
clearly wants no identification with Bernstein's
ambitions, and he is, after all, publishing in a
leading Social Democratic Journal. The claim he puts
forward is a very wide claim. What he proposes is
little less than a global re-interpretation of Marx,
one which is to affect the reading of every single
item of Marx's work, not excluding <u>Capital</u>.

Marcuse for once indicates the nature of the
difficulties and conveys some idea of the method to
be applied.

> "Not only does the fragmentary nature of the
> manuscripts (substantial sections seem to have
> been lost and the analysis often breaks off at
> the crucial points; there is no final draft
> ready for publication) necessitate a detailed
> interpretation constantly relating individual
> passages to the text in its entirety, but the
> text itself is technically exceptionally deman-
> ding, and, in particular, requires a very solid
> philosophical background of the reader" (17).

The warning, as we shall see, is not out of place.
As Marcuse's piece appeared so shortly after the
publication of these manuscripts, it may be tempting
to consider it essentially as a review, and in
places this is also what Marcuse's tone and style
suggest. Yet nothing could be more mistaken. If it
is a review it is a very curious one. It disregards
almost three quarters of the original text, barely
mentions the detailed economic considerations which
take up so much of the manuscript, and there is
virtually no reference to Marx's often vivid descriptions of mass poverty and exploitation. There is
virtually no comment upon the circumstances under

which the piece was written, no mention of the fact
that it was Marx's first serious encounter with
English economists such as Smith or Ricardo or that
at the time Marx was already breaking with Ruge and
the French Socialists, who were each alarmed by
Marx's radicalism. As to why the material gathered
by Marx was never published or taken up in later
works, or even the reasons for its reappearance so
long after Marx's death, Marcuse says not a word.

It is difficult to stress strongly enough just
how extraordinary Marcuse's treatment of these manuscripts must have been at the time. Out of a total
of 140 pages, Marcuse focuses on little more than a
dozen. The whole essay appears as if Marcuse only
wants us to read...and <u>Philosophical Manuscripts of
1844</u>. Philosphy, in this essay of 1932, appears to
be everywhere and to explain everything; it is the
key word for all the discussions; it is the medium
for all analyses; it is made to appear as Marx's
true mode of discourse: philosophy can be found
behind each word of the manuscript and philosophical
categories can be retraced in each and every one of
Marx's later concepts, be it labour, private property or communism. The contrast between the two texts
is astounding; so much so that at times it is difficult not to wonder whether Marcuse is really referring to the manuscripts in question. Yet all the
references I have been able to follow up are correct, all the quotations rigorously rendered, and
none of them are cited in such a way as to be gross-
ly at odds with the context. Heidegger's method of
working, Marcuse's most important debt to his former
mentor, if a strange one, is nevertheless a scrupulous one. The interpretation Marcuse puts forward in
this essay, however bold or farfetched it may appear, is one which finds firm support in the text,
and we have good reason to believe that it is one
which he found in the text itself.

3.3 From Concrete Philosophy to Alienated Labour

That Marcuse appears to present an interpretation
which is exclusively philosophical in character and
intent should not mislead us. This essay on "The
Foundation of Historical Materialism" constitutes a
crucial point in Marcuse's career, and it represents
a shift not toward, but away from philosophical
preoccupations as such. It is really possible to
speak of a new meeting with Marx. It constitutes a
second encounter with the founder of a tradition
which informs Marcuse's writings from the very be-

ginning, and which plays into virtually every single
piece Marcuse ever wrote (18). The subject of this
essay, the Paris manuscripts, represents far more to
Marcuse than some early writings. They illustrate a
whole new dimension to the entire marxist heritage.
It is this heritage Marcuse will be rethinking in a
process which will be echoed throughout all of his
later writings. The process starts and takes shape
in the essay of 1932.

Three points are essential in this context.
Marcuse now speaks of "the question of the historical conditions and the bearer of revolution", explicitly relates his interpretation to "the theory of
the class struggle" and to the "dictatorship of the
proletariat", and speaks of the "praxis of transcendence" as "the work of the working class" (19).
"Radical action" alone no longer forms the focal
point for his research, but is joined by the whole
body of revolutionary theory that Marx elaborates in
the course of a lifetime.

The second point is no less important. The few
commentators to have addressed themselves to this
1932 essay have invariably pointed to the presence
of Heideggerian undertones and Heideggerian philosophical categories (20). Yet the concepts and vocabulary used by Marcuse in this piece should not obscure the very different perspective in which they
are used, even in relation to the period 1928-32.
For example, the idea of "authentic existence" which
has been seen as central to the essay receives a
treatment which is radically different from anything
Heidegger may ever have intended and it bears no or
little resemblance to Marcuse's use of the concept
in the "Contributions..."(21).

The third point which makes this 1932 essay
different from any of Marcuse's previous work is the
introduction of the idea of human labour as the
fundamental category of a revised theory of liberation (22). According to Marcuse the manuscripts show
that the concept of labour in Marx is not merely a
technical term for political economy. It has definite and direct implications for a wider theory of
freedom. It is this new theory of liberation which
forms the directing perspective for Marcuse's original and powerful re-interpretation of Marx. Its key
elements are as follows. The idea of freedom itself
should be understood in relation to the explicit
definition of "true communism" given in these manuscripts. All the characteristics of a "reified" social order can now be seen as rooted in the fundamental social processes Marx describes as "alienated

labour". The development and character of these processes under late capitalism can in turn be retraced
to the crucial ontological role of labour. The further implications of this analysis of labour will
moreover yield a more definite outline of the potential for human freedom.

The theory of liberation which guides Marcuse's
interpretation does not appear as such in the text.
It is presented in table 3. Marcuse characteristically seeks to develop it from the text itself. The
argument consists largely of a dialogue between
orthodox marxism and a distinct reading of Hegel
through Feuerbach, a dialogue whose crucial elements
are provided by the newly recovered manuscripts -
and it is from this dialogue that the leading perspective progressively emerges.

Where the manuscripts are invaluable, says
Marcuse, is not in showing Marx dealing for the
first time with political economy in a sustained
manner. It is the way in which he does so and the
context in which this happens. What we see in the
manuscripts that we cannot see elsewhere is Marx
returning to the set of problems upon which Hegel
founds his whole philosophy and developing totally
new and original answers. These problems are those
with which Hegel deals in his The Phenomenology of
Mind, especially the famous section on "Domination
and Servitude" (23). Marx does not seek to provide
us with a new philosophy, but in the course of his
critique of classical political economy, the philosophical discussions have allowed him to forge the
conceptual tools needed for a theory of revolution -
a theory which allows him not only to transcend the
framework of political economy but also the stark
realities upon which it is founded. Marx's emerging
social theory is not philosophical, but it is rooted
in particular philosophical problems, and by grasp-
ing Marx's solution to these, we shall be better
able to grasp the full scope of his thinking. These
points are summarized by Marcuse as follows: "What
must be seen and understood is that economics and
politics have become the economico-political basis
of the theory of revolution through a quite particular, philosophical interpretation of human essence
and its historical realization" (24).

To emphasise the full scope of Marx's new theory of revolution and its clear philosophical origins, Marcuse brings up in his introductory remarks
the famous passage on "true communism" (25). In the
third manuscript Marx states that it is "the genuine
resolution of the conflict between man and nature

Table 3 (*)

Assumptions and logical implications of Marcuse's new theory
of liberation in "The Foundation of Historical Materialism".

ASS 1   Society is the totality of human activities and rela-
        tions as they stand at a particular point in history.

ASS 2   a) All different kinds of activities influence all
        others.
            b) No one set of activities fully determine all
        others.
            c) The activities performed as labour and the con-
        ditions in which they are performed are nevertheless
        decisive for the maintenance and/or evolution of socie-
        ty.

ASS 3   By labour is understood any purposeful and disciplined
        activity aiming at the transformation of a given envi-
        ronment (or part thereof) with a view to enhance the
        fulfilment of biological or acquired needs.

ASS 4   The overall setting for these activities is given at
        any particular point in history by:
            a) The natural environment in which the society is
        situated.
            b) The transformation of that environment by human
        labour up to that point in history.
            c) The mode of production of society.

ASS 5   Marx's statement that man is a species-being, and a
        natural sensuous and objective being, should be under-
        stood as follows:
            a) Man is free only if all men exist in the deve-
        loped wealth of their natural resources.
            b) More specifically, the development of each indi-
        vidual's intellectual and physical faculties is depen-
        dent upon a parallel development in all men; the wealth
        of developed humanity is thus dependent upon the very
        diverse and often unique combinations of powers, skills
        and talents developed by each single individual.
            c) Human needs and powers have all a natural foun-
        dation in man's basic biological make-up.
            d) Man's original and fundamental destitution for-
        ces him in a constant state of interaction with nature,
        first to satisfy his most elementary needs, later to
        develop his powers and faculties, as well as his origi-
        nal and acquired needs.
            e) Man has a unique potential, through labour, to
        act upon any part of his environment, limited only the

the operation of physical laws.

f) Human needs and powers are susceptible of considerable development through social and cultural forces, in turn dependent upon man's interaction with nature or derivatives thereof.

g) Human senses are susceptible of considerable development and refinement through the influence of social and cultural forces.

ASS 6   Labour is the nexus of all of man's fundamental interactions with nature.

ASS 7   The development of civilisation is dependent upon man's ability, in the individual or collective processes of labour, to:

a) recognise the alien character of nature, and of the laws governing it.

b) develop the powers and skills necessary to transform the given environment.

c) develop new or changed needs and sensitivities, directly, by virtue of the requirements and possibilities of the labour activities, or indirectly, as a consequence of the changes his labour has brought to the environment.

d) impart upon objects or any other part of the environment the mark of these powers and needs.

e) use and build upon the transformed environment to further the development of his powers and needs.

f) understand himself in the labour he performs upon the world and in the world as transformed by his labour.

Implication 1:   Human nature will at any point in history be primarily determined by:

a) the basic biological foundation as developed through labour up to that point in history.

b) the character of the environment as transformed by labour at that point in history (Ass 4 & 7).

Implication 2:   Human nature is in this sense both internal and external to man (Imp. 1).

Implication 3:   Similarly, man's potential for further development, his "historical essence", depends upon:

a) the potentialities for maintaining and for further transforming the natural and socialised environment of a given community or society.

b) The forms and modalities of the dominant labour activities performed by the members of the community or society (Ass 5, 6, & 7).

Implication 4: "Historical essence" in the above sense is the product of a historical development and is dependent upon the general evolution of the community or society. It is both internal and external to man (Ass 5 & Imp. 3).

Implication 5: The development of human nature implies that man to a very large extent had to "externalise" and "objectify" his powers, sensitivities and needs into a transformed environment (Ass 5, 6 & Imp. 1, 2, 3, 4).

ASS 8 In advanced societies, alongside the general processes listed in Assumption 10, labour potentially allows the individual to:

a) develop his own individual skills, talents, sensitivities and needs.

b) understand and recognize himself in the object of his labour.

c) understand and relate to others through the labour that is performed in co-operation with others.

d) understand and relate to others through the objects created by this labour,

e) understand and relate to the social world as a creation of fellow men, in history and in the present.

f) understand and directly participate through his own labour in the global process of maintenance and/or transformation of internal and external human nature carried out through the total labour of society.

ASS 9 Human freedom is a function of the character and conditions of the labour activities which are performed by the individual member of a community/society. In particular it depends upon:

a) the degree to which each individual chooses to engage in individual or collective labour out of his own needs and for the purpose of trying his own powers, skills and talents.

b) the degree to which each individual in the labour activities fulfills his existing needs and sensitivities, finds room for new needs and/or refined senses, as well as develops his powers, skills and talents.

c) possibly also the degree to which these labour activities sustain and to an extent fulfill the need to transform nature "in accordance with the laws of beauty".

d) the degree to which these labour activities allow for a full and equal participation in the collective freedom to maintain and develop the attained level of civilisation, either directly, through these labour activities themselves, or by other channels.

ASS 10 Freedom is the measure to which such free labour finds place, and the measure to which the processes described in Assumptions 7 and 8 subsequently take their full effect. Complete freedom is a society which allows such free labour to the full.

ASS 11   a)   The process of "externalization" and "objecti-fication", as described above, can lead men to regard their own creation as alien and beyond their control.
   b)   Widespread alienation is likely to occur in a society when its members, or a large majority thereof, are not in a position to engage freely in labour acti-vities, and to jointly determine the evolution of so-ciety.
   c)   When labour is alienated, none of the processes described in Assumption 10 and 11 will have their full and undistorted effect.
   d)   Widespread and extended alienation of labour will lead to a global process of reification, whereby all members of society progressively will be led to regard social objects and institutions as immutable and beyond human control altogether.
   e)   Widespread and extended alienation will affect the "historical essence", as defined above.

ASS 12 Post first world war capitalism (late capitalism, ad-vanced capitalism) is characterised by an unprecedented measure of reification, rooted in all round and extreme forms of alienated labour and in the particular insti-tution of private property.

ASS 13 Advanced capitalism fulfills all the necessary condi-tions for a successful transition to socialism, and has long done so. That a socialist revolution has not taken place is due to:
   a)   the unprecedented and pervasive power of the processes of alienation and reification.
   b)   insufficient knowledge of the processes leading to - and from - the attained level and form of civili-sation.
   c)   insufficient economic and historical analysis showing the concrete forms of such processes at the present point in history.

ASS 14 The widespread, extreme and long lasting process of alienation and reification characteristic of late capi-talism has progressively lead to a total perversion of man's historical essence as a "species being".

Implication 6: Hence a radical change in society can only

take place as a total change, and this must happen before long to revert the impact of the processes of alienation and reification (Ass 2, 13 & 14).

ASS 15 Men wish to have greater freedom, as defined in Assumptions 12 and 13.

Implication 7: The proletariat, if made aware:
        a) through better knowledge of the processes of civilisation
        b) through acquaintance with analyses showing these processes in relation to present history, that
        c) existing class societies frustrate the full fulfillment of their needs, sensitivities and powers, and
        d) threaten the very potential for such development in future, will engage or support radical collective action to change society as a whole; they will in other words engage in the praxis of transcendence. (Ass 5, 11, 12, 13 & 14)

Implication 8: For those who wish to change society, the most promising strategy is to spread this awareness by increasing the knowledge of the preceding propositions and by developing/supporting the economic and historical analyses that can underpin them. (All of the above)

(*) The differences with table 2 should make the radical shift from the earlier pro-Heideggerian positions immediately apparent. The "historical movement" disappears as a central concern. Labour enters as the all determining philosophical category, as is stated in Assumptions 3, 6, 7, 8, 9 and 10 in table 3. Instead of the immutable "existential needs" in Assumptions 6 to 9 in table 2, it is the concept of "species being" and "free labor" which serves to define human needs and human nature (Assumption 5 and the above). Freedom is now primarily defined in relation to labour (Assumptions 9 and 10 in table 3) as opposed to the "existential needs" (Assumptions 8 and 9 in table 2). Reification is now solely a function of alienated labour (Assumptions 11 and 12 in 3) as opposed to social factors (Assumption 11, t. 2), or Heidegger's phenomenological analyses (Assumptions 16 and 17, t. 2). The process of liberation rests no longer upon the Heideggerian "concern" or "care" (Assumption 17, t. 2) but uniquely on the Marxist theory of historical materialism (Assumption 13, t.3).

and between man and man - the true resolution of the strife between existence and essence, between objectification and self-confirmation, between freedom and necessity, between the individual and the species. Communism is the riddle of history solved, and

it knows itself to be this solution" (26). This
description of the freedom to come is certainly
different from anything Marx may have come upon in
reading Smith, Sismondi or Ricardo. The explicitly
philosophical formulation also suggests that Marx
has more in mind than a technical or scientific
critique of political economy. Marx's critique
points to a whole range of social processes characteristic of industrial capitalism. Competition,
private property and the division of labour are
elements of unfreedom in which "the historical-
social world of men is transformed into an alien
world of money and commodities" (27). This state of
affairs, according to Marcuse, "has often been described under the heading of 'alienation', 'estrangement' and 'reification' and is a widely known
element of Marxist theory" (28).

Having set the stage, Marcuse proceeds to provide a detailed analysis of the concept of labour,
which he sees as the central category of Marxist
economics, as it appears in the manuscripts. The
situation of general alienation, or reification,
Marcuse tells us, is rooted in "alienated labor",
and, furthermore, Marx thought so too. In fact it is
one of Marx's major discoveries brought out by the
confrontation between political economy and the
perspective of German idealist philosophy. This can
literally be seen in the text of the manuscripts.

> "The way in which Marx intends to bring out and
> demonstrate alienation and estrangement seems
> initially to proceed completely on the ground
> of traditional political economy and its theo-
> rems. Marx significantly starts by dividing his
> investigation into the three traditional con-
> cepts of political economy: 'The Wages of La-
> bour', 'The Profit of Capital' and 'The Rent of
> Land'. But more important, and a sign pointing
> in a completely new direction, is the fact that
> this division into three is soon exploded and
> abandoned: 'From page xxii to the end of the
> manuscript Marx wrote across the three columns,
> disregarding the headings. The text of these
> six pages (xxii to xxvii) is given in the
> present book under the title 'Estranged La-
> bor''" (29).

The new-found concept of "alienated labor" serves
Marx to regroup and re-organize a variety of material from political economy and his own observations
and judgements on the conditions of the working

class at the time. Marcuse briefly retraces the familiar analyses by Marx, brings up the inner relation of "estranged labor" with property, describes in one movement the degrading and inhuman working conditions and shows the alien, commodity character of the objects produced under such conditions.

Marcuse then asks whether this description of "alienated labor" should really be understood as "a simple economic fact", as Marx would have us believe. He answers, not unreasonably, that it should not. Marx speaks of "human essential powers", "man's essential being", of a "loss of realization", of labour producing "itself and the worker as a commodity" and describes the working man as forced to "sell himself and his human identity". Thus, "even in this depiction of the 'economic fact' of alienated labor, the simple economic description is constantly broken through: the economic 'condition' of labor is cast back into the 'existence' of the working man" (30). Marcuse develops similar considerations with respect to the analysis of "private property" as conceptualized in the Paris Manuscripts.

It is on this basis that Marcuse, through detailed analyses, is able to bring forth two major conclusions concerning the role of labour in Marx's writings. Firstly, given that alienated labour is the negation of all humanity in the worker, labour when non-alienated - labour that is truly "free" - must be seen "as the true expression and realisation of human essence" (31). Secondly, insofar as labour pertains to man's potentialities and creative powers in his relation to nature in entirety, labour in general can be understood as a fundamental ontological category of "human existence". Marcuse at this point explicitly warns his reader against the "often misused term ontology", but, finding support in two sentences from Marx himself, nevertheless asserts that the analysis of "alienated labor" reveals an underlying "human ontology" in Marx (32). It is this new Marxist ontology that Marcuse later develops. Marcuse's starting point, it should be noted, and one to which he constantly returns, is the idea of "free labor" implied in the concept of "alienated labor". The ontological determinations of man and "human essence" that Marcuse brings forth all rest on a distinctive interpretation of the concept of labour in Marx (33).

3.4 Ontology, Human Ontology and Political Praxis

Rarely have early research papers caused so much controversy as the Economic and Philosophical Manuscripts of 1844 (34). To do justice to both Marx's text and Marcuse's interpretation of it would be a hopelessly ambitious task, and it will not be attempted here (35). We shall consider only the high points of Marcuse's exposition, his method of research and presentation, and the difficulties and ambiguities of this first interpretation of the Paris Manuscripts.

It is essential to realise that Marcuse develops an argument directed against the predominant Kantian or Neo-Kantian reading of Marx of the last decades (36). The Hegelian roots of Marxism are again and again stressed in that essay, and it is Marx's debt to the Hegel of The Phenomenology which is constantly brought to the foreground. This approach allows Marcuse to project a particularly forceful image, and it also helps him to bring out several important facets of Hegel's considerable influence on Marx, not only in the manuscripts, but in his works as a whole. It does also suggest, however, a far greater measure of identity between Marx and Hegel than that actually argued by Marcuse. This comes out clearly in the context of Marcuse's other works, for instance Reason and Revolution, where a substantially unchanged argument serves to bring out what are also fundamental differences between the two thinkers and their respective overall approach (37). The distinctly non-Hegelian elements, aspects where Marx shows himself as an economist, a revolutionary or as a Feuerbachian rather than a Hegelian, tend to slide into the background in this 1932 essay. Yet those aspects constitute the main line of the interpretation - in this respect Marcuse remains much closer to the text itself than it would first appear (38).

This tension in Marcuse's interpretation is nowhere more marked than in his account of the famous category of "species being" where an essentially materialist, humanist, man-centred perspective is uneasily merged with elements which owe more to Hegel or Heidegger than either Marx or Feuerbach. Yet it is the latter who is brought out at the beginning of this discussion - Marcuse for instance stresses that "the 'establishment of true materialism and of real science' is described (by Marx) as Feuerbach's 'great achievement'" (39). The crucial passage chosen by Marcuse is also clearly Feuerbachian (40). "Man is a species-being, not only be-

cause in practice and in theory he adopts the species (his own as well as those of other things) as
his object, but - and this is only another way of
expressing it - also because he treats himself as
the actual, living species; because he treats himself as a _universal_ and therefore free being" (41).
What we are to understand by the phrase "species
being" (gattungswesen) has always been a little
mysterious. The underlying idea is that men are not
self-sufficient creatures, and are only fully human
by virtue of membership of the species mankind. Only
together, in communion with each other and with the
full awareness of their interdependence can they
exist as true individuals (42). To state that man is
species-being is to state that a given man or woman
is more than just that given individual, or rather
expresses in that individuality something of the
entire spectrum of potentialities and limitations of
human beings.

For Marcuse, the term species implies also
something more: "The species of a being is that
which this being is according to its 'stock' and
'origin'; it is the 'principle' of its being which
is common to all the particular features of what is:
the _general_, (common, all round) _being_ of all these
instances" (43). In other words, each category of
beings has a sort of internal mechanism, or set of
such mechanisms, which determines its potentialities
and limitations. What is specific and characteristic
of man as a species is his particular ability to
perceive, act upon and bring out such arrays of
potentialities and limitations in every object,
plant or animal, including himself. Man as a species
being appears as uniquely able to relate freely and
universally to beings. He is "free" in the sense
that he can use any avenue, any thinkable or conceivable way of acting upon or perceiving a given
being; he is "universal" in the sense that no being
is in principle inaccessible (given time) to him.

This unique ability, this freedom and this
universality, man realises through work, non-alienated, "free" work. It is through labour that he "is
not limited to the particular actual state of the
(given) being and his immediate relationship to it,
but can take the being as it is in its essence
beyond its immediate, particular, actual state; he
can recognise and grasp the _possibilities_ contained
in every being. He can exploit, alter, mould, treat
and take further ('pro-duce') any being according to
its 'inherent standard'" (44).

Marcuse argues that the conception of man as a

"species being" is contained and expressed within
Marx's description of "alienated labor", just as the
idea of "free labor" is implicit in Marx's negative
formulations of labour under the capitalist order.
But the latter also implies something more: man can
take any object according to its "inherent standards", and this includes himself qua "species
being". Here man attains his greatest and most potent freedom, and it is also there that his most
important mission lies - in the "'self-realization'
and 'self-creation' of man" (45).

Marcuse is ambiguous at this point in the argument. The logical progression from then on would be
to move to something akin to Hegelian cosmology,
whereby man could only complete his full and predetermined self-development through universal, god-
like contribution to the full development of every
object, plant or animal around him, with the end
product merging into a new "Absolute Spirit" or an
atheist version of the garden of Eden, with the lion
peacefully watching the lambs grazing nearby, and
the subject-object dualism finally overcome.

This is not the road Marcuse chooses to follow.
In the ontology he puts forward at this point, man
is at the centre, and his freedom is quite open-
ended, only determined by his/her own needs and
desires. Marcuse now states that man must "transform
the objects of this (objective) world into organs of
his life, which becomes effective in and through
them" (46). Elsewhere he explicitly speaks of "the
thesis that nature (is) a means for man" (47), and
the substance of his argument supports the idea of a
social ontology which is primarily man-centred.

The Hegelian trail is not left entirely behind,
however. Mankind has the power to re-create the
world to help and promote the varied needs of its
members; but these needs themselves are not simply
material or dictated by the imperative of sheer
survival. Mankind is to develop and satisfy equally
its intellectual, emotional and creative needs. This
includes artistic needs, and it is in this respect
that Marcuse comes closest to re-affirming the disregarded "inherent standards" in the objects shaped
by man's industry. Marcuse stresses that man "can
produce 'in accordance with the laws of beauty' and
not merely in accordance with the standard of his
own needs" (48). This is the first reference to an
idea which will play an increasing role in Marcuse's
later works, an idea which is most forcefully evoked
in Eros and Civilization. It is the ideal of beauty
and artistic sensibility that mankind has its best

hope for a civilization not dominated by an all-
pervasive and ultimately aimless "technological
rationality". For Marcuse there is no doubt that
"man does not have objects merely as the environment
of his immediate life activity and does not treat
them merely as objects of his immediate needs".
Moreover, "in this freedom man 'reproduces the whole
of nature', and through transformation and appropriation furthers it, along with its own life, even
when this production does not satisfy an immediate
need" (49).
    Let us consider this latter idea in more de-
tail. The difficulty in this passage is that Marcuse
describes all at once a future state of affairs and
its reality in an "alienated", distorted form under
the present state of affairs. "Free labor", as the
Feuerbachian idea of "species being", demands that
the present order should be totally transformed, for
only in a new and radically different societal organisation would such a co-operative and communitarian
form of work be possible. Yet it also expresses
something which already exists. It expresses man's
singular position in the animal order whereby he is,
on the one hand, totally dependent upon his physical
environment for the overwhelming majority of his
needs, and on the other hand, far more at liberty to
alter this physical environment than any other
living being. In this interdependence lies the "unity of man with nature". It is this idea that Marx
renders by saying that man "can only express his
life in real sensuous objects" (50).
    This same idea, however, can also be stated in
terms of more traditional philosophical categories,
such as the subject-object opposition and the idea
of "human essence". This terminology is partially
used by Marx. The Hegelian category of "objectification" refers in Hegel to the variety of processes
through which the Absolute Spirit achieves its eventual fusion with the world outside "pure thought".
The first step of that process is for a part of this
Absolute Spirit to become embodied in material objects, transforming them into new entities, different both from the original objects and the element
of thought entering them. The creative tension between the Spirit and the new object leads to further
transformation in both the object and the Spirit.
The synthesis which emerges constitutes a new stage
in the self-creation of the Absolute Spirit. After
several such stages the Absolute Spirit eventually
changes from mere potentiality to the actual reality
(51). In Marcuse's reading of Marx the same general

framework serves to describe the ascent of man
through history to his final (or at least qualitati-
vely different) stage of man as a full "species
being". It is the reality of this potential for a
deeper, conscious and total unity with nature that
Marcuse describes as "human-essence". Man, to become
fully himself, must invest the best of himself in
objects, leave his mark upon nature and develop his
talents in the struggle with nature. Only by becoming "objectified" in nature can he create the
material and spiritual civilisation upon which further advances toward his full realization as "species being" can be achieved. Yet in a way similar to
Hegel's ideas on the Absolute Spirit, this must
almost necessarily be done by first giving the social objects he has created a life of their own and
by "losing sight" of his own intimate relation with
the new objective world he has created out of nature. This is why the advance of civilisation so
easily can entail the "alienation" of creative man
and the subsequent "reification" of human artifacts
into alien objects outside of man's control. In this
transformation of the necessary "externalization"
into "alienation" and "objectification" into "reification" lies the general drama. Marcuse states these
ideas as follows: "In this division of human essence
- man being itself an objective being - is rooted
the fact that objectification can become reification, and that externalization can become alienation; it is what makes possible for man to completely 'lose' the objective world as part of his essence
and let it become independent and overpowering - a
possibility which has become a reality in alienated
labor and private property" (52).
      Marcuse develops the argument further by seek-
ing to show how Marx, with the help of Feuerbach,
reinterprets the insights gained from the German
Idealist tradition, insights which in Kant or Hegel
appear as ontological, epistemological or metaphysical statements. The reason that man can only develop
his essence through nature is that at bottom, he is
nature. It is no Hegelian "Spirit" which faces nature and transforms it, it is man as a physical,
natural, sensuous being with needs and desires. In
this discussion of man's "sensuous" nature, Marcuse
depicts Marx as reaching back, via Feuerbach and
Hegel, to Kant's idea of sensuousness as the totality of senses through which we can perceive the
world, and which alone determines the extent to
which objects "affect" man as they are given to him.
For Feuerbach as for Marx, the fact that man is in

this way posited by nature has implications which go beyond the question of the "a priori" of human knowledge. It conditions his entire relation to the world and to himself. Man is limited, dependent and conditioned by the objects affecting him. Man needs the objects outside him. His senses are not merely distorting lenses through which he simply looks at the world and attempts to apprehend it intellectually. They are necessary contact points with the world, and they are channels through which the world imposes itself upon man. For Marx man is a needy, suffering and passionate creature, and the object of his needs and his passions is something outside him, something beyond his immediate control and with which he has to interact. Marcuse at this point emphasises that "distress and neediness here do not describe individual modes of man's behaviour at all; they are features of his whole existence" (53).

Marcuse stresses that Marx's aim in insisting upon the physical and suffering aspects of man is to bring out "the concrete nature of man, united with the world, objective and natural, in opposition to Hegel's abstract and absolute 'being', detached from pre-established 'naturalness' and positing both itself and all objectivity" (54). He now argues that if Marx follows Feuerbach on this point, it is to Hegel he returns when dealing with the second and crucial aspects of man's interaction with nature, that brought about by his own activity.

Marcuse begins his analysis with reference to the famous theses on Feuerbach, written in 1845. These short considerations are usually understood as representing Marx's most definite break with all previous philosophical preoccupations, as well as the transition from the humanist and philosophical materialism of Feuerbach to an all-pervasive, unqualified and "scientific" materialism (55). What Marcuse proposes is an altogether different interpretation. These theses show Marx moving away from Feuerbach, but not towards a more radical philosophical materialism. Marx, on the contrary returns partially to Hegel and to the German idealist tradition, and adopts a position somewhere between materialism and idealism, a position wherein free, conscious and co-operative labour plays the crucial mediating role. This is how the central concept of "practice" - which so sharply opposes him to Feuerbach - should be understood. This is usually understood with reference to the eleventh and most widely quoted thesis: "The philosophers have only interpreted the world, and in various ways: the point, however, is to

change it" (56). Practical, revolutionary activity
will resolve philosophical problems by changing the
world in which these problems arise, and only in
such activity lie the real solutions for mankind's
problem.

This more common understanding of "practical
activity" is also present in Marcuse's essay under
the heading "practice of transcendence". But he
argues that a more fundamental sense must be attached to Marx's reflections on Feuerbach in these
theses. As we have just seen, Marcuse argues that
for Feuerbach as for Marx man as a "species being"
stands in a double relation to nature. He is able to
relate freely and universally to any being and he is
also posited by the objects existing outside of himself as a consequence of his limited natural being.
For Feuerbach, as interpreted by Marcuse, the central nexus of these multiple interactions between
man and nature and the potential for their full
unity is "intuition" ("Anschauung"). For Marx it is
labour. "Free labor" is the human practical activity
par excellence. It is the "vital activity" through
which man acts upon nature in a "free" and "universal" manner. Man's knowledge of the external world
does not come through a contemplative, passive,
theoretical attitude, but through interaction with
nature through labour, and in which man expresses
and fulfils his desires and his skills. In other
words, "objects are not ... primarily objects of
intuition, but of needs, and as such objects of the
powers, abilities and instincts of man" (57).

It is in labour that man meets the world; it is
through labour that man understands the world; and
it is with labour that man changes this world so as
to transform it into his world, one which bears his
mark and one in which he can recognise himself and
what he is. Labour is the fundamental ontological
relation between man and the world. It is in labour
and through labour that thought, ideas and creativity can be imparted to the world as a force capable
of altering this world. It is through labour that
man ultimately transforms himself. This, presumably,
is how Marcuse wants us to understand Marx's first
and in this context most important theses on Feuerbach.

"The chief defect of all hitherto existing
materialism - that of Feuerbach included - is
that the thing, reality, sensuousness, is
conceived only in the form of the object or of
contemplation, but not as human sensuous acti-

vity, practice, not subjectively. Hence it
happened that the active side, in contradis-
tinction to materialism, was developed by idealism - but only abstractly, since, of course,
idealism does not know real, sensuous activity
as such. Feuerbach wants sensuous objects,
really differentiated from the thought objects,
but he does not conceive human activity itself
as objective activity. Hence, in the Essence of
Christianity, he regards the theoretical attitude as the only genuinely human attitude,
while practice is conceived and fixed only in
its dirty-judaical form of appearance." (58)

Against the purely materialist Marx portrayed by
Engels, Marcuse opposes Marx visualising man expressing his humanity, - a mixture of desire, ambitions
and creative thinking - through his activity (epitomized in "free labor") which profoundly changes this
world. Ideas, ideologies and human meaning matter,
if translated into an action upon the world - primarily in the form of labour. Inversely, for Marcuse
to advance this position means that the world of
thought and meaning looming largely in "On the Problem of the Dialectic" must now be seen as profoundly limited in relation to the physical environment
that man must master. From this essay onwards,
alongside the centrality of labour in human existence, there will be a far greater attention in Marcuse's thinking to the material and biological dimension of life. Much of the later Freudian interpretation bears the mark of this second and decisive
encounter with Marx.
    As emphasised earlier, Marcuse aims in this
description to do more than depict a future state of
affairs where the full unity with nature will be
brought about by the communitarian and conscious
action of a united mankind. He also claims to uncover the underlying structures of the present social
organization. To establish firmly the true role and
character of labour in existing societies is already
an important step toward human liberation, insofar
as it makes possible the visualization of a potentially better society implied by the idea of "free
labor". The demystification of labour is a constant
concern in Marx's work. It is in and through labour
that man can see himself for what he is - the buil-
der of human material and intellectual civilization
which reflects his essential and collective powers.
"The object of labor is ... the objectification of
man's species life; for he duplicates himself not

only, as in consciousness, intellectually, but also
actively, in reality, and therefore he contemplates
himself in a world which he has created (59). This
in turn implies that all the things which constitute
our daily environment and which shape our lives are
neither simply given nor simply natural. The world
is socially created and socially maintained, and it
has emerged from the efforts of a succession of
human generations through a long historical struggle
with nature. Labour transforms the natural environment into a social and historical environment,
created and owned by men and women. Furthermore, the
objects that are created, all bring to light the
existence and reality of other men and women in the
given society, or beyond it. This Marcuse states as
follows: "The sphere of objects in which labor takes
place is precisely the sphere of common vital activity: it is in and through the objects of labor that
the other appears to man in his reality" (60).
Finally, the objects themselves constitute the most
real and essential bonds between men. It is in this
sense that we must understand Marx's statement in
The Holy Family that ".. the object as being for man
or as the objective being of man is at the same time
the existence of man for other men, his human relation to other man, the social relation of man to
man" (61). Labour as the expression of man's essential powers - qua species being - is a philosophical
tenet which runs through the whole of Marx.
    It is important to stress that Marcuse's "human
ontology" should perhaps be understood as "social
ontology" insofar as it is man-in-society, the real
focus of Marcuse's reconstruction of Marx's argument
in the manuscripts. This ontology does not deal with
man in general, but with man as struggling to build
and maintain with his fellow men a common and organised society of mutually dependent individuals.
Moreover, it is the sensuous, needy and passionate
man depicted by Marx which is at the centre of this
ontology; it is no longer the Heideggerian "Being
There". But the question arises, whether Marcuse is
primarily concerned with ontology, i.e. the branch
of philosophy aiming to discover fundamental relations and invariant structures enduring through all
times and all places? It is even doubtful whether
the term "social ontology", limiting ontological
considerations to social realities and to mankind's
history of living in society is adequate. In perhaps
the best researched article on the question Morton
Schoolman argues that the use of "ontological categories by Marcuse should only be understood in a

metaphorical sense, insofar that they do not refer
to ontology at all, but to a wider philosophy of
history, which is only fully comprehensible within a
marxist perspective" (62). This finds support in
various statements by Marcuse in the 1933 essay on
labour, upon which Schoolman in particular had focused: "It should have become clear to what extent
labor is a specifically _historical_ category of human
existence _as_ historical existence"; and a little
later: "The concept of domination and servitude,
used by Hegel as categories of human existence,
designate here a universal historical fact: servitude means the enduring and constant binding of the
praxis of the whole of human existence to material
production and reproduction, in the service and
under the direction of another existence... and its
needs" (63). Yet the final comments of the substantive sections of the 1932 essay point in another
direction: "From every point of approach and in all
directions this theory, arising out of the philosophical critique and foundation of political economy,
proves itself to be a practical theory, a theory
whose immanent meaning (required by the nature of
its object), is a particular praxis; only a particular praxis can solve the problems peculiar to that
theory (64). The "praxis of transcendence" to which
this refers is a political praxis. It is upon the
goals and methods of this political praxis that the
theory rests.

    This essay also reveals the main threads of a
project which will only come to fruition in _Reason
and Revolution_: a close re-examination of the relationship Hegel-Marx. There is no mistaking Marcuse's
genuine sense of a rediscovery of forgotten insights, and a tone of amazement on occasion emerges
through a reasonably sober academic style. This is
perhaps best conveyed by the short penultimate paragraph: "Thus Marx has expressed in all clarity the
inner connection between revolutionary theory and
Hegel's philosophy. What seems amazing, as measured
by the critique - which is the result of a _philoso-
phical_ discussion - is the decline of later interpretations of Marx (even - _sit venia verbio_ - those
of Engels!) by people who believed they could reduce
Marx's relation to Hegel to the familiar transformation of Hegel's 'dialectic', which they also completely emptied of all content" (65).

3.5 The Redefinition of Human Liberation
It would be difficult to overstress the dramatic

consequences of this interpretation of the <u>Paris Ma-nuscripts</u> for Marcuse's theory of freedom. We noted in the last chapter how Marcuse's initial bold at-tempt to fuse a re-interpreted Marx with more recent philosophical findings progressively gave way to a more pronounced Heideggerianism, with an emphasis upon a dialectic centered around the existential meanings of the social world; this was compounded with a radical, but vague socialist humanism as the prime motor for a "concrete philosophy". The extra-ordinary material brought forth in the manuscripts changes all that. Marcuse develops anew a theory of human liberation, but this time virtually all its elements derive from a distinctive reading of Marx in which previous philosophical concerns play a much diminished role.

As regards freedom, labour now serves as the defining characteristic: "labor is the real expres-sion of human freedom" (66). This, it should be noted, is only true for labour which is genuinely "free" and "universal". Only in such labour can man as a "species being" "freely realize himself in the object of his labor" (67). It is a form and organi-zation of labour which implies - in sharp contrast to any form of "alienated labor" - that the relation to nature thereby established is more than the pro-duct of simple physical needs, but, on the contrary, emerges as a process of conscious social and histo-rical "self-creation" and "self-generation". Man as a "species being" will for the time be able to direct, collectively and individually, the process of interaction with nature in which he shapes both himself and his environment. He will be at one with the civilization he has created and recognize him-self in that civilization. It is in this sense that we must understand the process of (free) objec-tification - as opposed to that of reification - whereby for "man in society ... all objects become the objectification of himself, become objects which confirm and realize his individuality, become <u>his</u> objects: that is, man <u>himself</u> becomes the object" (68). "Free labor" implies that he can "turn his existence into the 'means' of his essence, can give himself his own reality, and himself produce himself and his 'objectivity'"(69).

Similarly, "private property" is a necessary consequence rather than the prerequisite for the "de-possession" of the worker in his relation to the object of his labour. "Private property" is a frozen behaviour pattern originating in the workers' own activities - not an immutable state of affairs and

not even a given socio-political "fact". "True property" implies that the object becomes an extension
of man himself, a part of his "human nature" and
something which completes, complements and expands
his being beyond itself. Against the capitalist
world of "commodities" there will be a "human world"
possessed by all and for all (70).

The analysis of "reification" that Marcuse
previously derived from Lukács and Heidegger now
receives a very different foundation. The concept of
"alienated labor" is now at the root of that analysis, and the relation with Marx's later more economic descriptions of the exploitation of workers'
labour power as the motor of developing capitalism
is direct and obvious. It is in the area of life
determined by work, and the conditions under which
labour is carried out, where the central defining
characteristics of the capitalist mode of existence
are found. The alienation of the worker from the
object of his labour, from others, from labour as a
truly human activity ("free labor") and ultimately
from himself (qua potential "species being") leads
unavoidably to "the domination of dead matter over
man". The wider "reification" process begins with
and is rooted in the particular character of labour
under capitalism, and it begins with the working man
himself. But "it also affects the non-worker - the
capitalist" (71). The capitalist shows himself "in a
state of being possessed, or being had, slavery in
the service of property" (72). Rather than a wicked
class commanding the course of events, the capita-
lists themselves are in the play of the wider social
forces they almost unconsciously nurture.

The revolution should not be a mere reversing
of roles, nor will the simple economic or legal
abolition of private property suffice. It must entail a transformation of man's nature and the emergence of a new community of individuals. It is this
idea that Marcuse seeks to express more forcefully
by an interpretation of Marx's references to "essence" or "essential powers" in the manuscripts. Marcuse argues that the transformation of this concept
in the manuscripts reveals Marx's newly gained insights. Contrary to the impression of a superficial
reading of The German Ideology may convey, Marx does
not reject the idea of a "human essence" altogether.
He attacks the purely philosophical, speculative and
abstract conception of the Young Hegelian as just
another bourgeois illusion. The conception advanced
in the manuscripts, on the contrary, serves to com-
bine the traditional connotations of a better poten-

tial for humanity, a dynamic force within each individual with a specific and very concrete idea of how
it is to be realized; this can only be done by
acting collectively to change the historical and
social world to make a reality of "species being".
"Human essence" thus refers to the sum of skills,
needs and aspirations which have developed through
interactions with nature and the progressive building of a rich intellectual and material civilization. Capitalism - and the stages preceding it - has
not only brought about a certain type of social
reality, a given "facticity" and a particular form
of "existence" which shapes man in almost every way;
it has also brought about a potential for the good
life, opened new and untold possibilities for maste-
ring the natural environment and developed in man a
whole range of new needs and skills - in short, a
definite historical "human essence". This point is
stated in the following passage:

> "To play off essence (the determinants of "the"
> man) and facticity (his given concrete factici-
> ty) against each other is to miss completely
> the new standpoint which Marx had already as-
> sumed at the outset of his investigations. For
> Marx essence and facticity, the situation of
> essential theory and the situation of factual
> history, are no longer separate regions or
> levels independent of ech other: the historical
> experience of man is taken up into the defini-
> tion of his essence" (73).

This passage is extremely valuable because it shows
that in 1932 Marcuse already gave a specific social
and historical content to the idea of "human essence". And it is with this content in mind that we
should understand the often cited denunciation of
capitalism as "a catastrophe affecting human essence" which must "condemn any mere economic or political reform to failure from the outset" (74). Marcuse
refers in this context to the specific potential for
a good life and a transformed human nature that
historical development has made possible, a potential that further developments may endanger (75).
That given social developments can - in Marcuse's
words "pervert human essence" - will be shown only
too dramatically by the events in Germany in the
years that followed.
It remains to be seen how Marcuse was to sketch
a new conception of human liberation on the basis of
these ideas. Knowledge, which played such a determi-

ning role in previous writings, retains an essential place in this conception but it is now firmly reinserted into the broader Marxist framework, and becomes operative only within this framework. The knowledge that matters is again that which helps men see reality as social and historical and something which they have shaped and can therefore change. Thus, in order to "break through reification", "the objective conditions must become human" and "they must be recognized and preserved as such" (76). A particular type of insights is required ("man's coming-to-be-for-himself"). It is a knowledge which is practical and exercised in practice ("no mere theoretical cognition or arbitrary, passive intuition"). It is a committing knowledge - "the recognition of the historical-social situation is ... in itself the recognition of a <u>mission</u> which demands and imposes a definite goal: the practical realization of a reality which is "relly human" demanded by and within this situation (77). From this it follows, and this is different from Marcuse's previous positions, that "the insight which defines this task is by no means available to everyone: it can only be known by those who are actually <u>entrusted with this task</u> by their socio-historical situation" (78). In other words, only the proletariat, who are the most exploited and most alienated class are able to take such knowledge as their own and act upon it (79). Yet theory has a role to play. "The praxis of transcendence must, <u>in order to be genuine transcendence</u>, reveal the conditions (pre-established by history) and appropriate them. Insight into objectification as insight into the historical and social situation of man reveals the historical conditions of this situation and so achieves the <u>practical force and concrete form</u> through which alone it can become the level of the revolution" (80). The fundamental role of theory in activating and consolidating the "consciousness of the proletariat" through which alone it can become a reality is explicitly affirmed. This will remain a central trait of all of Marcuse's later writings, with the exception, perhaps, of <u>One Dimensional Man</u>. If theory can not do so it becomes "mere" philosophy or ideology, as Marcuse later asserts in <u>Soviet Marxism</u>.

This 1932 essay on "The Foundation of Historical Materialism" constitutes a turning point in Marcuse's thinking in more than one way. It indicates a substantial shift from the degree of influence that Heidegger held over his work in the period 1928 to 1932. It shows a return to the sources, the re-discovery of a powerful and multi-sided Marx, whose work - far from being alien to classical German philosophy, draws from it the inspiration for a bold para-sociological theory of the human liberation. It means also that Marcuse is now able to base a comprehensive idea of the good society upon Marx's own texts, and develop his own idea of freedom from his interpretation of these texts. To elucidate the more definite features of this idea of freedom is the task to which we shall now turn.

NOTES

1. See Maguire, Marx's Paris Writings: An Analysis, Dublin: Gill & Macmillan, 1972, p. 147.
2. An earlier, but incomplete Russian edition was published in 1927.
3. On these point see MacLellan, The Thought of Karl Marx, op. cit., pp. 16-30.
4. The edition used here will be Marx, K., Economic and Philosophical Manuscripts of 1844 (EPM), Moscow: Progress Publishers, 1974. The expressions Paris Manuscripts or 1844 Manuscripts will be used interchangeably.
5. Herbert Marcuse, "The Foundation of Historical Materialism", Studies in Critical Philosophy, London: New Left Books, 1972.
6. On these various points see for instance Colletti, "Introduction" in Marx, Early Writings, op. cit.
7. "The Foundation of Historical Materialism", op. cit., p. 3, p. 156. The first reference refers to the English text, the second to the German original.
8. Marcuse, "Transcendental Marxism?", op. cit., p. 5, p. 306 my translation.
9. MacIntyre, Marcuse, op. cit., p. 48.
10. See Jay, The Dialectical Imagination, op. cit., pp. 41-85.
11. See Mehta, Martin Heidegger: The Way and the Vision, op. cit., p. 39.
12. 1977 interview: "Heidegger's Politics", op. cit., p. 39.
13. On Eros and Civilisation, see for instance Paul Robinson's comments in his The Sexual Radicals, op. cit., pp. 200-201; as for Soviet Marxism we shall have the occasion to consider Marcuse's treatment of Marx and the marxist tradition in more detail below.
14. See for instance Mézáros, Marx's Theory of Alienation, op. cit.; Maguire, J., Marx's Paris

Writings, op. cit.; Colletti, "Introduction" in
Marx, Early Writings, op. cit.; Graeme Duncan, Marx
and Mill: Two Views of Social Conflict and Social
Harmony, Cambridge University Press, 1973; Mandel,
E., The Formation of the Economic Thought of Karl
Marx: 1843 to 'Capital', Monthly Review Press, 1971;
Librairie Francois Maspéro, 1967; Fromm, E., Marx's
Concept of Man, USA New York, 1961; MacLellan, The
Thought of Karl Marx, op. cit.; Avineri, S. (Ed.),
Marx's Socialism, USA, Lieber-Atherton, Inc., 1972.
    15. The Russian version has been preferred as
being the fullest, most detailed and best annotated.
The recently published Penguin version (Marx, Early Writings, op. cit.) although far easier to read,
does not indicate the deleted passages, omits much
contextual information and fails to convey the provisional quality of the text. All references in the
following will be the 1974 edition, and page numbers
in Marcuse's text have accordingly changed.
    16. "Foundations of Historical Materialism",
op. cit., p. 3, p. 136.
    17. Ibid., translation modified.
    18. This does not mean that he does so every-
where explicitly. Eros and Civilization is probably
the best example in this context - see Robinson,
The Sexual Radicals, op. cit. pp. 201-202.
    19. "The Foundation of Historical Materia-
lism", op. cit., p. 29, p. 158, and p. 35, and p.
163.
    20. See Frankel, "Herbert Marcuse, 'Studies in
Critical Philosophy'", (Review), in Telos, No. 16,
Summer 1973, pp. 156-160; Jay, M., The Dialectical
Imagination, op. cit., pp. 74-75; Kellner, D., "Introduction to 'On Philosophical Foundation of the
Concept of Labor'", in Telos: No. 16, Summer 1973,
pp. 2-37.
    21. See Frankel, Ibid., p. 152.
    22. The importance of the category of labour
for Marcuse's thought can hardly be overstressed. It
is also what distinguishes his marxism from that of
the other "Western Marxists". Kellner, in "Introduction to 'On the Philosophical Foundation of the
Concept of Labor'", op. cit., for instance points
out that neither Korsch nor Lukács gave much attention to the role of labour in Marx. As for Marcuse's
later colleagues at the Institute of Social Research, it is noteworthy that Jay points to Marcuse's attitude toward the centrality of labour as
one of the most significant differences between
Marcuse on the one hand, and Horkeimer and Adorno on
the other; see Jay, The Dialectical Imagination, op.

cit., p. 79.
    23. Also rendered as "lordship and bondage";
see Hegel, F., The Phenomenology of Mind, London:
Allen and Unwin, 1931, pp. 228-240.
    24. "The Foundation of Historical Materia-
lism", 4, 137, translation modified; emphasis in the
text.
    25. Marx, EPM, 90.
    26. Cited in "The Foundation of Historical
Materialism", p. 5, p. 138.
    27. Ibid., p. 5-6, p. 138, translation modi-
fied.
    28. Ibid., p. 6, p. 139.
    29. Marx, EPM, Publisher's note, p. 183; cited
in "The Foundation of Historical Materialism", p. 7,
p. 139.
    30. Ibid., p. 11, p.142, all expressions in
quotations from EPM.
    31. Ibid., p. 12, p. 144, translation modi-
fied.
    32. Ibid., p. 12-13, p. 144; translation modi-
fied or provided for this and much of the preceding.
The English translation is very weak at this junc-
ture of Marcuse's argument - to the point that one
passage and a whole paragraph is omitted altogether.
    33. Marcuse explicitly introduces this whole
discussion by a detailed analysis of three short
formulations in the text where the positive implications of the marxist concept of "alienated labor"
are particularly clear. These are: "'labor is man's
coming-to-be for himself within alienation, or as
alienated man (p. 131), it is 'man's act of self-
creation or self-objectification' (p. 188), 'life
activity, productive life itself'" (p. 133) from
"The Foundations of Historical Materialism", p. 13,
p. 144; all page numbers given here refer to the
1974 edition of EPM.
    34. See for instance Maguire, Marx's Paris
Writings, op. cit., for an account of some of these
debates; see also Martin Nicholaus for the further
implications that the Grundrisse brought for this
debate based upon the EPM, Nicholaus, M., "The Unknown Marx" in New Left Review, 1968.
    35. For a comprehensive account of Marx's
ontological perspective see Carol Gould's Marx's
Social Ontology, op. cit.. A simplified, if considerably tightened account of Marcuse's interpretation
can also be found in Habermas, Knowledge and Human
Interests, op. cit., pp. 25-64.
    36. See the discussion in Goldmann, Lukács and
Heidegger, op. cit.. See also Bernstein, E., Evolu-

tionary Socialism, USA New York: Schocken Books, 1961.

37. See Reason and Revolution, op. cit., pp. 258-322.

38. On Feuerbach's influence in the manuscripts see MacLellan, The Young Hegelians, op. cit., pp. 106-110.

39. "The Foundation of Historical Materialism", op. cit., p. 15, p. 146.

40. All of Marcuse's quotations in this discussion are from three pages in the section on "Estranged Labor" (pp. 67-70), and three pages in the section on the "Critique of the Hegelian Dialectic and Philosophy as a Whole" (pp. 133-136); the titles and page references given here are from the 1974 edition of EPM.

41. Marx, EPM, p. 67, emphasis in the text; "The Foundation of Historical Materialism", p. 15, p. 146.

42. See MacLellan, The Young Hegelians and Karl Marx, op. cit., p. 92.

43. "The Foundation of Historical Materialism", op. cit., p. 15, p. 147, translation modified.

44. Ibid., p. 16, p. 147.

45. Ibid.

46. Ibid.

47. Ibid.

48. Ibid., p. 17, p. 148.

49. Ibid.

50. Marx, EPM, p. 135; "The Foundation of Historical Materialism", op. cit., p. 18, p. 149.

51. On these points see for instance Taylor, C., Hegel, Cambridge: Cambridge University Press, 1975, pp. 127-221.

52. "The Foundation of Historical Materialism", p. 18, p. 149, translation modified.

53. Ibid., p. 21, p. 151 emphasis in the text.

54. Ibid., p. 29, p. 151, translation modified.

55. See Engels' Ludwig Feuerbach, op. cit., passim, for a discussion of these points along such lines.

56. Marx, Selected Works, op. cit., Vol. 1, p. 15.

57. "The Foundation of Historical Materialism", p. 23, p. 153, translation modified.

58. Marx, Selected Works, op. cit., Vol.1, p. 13.

59. Marx, EPM, p. 63; "The Foundation of Historical Materialism", op. cit., p. 23, p. 153.

60. "The Foundation of Historical Materialism", op. cit., p. 23, p. 153, translation modified.

61. Marx, The Holy Family, Moscow: Progress Publishers, p. 60.

62. See Schoolman, "Introduction of Marcuse's "On the Problem of the Dialectic", op. cit., p. 10.

63. "The Foundation of Historical Materialism", pp.39-40, p. 167.

64. "The Foundation of the Concept of Labor in Economics", op. cit., pp. 27 og 34, pp 34 og 44.

65. "The Foundation of Historical Materialism", op. cit., p. 48, p. 174.

66. Ibid., p. 25, p. 155.

67. Ibid.

68. Ibid., p. 25-26, p. 155, and Marx, EPM, p. 95, emphasis in the text.

69. Ibid., p. 25, p. 155, and Marx, EPM, p. 69.

70. All the quotes from "The Foundation of Historical Materialism", op. cit., pp. 30-34, pp. 159-162.

71. Ibid., p. 27, p. 156.

72. Ibid.

73. Ibid., p. 28, pp. 156-157, emphasis in the text.

74. Ibid., p. 29, p. 158.

75. For a different interpretation, see Shapiro, "The Dialectic of Theory in the Age of Technological Rationality", op. cit., p. 181.

76. "The Foundation of Historical Materialism", op. cit., p. 34, p. 162.

77. Ibid., p. 35, p. 163, emphasis in the text, text of last quotation omitted in English translation.

78. Ibid.

79. Marcuse explicitly refers to Marx's "Critique of Hegel's Philosophy of Right: Introduction"; see Marx, Early Writings, op. cit., pp. 243-258. This is where Marx for the first, and I believe only time, expounds the reasons which make the proletariat particularly suited for the task of bringing the communist revolution.

80. "The Foundation of Historical Materialism", op. cit., p. 35, 163, first emphasis mine, second emphasis in the text.

Chapter Four

THE CO-OPERATIVE SOCIETY

4.1 The Positive Philosophy of a Negative Philosopher

Marcuse has often been attacked for what one critic
has labelled his "one dimensional pessimism"(1).
This is more than a play on words - it refers to a
fundamental trait in Marcuse's whole approach which
is characterized as essentially negative and opposi-
ional per se. Marcuse is viewed primarily through
lenses provided by his own One Dimensional Man,
which leads his commentators to see his work as a
series of disjointed, yet constantly critical analyses of a twentieth century civilisation Marcuse
always refused to come to terms with (2). It is this
intrinsically negative attitude to present-day circumstances that MacIntyre means to capture with his
parallel to the Left Hegelians, which Marx ironical-
ly called "critical critics", only able to set themselves mentally outside or above a society against
which they could offer little or no constructive
alternatives (3). It is an attitude that Marcuse has
himself expressed in occasional references to the
"Great Refusal" of the Surrealists as the only open
avenue of protest. His frequent references to Nietzsche in recent years have also been understood by
one commentator to have overshadowed his original
marxism, which is replaced by a nihilistic demand
for an "explosion which will transvalue all values"
(4). Marcuse has also been accused of replacing the
subtle, multisided and transcending dialectic of
Marx and Hegel with a simplistic, one-sided and
thoroughly undialectical emphasis upon the "power of
the negative" (5). He has been understood to reject
all that is positive and valuable in our societies,
including the scientific methods of investigation,
the value of technological innovation or the political freedom of Western societies (6). What Marcuse
has to offer is an essentially negative philosophy,

and he has few or no alternatives, not even an overall standard by which to judge the present.

This perspective finds further support in Marcuse's chequered academic history. The years of
collaboration with other members of the "Frankfurt
School" would suggest that little can be found in
Marcuse concerning the reality of a different society. After all, as Martin Jay constantly emphasises,
the trade-mark of the body of research he regroups
under this heading is precisely its character of a
"critical theory". Following Horkheimer's own considerations, he argues that it should, first of all,
be understood as a critical weapon to fight the
established order and the established truths, and
that no overall vision can or should emerge from a
series of investigations always directed at the most
pressing problem of the moment, be it Nazism, the
growth of positivism or the instrumental rationality
inherited from the Enlightenment (7). What the main
figures of the School propose is neither a new
philosophy, nor a new image of the good society; its
work aims simply to preserve a "critical spirit" for
better times, when the task of human liberation will
again become actual, and even then "purely" critical
activity will still be justified. To this should be
added that the different intellectual and political
climates Marcuse experienced in the course of a long
academic career and from which output immediate
political considerations were never absent would
more than justify treating his work as a series of
separate stages. The distance between Freiburg and
the German exile community in New York cannot but
have been enormous, and so must the transition from
the American OSS to campus universities around the
States. The fight against Nazism necessarily placed
very different demands upon his philosophical thinking from those entailed by his opposition to the
much more subtle threats of post-war American liberal capitalism. All this would make it less than
plausible for us to find a coherent overall outlook
underlying his varied critiques of Hegel, Freud or
Soviet Marxism.

Yet, as I have argued earlier, it is difficult
not to be struck by the essential continuity in
Marcuse's works. This is something that many commentators have observed, and it can actualy be substantiated by comparing, for instance, an essay from the
thirties, such as "The Affirmative Character of
Culture" or "On Hedonism", with later works such as
Eros and Civilization or even Counterrevolution -
and Revolt (8). That Marcuse, in contrast to other

figures of the "Frankfurt School", is far more prepared to indicate the broad line of an alternative
to present day civilisation is undeniable. That the
essential continuity in Marcuse is to be found there
is less certain. Marcuse seems to have several conceptions of freedom, and they would appear to be
mutually incompatible. We have already seen that the
idea of "concern" borrowed from Heidegger, is considered by some as central to his thinking on the
question (9). The ambiguous notion of "true human
relationships" which figures prominently in the
writings of the thirties suggests another possible
path. The importance of the idea of "eroticised
reason" for the whole argument of <u>Eros and Civiliza-
tion</u> should need no emphasis; this again points in a
different direction, and to all appearances an unmarxist one. Yet another perspective seems to emerge
from his emphasis upon a "new sensibility" in the
late sixties, as the best hope for an overcalcula-
ting civilisation.

The extent of these difficulties is also reflected in those essays or articles which address
themselves to the nature of Marcuse's idea of freedom. For James Rhodes, "Pleasure" and "Reason" constitute the core of Marcuse's thinking on freedom,
with Freud and Heidegger as the main protagonists of
an ongoing battle of ideas in his writings (10).
Martin Jay, in an essay entitled "How Utopian is
Marcuse?", advances the view that Marcuse's vision
of the good society is best understood in terms of
two strains pulling in opposite directions: "first,
the stress on radical action, on the deed, on self-
creation as the only mode of authentic being; and
second, the unity of opposite, the harmony of paci-
fied existence, the end of conflict and contradiction" (11). David Kettler, in a sensitive treatment
of Marcuse as a critique of bourgeois civilisation,
argues for the importance of love and artistic sensibility as the two most permanent themes of Marcuse's varied intimations of a better world to come
(12). For Edward Andrew, what characterizes Marcuse's conception of freedom is a rejection of the
marxian idea of freedom as "non-alienated work";
this is replaced by a decidedly non-marxist vision
of freedom as idle play totally detached from any
active participation in a fully automated process of
production (13). Even when taking into account the
different approaches used to elucidate the various
aspects of Marcuse's (or Marx's) writing, it is
striking how little agreement prevails as to Marcuse's conception of the good society. Does this

mean that there is not, after all, a coherent and
continuous idea of freedom informing his analyses?
Should we understand his varied and frequent references to freedom and liberation as mainly the expressions of a generous, but vague commitment to
humanist ideals?

The nature and extent of the debates generated
by this facet of Marcuse's thought suggest otherwise. There is an essential continuity in Marcuse
and it revolves around a distinctive idea of freedom. To grasp the content and character of this
conception of freedom it is essential to realize
that his work is rooted in an original interpretation of Marx. Only in relation to Marcuse's earliest
work is it possible to capture the particular vision
of the good society which directs and informs each
of his analyses. It is furthermore in relation to
the marxist tradition as a whole that this interpretation should be understood.

Marcuse has a positive philosophy. It is best
described as a commitment to marxism and to all that
is important and alive within that tradition in
relation to contemporary problems and issues. Marcuse's particular contribution has been to re-inter-
pret this heritage as a broad theory of liberation
capable of guiding a wider political and philosophical critique of existing institutions. The centre-
piece of that theory is an idea of freedom which he
derives from Marx's original texts.

In order to grasp the nature and limitations of
this vision of the good society it is therefore
essential to recall Marx's own general position on
the question. It is not necessary to retrace in this
context the arguments Marx levelled against the
"Utopian Socialists" of his day, Owen, Fourier and
Saint-Simon (14). Yet it is of interest to consider
the reasons why Marx (and Engels) deliberately refrained from any explicit or detailed description of
the post-revolutionary society. (15). These reasons
are two-fold. There are, firstly, good theoretical
reasons for assuming it would be impossible to describe in any detail a future society whose socio-
economic conditions will differ so radically from
anything mankind has ever known. For the first time
humanity as a whole will be able to develop unfet-
tered by class antagonisms and the scarcity of ele-
mentary resources. There are, also, important normative reasons for such a caution. If the future
society is truly to be a "realm of freedom", it must
be up to the "freely associated producers" to decide
among themselves what the detailed organization of

that society should look like, and any substantive
or normative stand prior to the revolution to come
will only prejudge this right.
    Marcuse writes in the very different historical
context of the twentieth century. These arguments,
although still weighty, have to be balanced against
other considerations. In particular, Marcuse is
concerned from the start to develop marxism's ideological and philosophical dimensions in order to
meet the new challenges of the decades since Marx's
death in 1883. The question of the nature of the
future society becomes imperative again when it
becomes evident that capitalism has survived itself
- as Marcuse undoubtedly believes, as early as 1928
- for reasons which are partly to do with the lack
of a clear apprehension of the distinctive character
of a truly post-revolutionary society. Marx was
cautious but not entirely silent (16). To re-establish as firmly as possible the vision which, in
Marcuse's view, distinguishes marxism from all other
political or philosophical theories must become a
major concern for committed marxists. There is all
the more reason for such a limited departure from
the marxist taboo on the question when socialism of
a kind is being built in neighbouring Russia. A
clearer idea of the good society and an understanding of marxism as a comprehensive theory of freedom
would already be warranted by the need to fight the
scientific approach to marxism, the challenge of the
new social sciences or the appeal of more recent
bourgeois philosophies. Yet it is in relation to the
gradualist reformism of Social Democracy and the
complacency of socialists that such a revival of the
wider ideals informing marxism becomes crucial.
    The battle must be waged on the ideological
front, and it must concern not only the material
dimension of existence, but also questions which
affect the daily private as well as public life of
individuals in the society. The concern for the
ethical and personal dimension of marxist theory
most clearly animates Marcuse's earliest writings,
and it is reflected in the works of the thirties and
in those writings which led to Marcuse's fame as
"The Guru of the New Left"(17). These concerns are
best expressed in terms of various lines of attack,
which can be summarized as follows. Against the
predominance of material interests, it is necessary
to uphold the importance of wider ethical and political goals. Against the growing uniformization of
German society, which threatens this very goal, it
is imperative to maintain the demand for individual

happiness and individual lifestyle. Against the fostering of personal egoism, the narrow-mindedness of local issues and the retreat into private relations, it is necessary to affirm that the good society will not only be a world of plenty but also a different moral and political order. It will be one in which the personal and the social will not stand in perpetual confrontation, and one in which all individuals will be able to grow and develop in a world where material and cultural riches are there for all to use.

It is against such a background that we must understand Marcuse's reception of the newly rediscovered <u>Paris Manuscripts</u>. These provide invaluable material with respect to the philosophical context and human ideals which guide Marx's first attempts to develop a comprehensive theory of the coming socialist revolution. Alfred Schmidt has argued, not unconvincingly, that marxism served Marcuse as a "positive philosophy" answering Heidegger's question of "authentic existence" (18). This is perhaps most plausible for the years 1929-32 where the connection between Marcuse's philosophial concerns and the wider body of marxism was most tenuous. In the "Contributions to a Phenomenology of Historical Materialism", as I have shown, marxism re-interpreted as a wider theory of freedom constitutes the core problem. It is in relation to that problem that the manuscripts now provide Marcuse with a comprehensive "positive" philosophy - one in which a specific idea of freedom is articulated within the wider body of marxism understood as a theory of human liberation.

This perspective alone allows us to capture the inner continuity of Marcuse's diverse researches. At the centre of these various studies there is always, most often in between the lines, a distinctive idea of the good society, which derives from and belongs to the marxist tradition. Marcuse largely respects Marx's position with regard to the detailed organization of the post-revolutionary society. There are no blueprints for such a society in Marcuse's work, few precise indications of the new political, legal or constitutional provisions, and even less in the way of further historical development to take place within the new order. Marcuse suggests only broad ethical, political and existential guidelines for the alternative society based on the achievements of current capitalist development. Furthermore, Marcuse leaves unsaid everything considered trivial or obvious from the perspective of the marxist tradition.

In this as in other respects Marcuse assumes of his
readers a range of contextual information without
which his texts become, if not less suggestive, at
least far more difficult to pinpoint (19).

4.2 Liberalism, Freedom and the Marxist Tradition

The last observation points to the method of interpretation needed to bring out the underlying structure of Marcuse's work. To obtain a complete picture
of Marcuse's idea of freedom it is necessary to
formulate explicitly the unstated assumptions upon
which his work is built. The reconstruction of Marcuse's vision of the good society is made possible
by the above perspective and the analysis of preceding chapters: Marcuse's singular reading of the
Paris Manuscripts is directed by the concerns and
ideas developed in the years 1928-32; this interpretation of Marx's early work in turn reshapes those
concerns and those ideas into a definite theory of
freedom rooted in the marxist tradition. By re-
inserting the idea of freedom into its marxist context, it becomes possible to unfold the full picture
of this concept in Marcuse's thought. The reconstructed picture of the good society may be used as
the key to Marcuse's later and sometimes more explicitly utopian writings. Its ability to illuminate
these later texts will serve as a further test for
its validity.

However, rather than presenting a fully-fledged
exposition of marxist views on freedom, the approach
adopted here focuses on a few basic features clearly
differentiating marxism from other political or
philosophical doctrines (20). The most outstanding
feature in this respect is undoubtedly the relation
that both Marcuse and Marx establish between freedom
and work and will serve as the guiding thread of the
discussion. The idea that genuine freedom is only
possible in and through work is a central theme in
the early Marx and in the early Marcuse. It also
reappears in one form or another throughout both
writers' later works. We shall consider the question
for Marcuse in some details below; as for Marx, it
suffices to say for the moment that the idea of
freedom as work or labour appears as late as the
"Critique of the Gotha Programme", where Marx speaks
of a future society where "labor has become not only
a means of life but life's prime want" (21). While
other formulations appear throughout Marx's writings, it nevertheless remains that for Marx there
is no adequate treatment of freedom which fails to

view it as intimately related to work and defined in
relation to work (either positively or negatively)
(22). This applies both to work in capitalist societies and in the future society, and within the
latter to work deemed as "socially necessary" as
well as genuinely "free work" (23). The mere assertion that freedom is essentially related to work,
and inversely, that there can be no valid conception
of freedom failing to take into account the role of
work in human life, has important consequences for
traditional areas of concern for theories of freedom. The five areas with which we will deal are
freedom and legal and political rights, freedom and
constitutional arrangements, personal freedom, internal freedom and positive freedom (24).

The first of these areas, freedom understood in
terms of legal and political rights, is the most
prominent aspect of the question of freedom within
the field of political theory (25). It is certainly
the most common characterization of a distinctly
Western tradition of freedom, (which I have elsewhere discussed under the general heading of "the
legal-political tradition") and reappears in much
literature not primarily concerned with the question
of freedom (26). It is also the aspect of freedom
most frequently invoked in global East-West comparisons. In historical terms, the doctrine of unalie-
nable rights can be retraced as far back as the
schools of thought concerned with "natural rights",
as well as to Locke as the chief exponent of a
rising bourgeoisie, but it found its most vigorous
expression in the French Revolution and the foundation of the United States of America.

There is no need to dwell upon the general
marxist position on the question. Marx's attitude to
"bourgeois rights" is forcefully expressed in the
"Critique of the Gotha Programme" - reflecting positions developed as early as 1843 - and the traditional objections to the whole conception from the
marxist-leninist viewpoint are well known. These
rights are limited, formal and abstract. They fail
to include the most essential social rights; their
existence on paper is largely irrelevant to the
substance (or lack of such) of the guarantees they
proclaim; they rest upon and reinforce an illusory
legal world of justice and equality, divorced from
social and economic realities. They require no further comment in this context (27). More interesting
is the consideration of how this familiar critique
relates to freedom as dependent upon the role of
labour in human life. Two possible positions emerge

from this perspective. The first is the marxist demand that to the list of basic human rights should be added the right to work. The second position follows from Marx's general critique of a political community separate from or imposed upon a civil society rife with antagonisms (28). For Marx any conception of freedom in terms of human rights which fails to include the de facto inequalities of freedom with respect to property, economic or social power, will merely buttress the status quo without affecting any long term changes. The implication of that critique is that for freedom to be effectively protected or promoted through legal or political guarantees, it should first be assessed in relation to work. This also applies to the matter of distribution and arrangements for socially necessary work and "free work". This second position further implies that the whole structure of legal and political rights so forcefully advocated by radical movements in the eighteenth and nineteenth centuries is at best misconceived and at worst a deliberate diversion from the real problems of freedom.

The second traditional area of concern for theories of freedom is freedom conceived in terms of constitutional arrangements. This aspect has been the central concern of liberal movements for at least three centuries. The two central tenets are traditionally the parliamentary responsibility of government and the control of either parliament and/or the head of the state through electoral mechanisms (29). Again, it is clear that while Marx remained somewhat ambiguous, the general thrust of hiw views is highly critical (30). Recent discussions concerning the political forms of Eurocommunism have nevertheless tended to give the whole problem a somewhat different perspective (31).

The core idea of this particular form of freeom is perhaps best expressed in terms of "participatory rights" (32) where the emphasis is on the individual's guaranteed share of power in decisions affecting the community. Rephrased in such terms, it is easy to see why the traditional liberal democratic model suffers grave flaws from the standpoint of an idea of freedom committed to the central role of labour (33). The objections here are again of two kinds: one emphasising the limitation of purely constitutional-political guarantees; the second consisting in affirming the primacy of "work-democracy" as opposed to any other form of collective decision-making processes.

The third traditional area of concern for theories of freedom I will call "personal freedom", to distinguish it from the overworked "individual freedom" and from the "negative freedom" advocated by Berlin (34). Individual freedom has been used to designate a whole variety of freedoms which are in no way logically related. Thus individual freedom has been used to designate: 1) the system of political and legal guarantees against arbitrary state invervention as described above; 2) the related system of legal and political guarantees purporting to secure equal participation in collective decisions through electoral and constitutional mechanisms; 3) the area of personal freedom left to the individual within the network of legal prohibitions; 4) the sum of activities open to individuals within a given society, with the stress on the reality of social structures and the efficacy of the laws rather than their mere existence. It is in this sense 4) that I will define "personal freedom", as both the effective opportunities and the effective private space that the legal, economic and social institutions leave open or guarantee. This is a more restricted sense than the "negative freedom" advocated by many liberals which collapses the first and last two meanings of "individual freedom" into the same heading (35).

We have previously considered the arguments relating to the first two meanings of "individual freedom" as described above. For the last sense of "individual freedom", the bulk of the marxist argument has consisted in contrasting the social and economic realities of the individual's range of personal freedom with formalist definitions equating this freedom with the legal freedoms afforded by theoretically undiscriminating political and judicial institutions. Some marxist authors, including Marx himself, have focused on the class character of the legal system and forcefully denounced the pro-establishment character of an apparently egalitarian class system (36). Areas of attack have included the process of law application (arguments about judges' class background), the definition of offences (white collar crime) or wider questions of inequalities of power or opportunities (37). The general thrust of other arguments is that in capitalist or class societies it is impossible to enjoy genuine personal freedom, given the constraints of socio-economic forces. There is also much in Marx to suggest that the exclusive emphasis on personal freedom can only harm the pursuit of a truly human life oriented towards the community of others (38).

Similar conclusions flow from the notion that human freedom can only be understood with reference to work. This perspective implies that questions of legal rights and duties occupy a secondary, limited place. What matters is effective access to self-fulfilling work, or at least reasonable working conditions, a share in the decision-making directly relating to work, and possibilities for a varied and stimulating working life. Alternatively, if the focus is on "free labor" as opposed to "socially necessary labor", possibilities afforded by the society for individual self-actualization are what matter.

A fourth traditional area of concern for theories of freedom is the matter of internal freedom. Although it is difficult to identify a general marxist standpoint on all the issues involved, general agreement does seem to prevail on the question of "free will" and the related problem of adequate knowledge or "consciousness" (39). The overall emphasis upon the role of social forces as against the action, intuition or even self-perception of the individual clearly suggests that "free will" is at best a concept of dubious theoretical value for marxist writers. This applies most evidently to the second generation of marxists such as Kautsky or Plekanov, who gave a central positon in their writings to the inexorable "laws" of dialectical materialism. Yet even for these authors it seems difficult to reconcile a position akin to full determinism with the obvious stress upon the proper grasp and wide dissemination of not only marxist economics but also a whole conception of the world, as evidenced by such popular works as Ludwig Feuerbach or Anti-Dühring (40). This becomes even more problematic if we turn to Marx's own works, where the emphasis on the necessary and determining role of a self-enlightened and self-motivated proletariat is far stronger (41). The critique of the idea of "internal freedom", the purity of the concept of "free will" or the stress upon "consciousness" runs through the whole of Marx. Yet there is an equally constant emphasis upon "correct knowledge", presupposing a not unsubstantial measure of "free will" and a capacity for effective action. Rather than a simple rejection of "internal freedom" what we have is a rejection of freedom without practical consequence and knowledge without "praxis".

The same mixture of indifference to questions of "internal freedom" with a strong implicit belief in a measure of "free will" and action-oriented knowledge follows from the notion that freedom is primarily fulfilled through labour. Rather than an introspective or reflective attitude, it demands practical actions to be mastered by direct interactions. Nevertheless, it is difficult to imagine any form of "free labor" not implying a considerable capacity for "conscious" and self-directed knowledge.

A fifth traditional concern of theories of freedom is the idea of "positive freedom". This concept comes under attack in Berlin's brilliantly suggestive essay on "Two Concepts of Liberty" which still exerts a considerable influence upon much recent literature (42). Yet Berlin's account suffers from grave flaws. He defines "positive freedom" rather loosely as everything not falling under the rubric "negative liberty", itself defined in the most ambiguous manner. Partly as a consequence of this, the concept of "positive freedom" becomes the receptacle for different and often incompatible approches to the concept of freedom. The theory's original and most vigorous proponent, T.H. Green, intends freedom to be understood as "a positive power or capacity of doing or enjoying something worth doing or enjoying" (43). This definition is remarkable in two respects. First, freedom is defined in terms of powers or capacities as opposed to the absence of constraints, or the non-interference by the state or others in society, or again the abstract range of possibilities open to human or rational beings. Green does not advocate a return to nature, to a more natural order, the will of God or the forces of the market, all themes implied to a lesser or greater degree by liberal theories of freedom (44). Rather, he proposes a conception of freedom wherein the emphasis is on furthering new skills and needs, encouraging further growth and development in a society which is not "natural", "given", or merely reflecting (inadequately) the peace and justice of the past. Green's conception of "positive freedom" is resolutely modern, oriented towards progress and development, and it visualizes man growing within a dynamic society. The second striking feature of Green's conception is the emphasis on morally, ethically or politically acceptable goals. His formula (as opposed to those of other "new liberals") explicitly advances a substantive and goal-oriented definition of freedom (45). Freedom is no longer open-ended, but must clearly be compatible with other goals of the good society. It is difficult to comment specifically on a marxist

position toward positive freedom. Neither Marx (who
died before the "new liberals" emerged as a distinctive current of thought) nor later marxists have
commented much on Green and "positive liberals"
(46). It is not difficult, however, to see the
similarities of thought between the two traditions,
similarities which go beyond common Hegelian roots.
Freedom, for both marxists and positive liberals,
consists in the ability and power to alter one's
nature, to develop new skills, talents or needs
within the context of a rich and varied material and
cultural civilization. The second distinctive trait
of positive freedom, that freedom must be in some
way conducive to the development and further growth
of individuals in society, is also one to which both
Marx and marxists would be sympathetic. Marx clearly
pictures the free individual as one endowed with a
capacity for enjoying all things, developing equally
his mental and physical capacities, as well as ap-
preciating and needing the new cultural riches and
forms of enjoyment provided by the increasing material wealth of a fast-developing historical world.
    The idea that Marx's conception of freedom is
most distinctive insofar as it postulates an intimate relation between freedom and work also leads to
these conclusions. The similarities between this
understanding of the marxist view of freedom and
positive freedom are most evident in the notion of
freedom as power or capacity for doing things. Moreover, as I argued in relation to personal freedom,
the freedom which expresses itself in and through
work can never be entirely open-ended. All in all,
if we are prepared to accept with Marcuse that the
Marxist conception of freedom is chiefly characterised by the idea of "free labor", it is reasonable
to consider this conception as a special case of
Green's more extensive "positive freedom.
    A more detailed analysis of "free labor" and
its counterpart, "alienated labor", will allow us to
sharpen this picture and provide the elements for a
more specifically "Marcusian" vision of the good
society.

4.3 The Transcendence of Alienation and True Objec-
tification

In Chapter 4 we considered Marcuse's highly selective interpretation of Marx's Economic and Philosophical Manuscripts of 1844. It is, as we saw, the
relation to Hegel and the need to restore the philosophical dimension of marxism which dominate this

interpretation. The overall perspective of the es
say, however, is provided by the idea that from
Marx's analyses of "alienated labor" one may gain
considerable insight into the nature of his conception of freedom - a conception first of all characterized in terms of the "transcendence of alienation"
(48). The essay's open-ended character, its explicit
philosophical intention and the high level of abstraction at which the analysis is conducted all
help to account for this conception's evocation
rather than its full exposition. Yet the essay nevertheless contains all the elements for a comprehensive picture of Marcuse's understanding of the
"realm of freedom", if sometimes only by implication. With the help of the subsequent and more
detailed studies of this aspect of marxism, together
with Marcuse's own comments, it is possible to draw
the full picture from the text.

To do so adequately it is essential to respect
the text's perspective. Two points should be noted
in that context. The first is the importance that
Marcuse attaches throughout this piece to the idea
of the individual as the subject of freedom (49).
The second is Marcuse's deliberate stress on labour's consequences for the individual, as opposed
to the question of its wider outcome in creating and
maintaining the material and cultural civilization
(50). With these points firmly in mind, it is possible to develop those aspects of alienation crucial
to Marcuse's interpretation of the manuscripts. What
interests Marcuse is not the religious or the specific political alienation, but the social and economic aspects of this alienation.

Marcuse will thus stress the following five
facets of Marx's concept of alienation (51):

1. The worker is alienated from the object of
    his labour (52).
2. The worker is barred from any creative
    contribution to the transformation of
    nature into human civilization (53).
3. The worker is "estranged" from himself
    (54).
4. The worker is "estranged" from his fellow
    Man (55).
5. The worker is alienated from his essence
    as a "species being" (56).

Marcuse's interpretation of Marx should be understood with reference to these five now familiar
facets of alienation. The main argument is that the

manuscripts show that "the economico-political <u>basis</u> of the theory of revolution" emerges through a particular, philosophical interpretation of the ideas of human essence and its historical realization (57). The deliberate emphasis upon that philosophical dimension in Marx should not allow us to forget that Marcuse quite clearly takes other elements of Marx's theory into account. The economic and social aspects of the analyses in the manuscripts, the concrete historical setting in which they are presented, and the context provided by Marx's other works all enter into the perspective Marcuse derives from his distinctive reading of the manuscripts. This perspective, that of a new theory of freedom, guides the more detailed argumentation presented in the essay. It also constitutes the underlying structure for virtually all of Marcuse's later writings. The core of this new theory is an idea of freedom revolving around the idea of "free labor" implied by Marx's analyses of alienated labour. The full implications of Marcuse's interpretation of these analyses can be described as follows.

Marx's new social order should be understood with reference to "free labor". "True communism" requires firstly that the individual worker masters the object instead of being dominated by it. The individual decides what objects should be produced, in what order, at what speed and in what shape. He has a substantial influence upon the appearance and quality of the finished product, either directly (for smaller or less significant objects) or indirectly (for larger or more complex objects) through his association with other producers. Secondly, he participates fully in the creation, transformation and constant maintenance of the social and human world in which he lives. This applies equally to the material dimensions of the greatly accelerated process of "humanizing" nature and to the ideational and social aspects of that process - the "associated producer" is a full and equal participant in co-operative social institutions after the revolution. Thirdly, this new mode of individual and/or co-operative work opens a whole new range of possible "objectifications" for the individual's talents, creativity and individuality. Hitherto untapped potential will now be realised in the objects around him, in the co-operatively produced industrial objects for mass consumption and in the community's larger projects. Fourthly, the civilization after the revolution will see the emergence of altogether more varied personal modes of social intercourse,

promoting both a new increased sociability and new
patterns of individuality, and leading to a measure
of understanding of self and others never before
experienced. Blind, ruthless and dehumanizing competition will give way to radically different forms of
interaction, and the demand for work and material
goods will no longer be dominated by acquisitive-
ness, fear or desperation. The disappearance of dire
economic necessity, of the division of labour as
known under capitalism and of the all-pervasive
class system will mean that the human qualities will
enter into interactions between the "associated
producers" and will be recognised as such. The common ambition and effort to create a world reflecting
the individuality of each and the needs of all will
bind men/women more profoundly than ever before. The
social object produced by man's industry will reveal
each member of the community more clearly than any
long debate. The individual will see himself and
others in the world thus produced and this world
will be the objectification of the species as a
whole (58).
    This provisional picture of Marcuse's idea of
freedom I shall call "The co-operative society". As
it is presented here it follows quite closely Marx's
own text, and similar accounts can be found in the
previously cited studies by Maguire, Duncan or Mészáros (59). The centrality of labour singles out
Marcuse's interpretation of the manuscripts. The
idea of "free labor" which Marcuse derives from Marx
contributes to the distinctiveness of his analysis
of Marx's good society.

4.4 Marcuse and the Good Society
The provisional picture of the "co-operative society" helps clarify Marcuse's understanding of "free
labor" implied by the marxist concept of "alienated
labor". This is very different from any form of work
under capitalism, or in fact any previous stage of
mankind's historical development. "Free labor" is
other than and more than the sum of activities
socially necessary for the development or maintenance of the level of material and cultural civilization. It is essentially voluntary, a form of activity which individuals take upon themselves with the
sole objective of furthering their own goals and
pursuits in co-operation with others. These goals
can and will include socially useful objectives, but
this cannot be imposed upon them. The traditional
delimitations of work experienced under capitalism

will disappear. "Free labor" includes all these
activities by which the individual furthers his
self-development (and that of others) through deliberate and determined effort and by which the individual leaves his mark upon natural or social objects. Participating in community meetings, building
a chair, producing ball bearings or composing music
would presumably all fall under this heading. Labour
and play, work time and spare time, individual hob-
bies and co-operative activities will no longer be
sharply separated - there will be no necessity for
it. These are implications Marcuse will fully develop in later writings; similarly the presupposition
that all socially necessary labour will disappear
will receive more attention there.

Marcuse's shift from "concrete philosophy" to a
position much more akin to that of orthodox marxism
may suggest that his conception of freedom shifts
from the ideal of the committed philosopher - conception in which philosophical research guided by
humanistic ideals and a concern for the individual's
needs and aspirations would tend toward a radical
engagement in public affairs, as described in chapter 2 - to that of a liberated "homo faber". The
role he accords to work in a subsequent essay on the
concept of labour (60) as the fulfilment of the
individual's existence would support such a hypothesis. Following Hegel he there describes labour as
"an abiding event that constantly and continually
spans the whole of man's being and at the same time
evolves even man's 'world'" (61). The view that
labour is man's true field of self-realisation is
perfectly compatible with the idea of "free labor"
as labour which has become conscious, co-operative
and collectively directed. The good society would
then be a social order which allows a new "homo
faber" to devote himself fully to his share of the
collective social labour, to take a full part in
decisions to produce this or that social object and
participate on an equal basis in the allocation of
communal tasks.

The above discussion of "free labor" as it
emerges form Marcuse's analyses makes it clear,
however, that he envisions a far more radical break
with all previous forms of human interactions. The
free individual in the co-operative society is vastly different from any conscientious "homo faber",
sharing equally in the chores and the responsibili-
ties, however different they will be from those of a
capitalist order and however "conscious", able and
knowledgeable he may be (62). This new individual

will be an all round, hedonistic and loving person;
he expresses through labour a rich variety of skills
and talents; he also develops through this "free
labor" a new range of needs, passions and sensibilities which before would have been closed to him.
His relation to nature involves all the dimensions
of his physical being - "seeing, hearing, smelling,
tasting, feeling, thinking, observing, experiencing,
wanting, acting, loving" (63). This Marcuse sums up
by stating that "the whole man is at home in the
whole objective world which is 'his work and his
reality'" (64).

It may be useful at this point to retrace the
steps which lead Marcuse to that conclusion. His
starting point is Marx's concept of alienated labour
and its implication for the idea of "species-being".
He establishes that for Feuerbach it revolves around
the idea of "sensuousness" (Sinnlichkeit), a concept
which carries the dual notion of being affected
emotionally and being affected perceptually through
sensory stimuli. It is because of this "sensuousness" (in its dual sense) that "intuition" becomes
for Feuerbach the most complete relation that man as
a "species-being" can establish with the world. The
categories of "sensuousness" and "intuition" describe man's ontological relation to the world, and
"intuition" becomes the foundation for any well-
understood epistemology. By explicitly drawing the
parallel with Kant's theory of "affects", Marcuse
not only stresses the epistemological dimension, he
furthermore points to a concept of reason which in
contrast to the ideal of "pure reason" will encompass a whole world of human feelings and passions
(65). When Marcuse then argues that for Marx it is
labour that constitutes man's fundamental ontological relation to the world, he insists that the
theoretical mode of apprehension of the world implied by the Feuerbachian "intuition" does not simply disappear; on the contrary "it is combined with
labor in a relationship of founding interpenetra-
tion" (66). "Free labor" in Marcuse's interpretation
describes all of man's essential relations with the
world, a potential which once liberated allows each
individual to relate to others and the world so that
reason, passions, needs and creative activities are
all fused in one.

This should also make clear that the idea of
the co-operative society in Marcuse's 1932 essay is
not void of moral or ethical implication. By retracing the Feuerbachian and Hegelian roots of Marx's
conception of "species-being", and by insisting that

the redefined concept in Marx retains its original connotations, Marcuse implicitly argues that some of the original humanist dimension should be retained. Yet he does no more than that. Marcuse's account makes clear that there are no "lower" pleasures as opposed to the "higher" pleasures of the mind. If anything, the body, the "human <u>nature</u>" and the idea of man's multiple needs and passions reappears through Marcuse's otherwise technical account of Marx. What may have been a rather intellectual and passive ideal in Marcuse's early essays appears now, under the impulse of Marx's radical denunciation of all "detached" idealism, as a central tenet of his thinking (67).

The extensive definition of "free labor" has also definite epistemological implications for the idea of the "co-operative society". The rationality which is to guide its members is radically different from the cold calculus implied by political economy and fostered by the wider social order of capitalism; nor is there any room in Marcuse's vision for any "pure" technological rationality disassociated from the ends it is meant to serve. The directing rationality and the knowledge to strive for are informed and supported by a respect for basic human values and a commitment to the happiness of others as well as one's own. This would not deny that purely technical knowledge also exists, but it will only appear as knowledge in the context of the wider rationality of a new humane civilization.

Finally, it should be stressed once more that Marcuse's interpretation of the <u>Paris Manuscripts</u> has important implications for the notion of human needs and the whole idea of "human nature". Marcuse's explicit return to Feuerbach makes clear that the qualities emphasised by Feuerbach as distinctly human receive a central place in his own vision of the "co-operative society". Such feelings as love, affection and compassion will be given different opportunities for development under the new material and cultural civilization after the revolution. With the abolition of the restraints imposed by economic necessity and the capitalist order, a whole new world of human needs and feelings will furthermore become part of daily reality. A new type of man will emerge, the all-round individual capable of re-appropriating the products of a thousand years' long historical struggle with nature as the expression of his own labour. He will do so as the member of a new community, with which he is at one while remaining his very own self.

The resulting overall picture of the "co-operative society" can be summarized by the following
table 4.

The broad features of this utopian vision of
the good society emerge most clearly in Marcuse's
much later _Eros and Civilization_. Yet it is important to emphasise that this idea of the "co-operative society" is already largely spelled out in
Marcuse's 1932 essay, read in the context of his
previous work and with due reference to a marxist
tradition that Marcuse there claims as his own. This
idea will also serve as the guiding thread for the
works of the thirties and forties, and it can be
retraced in virtually every one of Marcuse's post-
1932 writings, with the notable exception of
One Dimensional Man. In order to fully understand
the position of the idea of the "co-operative society" in these later writings, it may be useful to
recall the very different role similar utopian elements play in respectively Marx and Marcuse's overall thinking. For reasons discussed above, i.e. that
it is impossible to describe a society so radically
different from anything mankind has ever known and
that we should not prejudge the right of the free
man of that society to decide upon its organisation,
Marx never elaborates upon the ideas contained in
these manuscripts, and the picture which results
from them will always remain a hidden presence in
his work. The task as he sees it is more immediate
and specific. It is necessary to first tackle the
obvious and pressing freedoms from poverty, from
lack of education, from lack of self-respect or even
from simple starvation (68). With respect to the
wider prospect for revolution, under the circumstances, rather than sketch a full and well-argued conception of the good society, it is more important to
show that this state of affairs follows from the
internal logic of a capitalist system rather than
any "natural" causes. The question for Marx thus
becomes to "prove concretely" that capitalism is
necessarily unviable and that the only "realistic"
solution is the complete overthrow of that order by
a proletariat conscious of its powers and of its
extraordinary position in the historical development
leading to industrial capitalism (69).

The situation is altogether different for Marcuse who must affirm the specificity of the marxist
revolution not only against a capitalist social
order which appears to have survived itself, but
also against the piecemeal, reformist and compromi-
sing politics of a new well-developed socialist

Table 4 (*)

Assumptions and logical implications of Marcuse's conception of a free society.

A. The Co-operative Society.

ASS 1   Genuine human freedom is only to be obtained in and through labour.

ASS 2   By labour is understood any purposeful and disciplined activity aiming at the transformation of a given environment (or part thereof) with a view to enhance the fulfilment of biological or acquired needs.

ASS 3   Human freedom is the measure to which free labour takes place. Complete freedom is a society which facilitates such free labour to the full for all its members. The co-operative society is such a society. It is described by the assumptions that follow.

ASS 4   The co-operative society is a society where the individual fully dominates the object of his labour and where he is able to shape it in accordance with the most satisfactory combination of the constraints imposed by the object's "inner laws" and of the needs he feels most express his individual personality. He understands himself through such labour and others through their labour.

ASS 5   In the co-operative society, this relation holds true not only for the individually created or shaped objects, or for those "worked upon" in collaboration with a few others; it is equally valid for all the achievements of that society at large, be it in terms of the wider material production, the world of culture or the social institutions. In all these areas it will be possible to see not only the mark of the "co-operative" man, but also that of each individual. The world will thus be a testimony to all of man's powers and needs, and of those of all the individuals composing that society.

ASS 6   The individual's self-realisation occurs through the work he performs upon the object and in relation to the collectively created social world of which he is an integral part.

ASS 7   Labour is primarily determined in terms of the direct, immediate and "subjective" impact it has upon the individual performing it; this impact is different from

127

anything conceivable in contemporary capitalistic societies. Work in the co-operative society is the sum of
all those activitie upon objects (social and natural)
which promotes the full development of the individual's
powers and capacities, allows him to express a rich
variety of social and individual needs, and afford him
varied emotional and sensory experiences.

ASS 8   The extent to which labour in the co-operative society
is determined by criteria other than those involving
the direct influence of work upon the individual's full
development - other than those arising from the objects
themselves - is limited to those few clear instances
where the long term benefits of such activities are
indisputably greater than the provisional harm caused
by the deviation from the definition of work in assumption 7.

ASS 9   Where and how such indirect criteria should be applied
is decided by the "associated producers" participating
fully and equally in joint planning decisions. The
overriding concern is always the best possible satisfaction of the individual's needs and powers.

ASS 10 The individual himself alone chooses to engage in labour, be it individual or collective. He determines,
alone or in co-operation with others, the character and
conditions of that labour. Only the exceptions which
assumptions 8 and 9 fuly describe can be enforced in
the co-operative society. This, however, is not incompatible with mild social pressure directly following
from the ethical ends described below.

ASS 11 Given that human nature is essentially a social creation, the human needs and powers to be found in the co-
operative society are not ascertainable from within the
present order of things, but for two exceptions. Firstly, the whole range of human emotions, senses and needs
is to be developed. Secondly, the co-operative society
is likely to give due attention to the need to transform the environment "in accordance with the laws of
beauty".

ASS 12 The rationality guiding the activities of the men and
women of the co-operative society is not the cold
instrumental rationality implied by economic theory or
the physical sciences. It is a rationality which is
always informed by and supportive of the above-mentioned goals.

ASS 13 The co-operative society is guided by ethical ends.

These ends are fully described in the overriding concern for the full development of all the individuals
constituting that society. No other moral value or
ethical ends can be invoked against this goal, and the
freedom of all is as unrestrained as possible within
the limits set by this goal.

ASS 14 Those aspects of human relations not falling under the
enlarged and enriched definition of labour as defined
above are similarly solely governed by the above ethical goals.

B. On Freedom

It is possible to further define the goals of the co-operative
society in relation to the existing literature. From the above
it follows that:

Implication 1:   Individual rights and legal guarantees do not
in themselves constitute freedom. Their validity and
importance in this context is fully dependent upon the
degree to which they may serve or not serve to promote
the full development of all individuals within the good
society.

Implication 2:   Legal and constitutional guarantees of participatory freedom are essentially empty. Their contribution to freedom is determined by the extent to which
they make possible/impossible the maximum development
of all individual needs and powers; or alternatively,
help to promote the goal of full and equal participation in the planning decisions in those limited areas
where individual needs and emotions cannot fully prevail.

Implication 3:   Individual freedom can never be a goal per se.
The only form of individual freedom worth this name is
the freedom of self-fulfilling work in co-operation
with others, and all the other aspects of individual or
personal freedom are ultimately dependent upon this
goal.

Implication 4:   Internal freedom as such is a vacuous freedom.
It is a freedom which can only be achieved in relation
of the wider goals of the co-operative society.

Implication 5:   The positive freedom advocated by T.H. Green
is in many respects the most similar to Marcuse's conception of a genuinely "co-operative" society. What

distinguishes Marcuse's conception is the very broad
and open definition of the individual's needs, and the
unconventional conception of the ethical ends of the
co-operative society.

(*) Table 4, section A is derived in part from table 3 and in
part from the text itself. The correspondences with table 3
are as follow.

Table 4	Table 3
ASS 1 is derived from	ASS 6
ASS 2 is identical with	ASS 3
ASS 3 is derived from	ASS 10
ASS 4 is derived from	ASS 7, a, b, d, f, and
	ASS 8, a, b, c, d, and
	ASS 9, b
ASS 5 is derived from	ASS 7, a, b, c, e, f, and
	ASS 8, d, e, f, and
	ASS 9, d
ASS 6 is derived from	ASS 8 and 10
ASS 7 is derived from	ASS 10 combined with 14, b, c
ASS 8 is derived from	ASS 10 combined with 7, a and 8, f
ASS 9 is derived from	ASS 9, b and d
ASS 10 is derived from	ASS 9, a and 2, c
ASS 11 is derived from	ASS 5 and Imp. 1 a, and b
ASS 12 is derived from	ASS 5, 7, f, 8, b, c, e, f, and 9, c
ASS 13 is derived from	ASS 10 and text in general
ASS 14 is derived from	ASS 10

Table 4, section B corresponds to section 4.2 in the text.

establishment. Freedom from poverty is now less
pressing, and it becomes imperative to recapture the
initial impetus of a theory with not only scientific, but also philosophical and humanist claims. The
wider freedom of mankind again comes up on the
agenda, and while the objections against too specific a picture of the society to come are still
valid, such a comprehensive picture of freedom can
at least serve to denounce the thousand influences
that contribute to the absurd persistence of the
capitalist mode of production. Marcuse's post-1932
writings are thus devoted to a dual task. The first
consists in developing cautiously, most often implicitly, the idea of the "co-operative society" derived from Marx. To retrace the continuity and change in this picture through Marcuse's work is the
concern of chapters 5 and 6. The second consists in

applying those ideas to a wider critique of contemporary civilization, marked as it is by the anachro-
nism of a surviving capitalism. That this provides
the surest approach to Marcuse's particular brand of
"critical theory" will be shown in chapter 8. The
overall theory of freedom articulating these two
central aspects of his thought will be examined
separately in chapter 9. Let us now turn to the
period 1932-41 for a closer look at the "co-operative society".

NOTES

1. See Graubard, A., "One-Dimensional Pessimism - A Critique of Herbert Marcuse's Theories", in
Dissent: No. XV, May-June 1968, pp. 216-228; a similar perspective can be found in Gray, J., "Dialectic
of Despair", in Meanjin Quarterly, Australia: Winter
1974, pp. 146-56.
2. This view is nowhere expressed more squarely than in Michel Ambacher, Marcuse et la civilisation américaine, op. cit., who sees Marcuse as an
unsuccessfully integrated German emigrant to an
America he never accepts. More subtle versions of
this crude psychologism can be found in other commentaries on Marcuse's works.
3. See MacIntyre, Marcuse, op. cit., passim;
see also his "Herbert Marcuse - From Marxism to
Pessimism", in Survey: No. 62, January 1967, pp. 38-
44.
4. See Feuer, L., Ideology and the Ideolo-
gists, New York: Harper & Row, 1975.
5. See Bykhowskii, B., "Marcusianism against
Marxism: A critique of uncritical criticism", in
Philosophy and Phenomenological Research, Vol. 30,
1969, pp. 203-218.
6. See for instance Vivas, Contra Marcuse, New
York: Delta Publishing Company Incorporated, 1971; a
much more thoughtful critique can be found in Sedgwick, P., "Natural Science and Human Theory - A
Critique of Herbert Marcuse", in Socialist Register:
1966, pp. 163-192; the contrast between Popper on
most of these points is well brought out in the
little book edited by Ferguson on Marcuse and Popper; see Marcuse, H. and Popper, K., Revolution
or Reform: A Confrontation, edited by A.T. Ferguson,
Chicago: New University Press, 1976.
7. See Martin Jay, The Dialectical Imagination
op. cit., passim; a similar perspective is also
adopted by Therborn, "The Frankfurt School", op.
cit.

8.   Marcuse, H., "The Affirmative Character of Culture", Negations, Boston: Beacon Press, 1968; "On Hedonism", Negations, Boston: Beacon Press, 1968; Eros and Civilization op. cit.; Counterrevolution and Revolt, op. cit.

9.   See Delfini and Piccone, "Marcuse's Heideggerian Marxism", op. cit., and also Franklin "The Irony of the Beautiful Soul of Herbert Marcuse", op. cit., both passim.

10.   See Rhodes, J., "Pleasure and Reason: Marcuse's Idea of Freedom", in Interpretation, Vol. 2, Winter 1971, pp. 79-104.

11.   See Jay, M., "How Utopian is Marcuse?", in The Revival of American Socialism, edited by G. Fischer, New York: Oxford University Press, p. 251.

12.   Kettler, D., "Herbert Marcuse; The Critique of Bourgeois Civilization and its Transcendence" in Crespigny, A. and Minogue, K., (Eds.) Contemporary Political Philosophers, London: Methuen and Co., 1976.

13.   Andrew, E., "Work and Freedom in Marcuse and Marx", in Canadian Journal of Political Science Canada: Vol. 3, No. 2, 1970, pp. 241-256. This article itself sparked off a lively controversy in the pages of the journal, with many excellent contributions on Marx and Marcuse's respective positions on freedom. See Baron, B. Le., "Marx on Human Emancipation", in Canadian Journal of Political Science, no. 4, December 1971, pp. 559-570; Clarke, J.J., "'The End of History': A Reappraisal of Marx's Views on Alienation and Human Emancipation", in Canadian Journal of Political Science, Canada: Vol 4, No. 3, september 1971, pp. 365-380; Solasse, B., "La Démarche critique d'Herbert Marcuse ou un nouveau type de critique social", in Canadian Journal of Political Science, Canada: Vol. II, No. 4, December 1969, pp. 448-470; Leiss, W., "Technological Rationality: Notes on 'Work and Freedom in Marcuse and Marx'", in Canadian Journal of Political Science, Vol IV, No. 3, September 1971, pp. 398-404; Schoolman, M., "Further Reflections on Work, Alienation, and Freedom in Marcuse and Marx", in Canadian Journal of Political Science, Vol. VI, No. 2, June 1973, pp. 293-302.

14.   Marx, K., The Communist Manifesto, in Selected Writings, Vol. 1, op. cit., pp. 134-136.

15.   On these points see Duncan, Marx and Mill op. cit., p. 167.

16.   See Duncan, Ibid., for a good picture of this vision, especially pp. 166-207.

17.   See Breines' article on "Marcuse and the

New Left", in The Revival of American Socialism,
edited by G. Fischer, New York: Oxford University
Press, 1971, pp. 1-21. He provides a reasonably
balanced picture on the impetus provided by Marcuse
and the distance felt by many in this movement
towards the grand old man.
    18. See Schmidt, A., "Existential-Ontologie
und historischer Materialismus bei Herbert Marcuse",
op. cit., passim; cited by Jay, m., "How Utopian is
Marcuse?", op. cit., p. 246.
    19. That this aspect has escaped an otherwise
astute observer such as MacIntyre may be due to his
own idiosyncratic interpretation of marxism; on
these points see above section 1.2 and 1.5.
    20. Regarding the marxist view on freedom, see
Duncan, Marx and Mill, op. cit., pp. 55-209; O'Rourke, The Problem of Freedom in Marxist Thought, op.
cit., especially pp. 11-78; Rays Dunayeskaya, Marxism and Freedom, op. cit., passim; Carol Gould,
Marx's Social Ontology, op. cit., pp. 101-128.
    21. Marx, Critique of the Gotha Programme, in
Selected Works op. cit., vol. 1, p. 19. See also
Andrew, "Work and Freedom in Marcuse and Marx", op.
cit., passim.
    22. See Andrew, ibid.; see also Duncan, op.
cit. and MacFarlane, Modern Political Theory, op.
cit., pp. 172-177.
    23. MacFarlane, ibid.
    24. This corresponds to major areas of inte-
rest within the field. On this point see for instance Feinberg, J., "The idea of a free man" in Doyle,
J.F. (Ed.) Educational Judgements, London and Boston: Routledge & Kegan Paul, 1973; see also Feinberg's Social Philosophy, Prentice Hall, 1973, especially chapter 1 and 2, and, with all due caution,
Berlin's "Two Concepts of Liberty", op. cit..
    25. See Feinberg, "The Idea of a Free Man",
op. cit., and section 1.1 above.
    26. See for instance Merkl, P.H., Modern Com-
parative Politics, USA - Illinois: Hinsdale, The
Dryden Press, 1977.
    27. On these points see Garaudy, La Liberté,
op. cit., pp. 262-366.
    28. See Marx, "On the Jewish Question" and
Critique of Hegel's Doctrine of the State", both in
Marx, Early Writings, op. cit., pp. 211-241 and pp.
57-198 respectively.
    29. On these points see for instance Gordon
Smith, Politics in Western Europe, London: Heinemann, 1972, 1976, pp. 99-122; see also Ruggiero,
The History of European Liberalism, op. cit..

30. Marx was certainly far more sceptical than for instance MacIntyre would like to portray him; see again on this point Marx's "Critique of the Gotha Programme", op. cit., Duncan again seems to me to capture best the ambivalent feelings that Marx entertained towards the "bourgeois" institutions of political democracy; see Duncan, Marx and Mill, op. cit., pp. 152-165.

31. See for instance Poulantzas' "Dual Power and the State" in New Left Review, vol. 109, May-June 1978, pp. 75-87.

32. See the discussion of that concept in Lind, P., The Idea of Freedom, op. cit., pp. 124-128.

33 See MacPherson, The Real World of Democracy, op. cit..

34. See Berlin, "Two Concepts of Liberty", op. cit., and Cohen, "Berlin and the liberal tradition", op. cit..

35. On this point see Gray, "Liberty, Autonomy and Human Nature", op. cit.

36. On Marx, see Duncan, Marx and Mill, op. cit.; see also Kirchheimer, O., Political Justice, USA - New Jersey, Princeton: Princeton University Press, 1961.

37. The basic argument is already to be found in "On the Jewish Question", in Early Writings, op. cit., pp. 211-242; on the judicial system, see for instance Griffith, J., The Politics of the Judiciary, London: Fontana, 1977; on the question of power inequalities see Westergaard and Resler, Class in a Capitalist Society, London: Heinemann Educational Books, 1975; on inequalities of opportunity see Schaar, J.H., "Equality of Opportunity and Beyond" in Crespigny & Wertheimer (Eds.) Contemporary Political Theory, London: Methuen & Co., 1976.

38. See for instance Duncan Marx and Mill, op. cit., and Berlin, Karl Marx, op. cit.; see also MacLellan, The Young Hegelians and Marx, op. cit.

39. By far the clearest account on such questions is to be found in O'Rourke, The Problem of Freedom in Marxist Thought, op. cit., passim; see however also Garaudy, La Liberté, op. cit., pp. 180-251.

40. Engels, F., Ludwig Feuerbach and the End of Classical German Philosophy, in Marx-Engels, Selected Writings, op. cit., vol. 3, pp. 365-376; Engels, Anti-Dühring, Peking: Foreign Language Press, 1976.

41. See in particular Wage, Labour and Capital, in Marx, Selected Works, op. cit., vol. 3, pp.

9-30.
42. See Berlin, "Two Concepts of Liberty", op.
cit., as well as the long introduction to his Four
Essays on Liberty, op. cit.. For a measure of Berlin's influence see MacCallum, "Negative and Positive Freedom", op. cit., and Gray, "Liberty, Autonomy and Human Nature", op. cit.
43. See Nicholls, "Positive Liberty, 1880-
1941" in the American Political Science Review, vol.
56, 1962, p. 121.
44. See Berlin, op. cit., Nicholls, Ibid.;
Sibley, M.Q., "The Modern Liberal Tradition" in his
Political Ideas and Ideologies, USA - New York:
1970.
45. On the "New Liberals", see Freeden, The
New Liberalism, England - Oxford: Clarendon Press,
1978.
46. Ibid.; Marcuse in fact comments on Green
and favourably so, in Reason and Revolution, op.
cit., pp. 391-393.
48. It should be noted that much of Marcuse's
interpretation is based upon the following comments
in Marx's "Critique of the Hegelian Dialectic and
Philosophy as a Whole", in the third manuscripts
(EPM, op. cit., p. 131): "The outstanding achievement of Hegel's Phenomenology and its final outcome,
the dialectic of negativity as the moving and gene-
rative principle, is thus first that Hegel conceives
the self-creation of man as a process, conceives
objectification as loss of the object, as alienation
and as transcendence of this alienation; that he
thus grasps the essence of labor and comprehends
objective man ... as the outcome of man's own labor"
(emphasis in Marx's text; cited in "The Foundation
of Historical Materialism", op. cit., p. 44, p.
171).
49. This is perhaps shown most clearly in the
essay on p. 34, p. 163; Marcuse there states that
"there is no such thing as 'society' as a subject
outside the individual", see "The Foundation of
Historical Materialism", op.cit.
50. This should not be understood - as Douglas
Kellner for instance argues - that Marcuse is unaware of this wider impact and its indirect repercussions upon the worker qua member of the society
he helps to maintain. On the contrary, this for
Marcuse must be axiomatic, having been brought up in
a fast industrializing Imperial Germany as well as
familiar with the analysis of Capital. This very
point is furthermore explicitly developed in the
"Contributions to a Phenomenology of Historical

Materialism", op. cit., pp. 9-10, pp. 49-50, see
Kellner, "Introduction to Marcuse's 'On the Philosophical Foundation of the Concept of Labor'", op.
cit., pp. 5-6.
    51.   In addition to Marcuse's own text and the
analysis in chapter four, see MacLellan, Karl Marx:
His Life and Thought, op. cit., pp. 110-111, Graeme
Duncan, Marx and Mill, op. cit., passim., and Mézáros, Marx's Theory of Alienation, op. cit., passim.
See also the less specific, but imaginative analyses
of Mandel's The Formation of the Economic Thought of
Karl Marx, op. cit., pp. 154-186.
    52.   On this point see in particular Blaumer,
R., Alienation and Freedom, USA: University of Chicago Press, 1964, pp. 16-22.
    53.   On these points see in addition to Mar-
cuse, Duncan, Marx and Mill, op. cit., pp. 72-91.
    54.   For this passage see Blauer, Alienation
and Freedom, op. cit., pp. 26-32, and Maguire,
Marx's Paris Writings, op. cit., pp. 75-76.
    55.   On the reserve army of labour, see for
instance Nicholaus' comments in his "Foreword" to
Marx's Grundrisse, op. cit., pp. 62-63; on this
aspect of alienation generally see Marx's own considerations in "Excerpts from James Mill's Elements
of Political Economy" in Early Writings, op. cit.,
p. 227; these are cited in MacLellan, The Thought
of Karl Marx, op. cit., p. 25, and in Maguire,
Marx's Paris Writings, op. cit., p. 77; see also and
compare with Marcuse's discussion of the idea of
"private property" in "The Foundation of Historical
Materialism", op. cit., pp. 30-34, pp. 159-162.
    56.   On this point see the relevant comments in
C. Taylor's "Feuerbach and the Roots of Materialism", in Political Studies, Volume XXVI, Number 3,
September 1978, pp. 417-421. See also Jean Hyppo-
lite's discussion of these points in his essay "A-
lienation et objectification", in Etudes sur Marx et
Hegel, Paris; Editions Marcel Rivière et Cie, 1955,
pp. 82-104.
    57.   Marcuse, "The Foundation of Historical
Materialism", op. cit., p. 4, p. 137, emphasis in
the text.
    58.   It is important in this context to recall
the Marcuse emphasises in his 1932 essay (footnote,
p. 12, 141 and on p. 20, p. 151) that "species-
being" should not be understood as man's "true"
nature in any empirical, biological or natural sense; Marcuse visualizes man as eminently plastic, and
the crucial dimension of human nature becomes therefore the cultural and historical "layers" left by

successive stages of development, as they are transformed in the course of an increasingly sophisti-
cated and complex civilization. This eminently social and historical perspective - and it is one that
finds support in the manuscripts themselves (most
clearly on p. 96, but also on p. 67, and p. 69) does
make it possible to visualize very radical changes
in terms of the sensibilities, emotions and powers
of men.

59.   This vision of the future society also
reappears at various points in Marx's later texts,
as for instance in the famous passages on "The free
development of individuals" in The German Ideology
(op. cit., pp. 116-117) or in the much later discussion on automation and the reduction of necessary
labour time in the Grundrisse (op. cit., pp. 116-
117); the power of that fantastic picture of a new
era for mankind can still be seen in such texts as
Bahro's 1977 forceful denunciation of the phenomenon
of "subalternity" and his condemnation of a party
which has forgotten the days of stronger hope and
greater solidarity. (See Bahro, "The Alternative in
Eastern Europe", New Left Review, 106, December
1977, pp. 3-37.)

60.   Marcuse, "On Philosophical Foundation of
the Concept of Labor in Economics", Telos, no. 16,
Summer 1973, pp. 9-37.

61.   Ibid., p. 13.

62.   This contrast will form one of the major
themes in Eros and Civilization; it will also play a
central role in Marcuse's denunciation of the Soviet
work ethic in Soviet Marxism.

63.   Marx, EPM, op. cit., p. 93; cited in Marcuse, "The Foundation of Historical Materialism",
op. cit., p. 33, p. 161.

64.   Marcuse, Ibid., p. 33, pp. 161-162, emphasis in the text.

65.   See the discussion in "The Foundation of
Historical Materialism", op. cit., pp. 19-20, pp.
150-151; this notion of a sensual, humane reason
will become a major development in Eros and Civilization; Marcuse there, paradoxically, returns to
Kant, but this time to his Critique of Judgement,
from which he develops through Schiller and Baumgar-
ten the notion of an aesthetic civilization based
around sensuality; from there there is but one step
to the conception of "eroticized reason" advanced at
the end of the book; see Eros and Civilization, op.
cit., pp. 127-141.

66.   Marcuse, "The Foundation of Historical
Materialism", p. 22, p. 152.

67. The description of "true humanism" given
at the end of the 1932 essay should not in my view
be taken entirely as a pure ontological statement.
Marcuse states that: "the 'practical theory' which
Marx sketches in these manuscripts is neither materialist nor idealist, but a fusion of the two.
Marx's description of this theory as 'real humanism'
should be understood in the sense that it 'places at
the centre of the theory man in the concreteness of
his historical and social nature (Wesen). That he
identifies with 'naturalism' here means that, if
carried through, it is an 'humanism' which leads to
the unity of man and nature; it means that we must
visualize both 'the naturalness of man' and the
'humanity of nature' as an integral part of that
'humanism'" ("The Foundation of Historical Materialism", p. 40, pp. 167-168, translation modified).

68. See Lubasz, H., "Marx's initial problematic: the problem of poverty" in Political Studies,
vol. XXIV, March 1976, pp. 24-42.

69. Marx, "The Critique of the Gotha Programme", in Selected Works, op. cit., vol. 3, pp. 15 and
19, and passim.

Chapter Five

THE IDEA OF THE CO-OPERATIVE SOCIETY IN THE THIRTIES
AND FORTIES

5.1 The New York Years

No period in Marcuse's intellectual history corresponds more closely to the image of a "negative"
philosopher than the years 1933-41 (1), when he was
concerned exclusively with the "critical" function
that Martin Jay considers the distinctive trademark
of the "Frankfurt School". In those years Marcuse
published in the Institute's journal, Zeitschrift
für Sozialforschung, a series of critical essays in
which he attacks several dominant features of bour-
eois philosophy and culture, alongside the magistral
critique of Hegel's philosophy in Reason and Revolution which appeared at the end of this period. He
devotes a long essay to the bourgeois concept of
authority from the Reformation to Sorel and Pareto,
discusses in another essay the parallels between
fascist political philosophy and liberal market
ideology and retraces in a forceful critique the
origin and development of the concept of essence in
traditional and bourgeois philosophy (2). Another
piece is devoted to a vigorous attack on the "affirmative character" of traditional culture, where the
quietist implication of that culture and its unconditional affirmation of a higher realm of beauty and
love are denounced in no uncertain terms (3). His
essay on hedonism is likewise an attack on ancient
and modern philosophical doctrines and their coun-
terparts in men's daily attitudes (4). In the discussion of "Philosophy and Critical Theory" the
negative elements of the former are most sharply
drawn out, and little is said of the positive elements of either this philosophy or the theory which
is to replace it (5).

Yet even during this period of intense collaboration with other members of the "Institut für Sozialforschung" Marcuse displays a greater willing-

ness than his colleagues to suggest the positive
implications of "critical theory". He does so in two
ways. Firstly, in most of these essays and critiques, Marcuse includes a short section on Marx,
Engels or marxism in general. These accounts are
rarely those of conventional marxist textbooks, but
present the reader with a distinctively "Marcusian"
interpretation of marxism, one in which much of the
elements of his early interpretation of the Marxian
legacy shows through. In contrast to Horkheimer or
Adorno, or the more orthodox Grünberg, there is
nearly always in these essays a sketch of the marxist answer to the question, as interpreted and
developed by Marcuse. The picture he presents in
these essays is seldom complete; it must constantly
be related to earlier positions and especially to
classical marxism without which much of what Marcuse
has to say becomes unintelligible (6).

The second way in which Marcuse advances the
positive implications of his various critiques is
best understood with reference to his first article,
"The Contributions...." (7). Marcuse there draws a
sharp distinction between what he called the "historical sense" of a given ideology and its "immanent
meaning"(8). The first of these expressions refers
to the classical understanding of an "ideology" as
no more than a reflection of a given state of affairs in the society, a reflection whose contents
can be described by its function within the totality
of social relations. This is the sense in which
"bourgeois ideology" is usually understood in marxist writings (9). The "immanent meaning", in contrast, refers to these elements of an ideology which
cannot be adequately so described. While Marcuse
never returns to the terminology he employed then,
the idea reappears as a constant feature of the
later works. There is always a certain ambiguity in
Marcuse's treatment of classical bourgeois thought.
This ambiguity comes across most clearly in his
sympathetic account of the "bourgeois" philosopher
Hegel in his Reason and Revolution, but also in his
treatment of much German philosophy in these essays
from the thirties. To some extent it is an ambiguity
he shares with the other members of the Institute
(10). What distinguishes Marcuse's position in this
respect, however, is a far greater commitment to the
idea of truth as absolute - in the sense that some
truths are unquestionable and real in relation to
the wider goal of human progress. This is the position he advocated in the essay "On Concrete Philosophy" and it is reaffirmed in the 1937 article on

"Philosophy and Critical Theory" in the context of
an argument against the absolute relativism of Mannheim's sociology of knowledge (11). Marcuse states
that when "critical theory" concerns itself with
"fundamental concepts of philosophy", they are not:

> "merely analysed sociologically in order to
> correlate philosophical dogmas with social
> loci...To the extent that philosophy is more
> than ideology, every such attempt must come to
> nought. When critical theory comes to terms
> with philosophy, it is interested in the truth
> content of philosophical concepts and problems.
> It presupposes that they really contain truth"
> (12)

Even in these most "negative" essays, there is thus
always an underlying search for a "positive philosophy". This philosophy comes forth in Marcuse's very
personal treatment of classical marxism, but it also
emerges from an independent treatment of the issues
involved. The core of this philosophy consists in an
elaboration of the idea of the "co-operative society".

The importance of these essays of the thirties
in relation to the wider body of Marcuse's works can
hardly be overstated. This is so for a variety of
reasons. Firstly, these writings constitute an invaluable link between the foundation years in Freiburg
and the later work in the fifties and sixties which
was to make Marcuse famous far beyond the limits of
academic repute. Without these essays it would be
difficult to comprehend the underlying unity of his
thought, and the development from the essay on the
Paris Manuscripts to the overt utopianism of Eros
and Civilization. Secondly, these essays, together
with Reason and Revolution, form the most powerful,
creative and convincing part of Marcuse's written
works. Many of the ideas developed in later articles, large parts of Eros and Civilization and even
parts of the more conventional Soviet Marxism, found
their first expression during this period. Thirdly,
it is in these writings, and in particular in the
essays, that the fruits of the extraordinary interdisciplinary collaboration characteristic of the
"Institut für Sozialforschung" are most clearly seen.
While the influence of this collaboration has been
greatly exaggerated as far as the core elements of
Marcuse's "positive philosophy" are concerned, there
is no doubt that it served as a tremendous intellectual stimulant and that in terms of creative impul-

ses and detailed analyses his work owes much to this period (13). Fourthly, this period also witnessed important changes with respect to Marcuse's relation to marxism, his attitude toward Heidegger and the development of the idea of freedom.

It is only with respect to the first of these changes that Marcuse's new membership of the institute can be said to be decisive. Following his departure from Freiburg, where his relationship with Heidegger had become more and more strained (on academic, but perhaps also on personal or political grounds), he went to Frankfurt, where a friend recommended him to Horkheimer. He arrived shortly thereafter in the USA, after a short stay in Geneva, and began to work in the new team (14). He has himself acknowledged how much this new milieu meant in terms of a renewed interest in political issues, and how it helped to strengthen his marxist convictions. Even in relation to the 1932 essay the shift from a philosophical to a more political commitment is marked. For instance, in Reason and Revolution, he now states that "all the philosophical concepts of Marxian theory are social and economic categories cal" (15). Elsewhere, in the section entitled "The Revision of the Dialectic", while Bernstein and Kautsky are equally blamed, both Plekanov and Lenin meet with approval for their insistence upon the centrality of the dialectic in Marx (16). An orthodox, if imaginative reliance upon marxist theory is also revealed in the analysis of fascism interpreted as an extreme, but plausible development from the bourgeois liberalism of an earlier age, and one more compatible with the demands of monopoly capitalism (17). It should be noted that in some respects this more clear-cut political stance went beyond the positions advocated by Horkheimer and Adorno, the two leading figures most often associated with Marcuse, and that these divergences reflect more fundamental differences in outlook (18).

The second of these changes is partly a result of these developments and the general situation in Germany. Its immediate cause was Heidegger's extraordinary pro-Hitler speech as newly constituted rector of Freiburg. Marcuse only recently re-affirmed the importance he attached to the event, and the highly personal character of Heidegger's philosophy tends to support his view that this constituted the most damaging indictment of this whole approach (19). There are reasons to doubt that this was more than a temporary aberration on the part of Heidegger, who resigned shortly afterward (20). Whatever the case may be, Marcuse was now firmly set against a body of ideas he once admired; the following year, in the context of a larger essay on the nature of Nazism, he roundly condemned the "philosophical existentialism" of Heidegger for providing support and inspiration to its infamous policitcal counter-part epitomized by the writings of the leading Nazi theoretician Carl Schmidt (21).

Concomitant with these changes, both already initiated in the essay on "The Foundation of Histo-rical Materialism", was a far greater support for materialism, whether philosophical, sociological or anthropological. This was partly terminological - marxism was henceforth referred to as "the materia-list theory of society". But it was also expressed in a greater reliance upon economic analyses, and in far more attention to this dimension of daily exis-tence under capitalism. The place of Heidegger in Marcuse's work was taken by Hegel and Kant to some extent, but also by sociologists such as Max Weber, and more attention was paid to the social sciences, in particular through an extended critique of posi-tivism (22). One important development of this pe-riod is the not unrelated appearance of a number of Freudian themes in the lates thirties (23). These various changes and developments took place in a context dominated largely by the events in Germany (24). Yet for the most part they were already con-tained in or implied by the idea of the "co-opera-tive society" derived from Marx the year before Marcuse's exile to the USA and prior to this period of collaborative research within the Institute for Social Research.

5.2. The Analysis of Labour

The continuity of Marcuse's idea of freedom is no-where more clearly expressed than in the fundamental role that the notion of labour plays in the post-1932 writings. In Reason and Revolution, published in 1941, he states that "labour in its true form is the medium for man's self-fulfilment, for the full development of his potentialities; the conscious utilization of the forces of nature should thus take place for his satisfaction and enjoyment" (25). La-bour once more is defined as that all-round activity which has no aims other than the full development of individual and communitarian potentialities. It is that which characterizes the good society. It is what allows men in the "co-operative society" to give to nature the distinctive imprint of their

Table 5 (*)

Assumptions and logical implications of Marcuse's conception of a free society as developed between 1932 and 1941.

The Co-operative society (2nd Version)

ASS 1   Genuine human freedom is only to be obtained in and through labour in its true form.

ASS 2   a) Labour in its true form is the "abolition" of labour as it exists in capitalistic society. A reasonable approximation would be to describe it as any sustained, deliberate and well-understood activity whereby the individual or collectivity seeks to develop human powers and capacities, with no other aims than human satisfaction, happiness and development. It takes place within the realm of freedom.
        b) Necessary rational labour is any purposeful and disciplined activity directly aiming at the transformation of the environment (or part thereof) with a view to promote the best conditions for all to be able to engage in true labour. This only takes place within the realm of necessity.

ASS 3   The extent of human freedom is the extent to which true labour becomes possible. Complete freedom is a society which allows for the possibility of such labour to the full. The co-operative society is such a society. It is described by the assumptions that follow.

ASS 4   The co-operative society is a society where the individual both:
        a)   participates on a full and equal basis in the necessary rational labour aiming to establish the best conditions for human happiness in the realm of freedom.
        b)   participates on a full and equal basis in labour in its true form, where he fully dominates the object of his labour and where he is able to shape it in accor-dance with the most satisfactory combination of the constraints imposed by the object's "inner laws" and of the needs he feels most expresses his individual personality. He understands himself through such labour and understands others through their labour (in its true form).

ASS 5   In the co-operative society, outside the realm of necessity this relation holds true not only for the individually created or shaped objects, or for those "worked upon" in collaboration with a few others; it is equally valid for all the achievements of that society at large, be it in terms of the wider material production, the world of culture or the social institutions. In all these areas it will be possible to see not only the mark of the "co-operative" man, but also that of each individual. The world will thus be a testimony of all of man's powers and needs, and of those of all individuals composing that society.

ASS 6   The individual's self-realisation occurs primarily through the direct impact upon his being of labour in its true form. It also takes place via the collective transformation of the world by necessary and true labour into a more human civilisation.

ASS 7   a) Necessary labour is determined in terms of the indirect, long term and "objective" impact it has upon the development of the co-operative society and thereby upon the "co-operative" man. It is rational in the sense that it is organised so as to require a minimum of time and resources, while taking full account of the abilities and needs of the individual performing it.
    b) Labour in its true form is almost wholly determined in terms of the direct, immediate and "subjective" impact it has upon the individual performing it: this impact is different from anything conceivable in contemporary capitalistic societies. True labour in the co-operative society is the sum of all of those activities upon objects (social and natural) which directly promotes the full development of the individual's powers and capacities, allows him to express a rich variety of social and individual needs, and affords him varied emotional and sensory experiences.

ASS 8   The extent of necessary labour in the co-operative society is limited to those clear instances where the long term benefits of such activities are indisputably greater than the provisional harm caused by the deviation from the definition of true labour in assumption 7 b).

ASS 9   When necessary labour is to be performed, and how it is to be organized, is decided by the "associated producers" participating fully and equally in joint planning decisions. The overriding concern is always the best possible satisfaction of the individual's needs and powers.

ASS 10 The individual himself alone chooses to engage in true labour, be it individual or collective. He determines, alone or in co-operation with others, the character and conditions of this form of work. Only necessary labour, under the conditions which assumptions 8 and 9 fully describe, can be enforced in the co-operative society. This, however, is not incompatible with mild social pressure directly following from the ethical ends described below.

ASS 11 Given that human nature is essentially a social creation, the human needs and powers to be found in the co-operative society are not ascertainable from within the present order of things, but for the following exceptions.

a) Firstly, the whole range of human emotions, senses and needs will be developed. This will include all of man's senses and bodily pleasures, inclusive sexual masochism and sadism, when it results in heightened pleasure between consenting and equal partners.

b) Secondly, there will be no room for any other form of self-abasement or abasement of another under human will, no meaningless sacrifice as a surrogate of sexuality, no heroism of war, or for any of the needs and wants which are based upon oppression, injustice and poverty.

c) Thirdly, the needs for beauty and for a culture concerned with the aspirations, joys and sorrows of the community, as well as the memories of the past, are likely to play an altogether more central role in the daily life of all in the co-operative society than in any existing society up to this point in history.

ASS 12 Happiness and knowledge will no longer be incompatible; love and affection for others will be able to rest on full knowledge of that other.

ASS 13 The rationality guiding the activities of the men and women in the co-operative society is never simply the cold instrumental rationality implied by economic theory or the physical sciences. Such forms of rationality are applied to the organisation of necessary labour and within the confines of the realm of necessity. Even there, it is a rationality which is informed by and supportive of the overriding goal of the co-operative society, namely the best possible satisfaction of all the individual's needs and powers.

ASS 14 The co-operative society is guided by ethical ends. These ends are fully described in the overriding concern for the full development of all the individuals constituting that society. No other moral value or ethical ends can be invoked against this goal, and the freedom of all is as unrestrained as possible within the limits set by this goal.

THE THIRTIES AND FORTIES

ASS 15 Those aspects of human relations not falling under the
limited sphere of necessary labour or the sphere of
true labour as defined above are similarly solely governed by the above ethical goals.

(*) Table 5 should be seen in relation to table 4. The
main differences between the two tables concern the concept of
labour and the definition of human needs in the co-operative
society. Labour is now divided between "labor in its true
form" and "necessary labor". The distinction applies to assumptions 1-10, 13 and 15. The human needs characteristic of
the co-operative society differ from the previous table by
including sexuality and sexual deviations, in explicitly eli-
minating heroism and other forms of social masochism and in
placing greater emphasis upon culture and beauty. Assumptiom
12 furthermore specifies that happiness and knowledge no longer will be incompatible.

personalities and cultural and material aspirations.
And it is how we should understand Marx when he
states that "man is free 'if nature is his work and
his reality' so that he 'recognizes himself in a
world he himself has made'" (26).
     Reason and Revolution is the major work of this
period, and it is probably the best, certainly the
most respected, of his full length written works
(27). It is a book with many aims. It is most often
thought of as a brilliant and scholarly interpretation of Hegel; it undoubtedly deserves to stand out
for its bold, vivid and well researched philosophical interpretation of the old master. It is often
forgotten that it was also conceived as a work with
an immediate political aim - that of rescuing Hegel
from his association with Nazism in American minds
(28). Its broader perspective consists in presenting
Hegel as the heir of the Enlightment and of the
radical liberal aspirations of the French Revolution; Hegel's later explicit conservatism thus con-
tradicts the overall thrust of his entire philosophy
(29).
     The main aim of Reason and Revolution, however,
is to bring to light the inner continuity between
Hegel thus understood and the revolutionary theory
of Marx. A number of things make this perfectly
clear. The subtitle of Reason and Revolution is
"Hegel and the Rise of Social Theory"; the section
on Marx occupies the central place between the exposition of Hegel's philosophy and the later sections

on positivism, neo-Hegelianism and Fascism; the
section on Marx as well as the interpretation of
Hegel are presented in terms of a continual Marx-
Hegel dialogue; the introduction to Part II explicitly presents Marx as the only true heir of Hegel;
inversely, Hegel's philosophy is seen as the philosophical and idealist prefiguration for the only
viable way to transform and understand the social
world, namely the Marxist revolutionary theory and
its implications for collective action.

The parallel between <u>Reason and Revolution</u> and
the last section of Marcuse's 1932 essay is immediately obvious. The programme outlined in this section
will, with modifications and some important changes,
develop into the full scale project whose culmination will be the publication, some nine years later,
of the book we know today.

The role played by the concept of labour in
this context is a paramount one. In contrast to the
other commentators Marcuse accords an unusually
large place to the role of labour in Hegel's thinking, and he systematically strives to present its
similarities with the later Marxian usages of the
concept, especially in <u>Capital</u> (30). In the context
of Hegel's "first system", elaborated during the
later part of his stay at Jena, Marcuse states that:

"The concept of labor is not peripheral in
Hegel's thinking, but is the central notion
through which he conceives the development of
society. Driven by the insight that opened this
dimension to him, Hegel describes the mode of
integration (i.e. alienated labor) prevailing
in commodity production society in terms that
clearly foreshadow Marx's critical approach."
(31).

Later in the text he brings up the central theme of
the 1932 essay:

"Marx was not familiar with the stages of Hegel's philosophy prior to the 'Phenomenology',
but he nevertheless caught the critical impact
of Hegel's analysis, even in the attenuated
form in which social problems were permitted to
enter the 'Phenomenology of Mind'. The great-
ness of that work he saw in the fact that Hegel
conceived the 'self creation' of man (that is,
the creation of a reasonable social order
through man's free action) as the process of
'reification' and its 'negation', in short,

that he grasped the 'nature of labor' and saw
man to be 'the result of his labor'." (32).

The concept of labour is also what divides Marx from
Feuerbach's philosophy: "Labor transforms the natural conditions of human existence into social ones.
By omitting the labour process from his <u>Philoso-
phy of Freedom</u>, therefore, Feuerbach omitted the
decisive factor through which nature may become the
medium for freedom" (33). Marcuse here sees Marx
siding with Hegel and points to the wider epistemological implications of labour as against Feuerbach's orientation toward "senses, perception and
sensation" (34).
    We shall not enter into details about the va-
rious ways in which Marcuse seeks to strengthen his
overall argument (35); nor shall we concern ourselves with the various other features of the "co-
operative society" as they reappear in this work.
Suffice it to say in this context that the category
of "species-being" is again presented as a fundamental concept for Marxian theory; that Marcuse reaffirms in the strongest possible terms that the goal
can only be understood in terms of "free individuals"; and that "this individualist trend is fundamental as an interest of the Marxian theory" (36).
    One important new development concerns the idea
of labour itself. Marcuse no longer speaks of "free
labor", but refers instead to the "abolition of
labor" as the goal of the Marxian revolution (37).
In part it is to allow "free labor" to describe
unambiguously, for better and for worse, a liberal
goal and a distinct capitalist achievement. Although
Max Weber's name is not mentioned Marcuse in this
passage clearly has in mind the German sociologist's
detailed analyses of the "free laborer", detached
from the ties of an often supportive feudal order
(38). Moreover, the new formulation enables Marcuse
to highlight the Hegelian idea of "abolition" (aufhebung) as an integral element in Marx's conception
of the new order the revolution will bring: "Abolition ... carries the meaning that a content is res-
tored to its true form" (39). True objectification
will replace the alienated form of labour which has
been known hitherto, i.e. that activity which creates surplus value and "produces capital" (40).
    Yet the new formulation also reflects Marcuse's
new thinking on the subject. He stresses that "Marx
ferent from the prevailing one that he hesitated to
use the same term 'labor' to designate alike the
material process of capitalist and communist socie-

ty" (41). Other passages in the text also strongly
suggest that the alternative to labour is now seen
as more akin to play than to any form of work as
commonly understood. To understand the evolution of
Marcuse's position on the question it is necessary
to return to the analysis in a 1933 essay entitled
"On the Philosophical Foundation of the Concept of
Labor in Economics" (42). Marcuse there develops
more fully the conclusions he derives from his essay
on the Paris Manuscripts in the context of then
current theories of labour in economic and social
theory. The main interest of the piece lies in the
contrast he draws between these conceptualizations
and an extensive and explicitly Hegelian apprehension of labour as a crucial, if thwarted, dimension
of individual existence.

Marcuse broadens Marx's analysis to include all
types of work necessary for industrial civilization
and suggests, if only tentatively, that Hegel's notion of the superiority of intellectual, creative
work may contain a pointer to the future (43). He
then develops three concepts of labour. Firstly,
there is that labour which has as its only goal the
development of individual co-operative existence.
Marcuse describes this form of labour by stating
that the true goal of labour is "real fulfilment of
human existence in its duration and permanence"
(44). Such labour can only develop in the region
beyond material production and reproduction, beyond
any mere "necessities", and it corresponds to what
Marx calls "the realm of freedom". This is "labor in
its true form". It will only arise from the "abolition" of present forms of labour, in a free society
such as the "co-operative society". The second is
that form of activity which has no other rationale
than the procurement and maintenance of vital necessities for all concerned. It can take many different
forms, and these can vary greatly in the degree of
freedom and enjoyment they afford to the individual.
Yet ultimately it is something which is imposed from
the outside, and not something which has the full
development of the individual as its prime goal.
This is necessary rational labour. It is that labour
which, in a free and jointly planned society, cannot
be performed as labour in its true form. Thirdly,
there are those activities which serve neither of
these goals, and which are solely the result of an
ineffective organization of society and a consequence of the prevailing class structure. This is alienated labour, as it has existed in all societies to
the present.

Marcuse uses these three concepts when re-
examining the question of the division of labour.
There is a natural division of labour, which can
also be a rational one. This is true for both labour
"in its true form" and necessary rational labour. It
is only through his interaction with others that the
individual fulfils his needs and becomes himself
(45). Labour is "naturally" to be divided according
to age, sex, talents, physical constitution and the
and the like. Moreover, this division of labour can
also involve elements of subordination which result
from the demands of task. Historically, however, the
evolution has been otherwise, and virtually all
forms of division of labour in the past have been
rooted in a relation of "domination and servitude"
as described by Hegel (46). It is this relation
which historically has constituted the foundation
for all "further division of labor among groups,
classes, occupations, etc., which are connected with
the socio-economic appropriation of labor" (47). It
has also meant that the measure of "conscious cir-
cumspection and foresight" inherent in all labour
has been restricted to the few and the privileged.
They alone could approach work in such a manner.
Furthermore, they alone were able to detach themselves sufficiently from immediate needs by virtue of
their social and economic security, enabling them to
make the integrity and fulfilment of their being a
goal in itself. For the subordinate classes, however
(and this Marcuse claims as Hegel's and Marx's most
profound insight), the nature of their work prevents
any such possibility.

> "Their existence is forever linked to the mate-
> rial production and reproduction and it is cut
> off at the root from the acquisition of the
> conscious foresight and circumspection that
> corresponds to their own inner potential. The
> social 'status' and the appropriation of la-
> bour, instead of being the expression of the
> power of their own existence, becomes instead
> the socio-economic chains to which the indivi-
> dual is riveted/bolted at birth or through
> circumstances." (48)

Overcoming this situation necessitates a total
transformation of labour, so it becomes free from
alienation and reification. This will only be possible by a revolution as envisioned by Marx, and this
is how the famous passage from Capital given below
should be understood:

> "In fact, the realm of freedom begins only
> where labor determined by necessity and exter-
> nal purpose stops. Therefore, it lies by defi-
> nition beyond the sphere of actual material
> production... Freedom in this realm can only
> consist in that socialized man, i.e. the asso-
> ciated producers, rationally control their
> material exchange with nature, bringing it
> under their common control, instead of being
> controlled by it as a blind force, performing
> it with the least expenditure of energy and
> under conditions most worthy and adequate to
> their human nature. But this always remains a
> realm of necessity. Beyond it begins the deve-
> lopment of human powers, which is an end in
> itself, the true realm of freedom. This, howe-
> ver, can only unfold on the basis of the realm
> of necessity." (49)

Marx's "realm of freedom" should be understood as
that where need and external necessity no longer
prevail, and "the shortening of the working day is
its basic prerequisite" (50). The "development of
human forces" is its only goal. How, where and when
this is achieved is for the individual and community
within the "co-operative society" to decide. A further step toward an easy-going, playful and hedonistic antithesis to "alienated labor" is then taken in
Reason and Revolution. Marcuse now speaks of a revolution to "set free all the potentialities for general satisfaction that have developed in the (capitalist) system" (51). He argues for the "abolition of
labor as such" (52). Elsewhere, in relation to the
class system under capitalism, he discusses "the
arena of free play still open to the individual"
(53).

The transition is nowhere sharply marked. Marx,
as is well-known, was himself ambiguous on this
point (54). Yet there is a definite progression from
the idea of "free labor" to an easier, self-inspired
and culturally well-supported gratification of needs
and talents. It is a progression which is already
latent in Marcuse's interpretation of the Paris Manuscripts. It is in this respect possible to see a
direct line of continuity between the 1932 essay and
the more utopian writings of post-war years; and, as
we shall see, it is with a mostly hidden Marx in
mind that these writings should be read.

152

5.3 Reason and Rationality

The second important development during the thirties is the emergence of reason as a central category of Marcuse's thinking. Among the factors which help to account for this is Marcuse's final disenchantment with Heidegger. Although the crucial turning point occurred with the rediscovery of Marx's <u>Paris Manuscripts</u>, much of Heidegger's style and terminology remained in evidence even thereafter. Heidegger's 1933 speech marked the end of the residual influence, and this shift, as well as Marcuse's new concerns, found expression in the new prominence of the concept of reason (55). An important influence is certainly that of his colleagues at the Institute for Social Research. It would be difficult to overstate the role played by the concept of reason for Horkheimer and Adorno in particular (56). Martin Jay goes as far as stating that "the Frankfurt School's stress of reason was one of the salient characteristics of its work" (57).

More decisive still was the advent of Nazism in Germany, and the events that followed it. The blatant combination of the most advanced and rigorous technological and economic rationality with the overt irrationalism of the regime itself demanded a re-examination of the traditional philosophical conception of rationality. In Marcuse's first article dealing with these questions, "The Struggle Against the Totalitarian View of the State", published in 1934, we can find the most comprehensive definition of the new idea of reason:

> "A theory of society is <u>rationalist</u> when the practice it enjoins is subject to the idea of autonomous reason, i.e. to the human faculty of comprehending, through conceptual thought, the true, the good and the right. Within society, every action and every determination of goals as well as the social organization as a whole has to legitimate itself before the decisive judgement of reason, and everything, in order to subsist as a fact or goal, stands in need of rational justification." (58)

Marcuse sketches in that passage a conception of reason akin to the idea of "Vernunft" as understood by Kant, and later developed by Hegel. As opposed to the commonsensical view of the world as a simple collection of disparate "givens" or mere facts, "Vernunft" is able to perceive and articulate the underlying relations. Hegel furthermore saw these

153

relations as interrelated in a wider dialectical
network which eventually would reveal itself to the
searching mind as the fundamental unity of the
world. This underlying unity includes both phenomena
and noumena, irreconciliable in the Kantian system.
The reason which ultimately becomes this dialectic
is a reason which is both "practical" and "theoretical"; the distinction between the "ought" and the
"is" will prove itself to be a superficial distinction (59).

Marcuse does not subscribe to the final identity of the subject and the object as envisioned by
Hegel. He adopts from Hegel the idea of reason as an
ethical and an epistemological tool. In other words,
reason is to show what is right as well as what is
true. Furthermore, he fully subscribes to the idea
that reason must aim to grasp what is present in its
totality in order to uncover the underlying structures that determine that present. He shares with
Hegel the fundamental distinction between essence
and appearance, even if the field of application
(the ontological status and ultimate goal of the
dialectical method) which follow from this conception differs radically from that of Hegel from 1932
onward. A further parallel with the Hegelian understanding of reason is that it is this essence, or
rather the potential it reveals, that ultimately
must constitute the ground upon which the present
must be judged. It is with respect to this potential
that every fact must be re-examined and re-interpreted, and it is in relation to that same potential
that its value for mankind must be assessed.

All this becomes clearer when placed in the
context of Marcuse's previous writings. It is reason
thus defined which is now to provide the "insight
that shatters reification" (60). Reason as redefined
by Marcuse now plays the fundamental role of providing the basis for the "consciousness" which is to
guide the "praxis of transcendence"(61). It is a
concept of reason which is to provide truths not
merely valid for effective actions upon the physical
world, but primarily aims at truths which are valid
for the existence of individuals in society. The
rationale for this concept of reason is the liberation of these individuals.

Marcuse sees the source and inspiration for
this substantive reason in classical German and European philosophy:

"Reason is the fundamental category of philosophical thought, the only one by means of which

it has bound itself to human destiny. Philosophy wanted to discover the ultimate and most
general grounds of Being. Under the name of
reason it conceived the idea of an authentic
Being in which all significant antitheses (of
subject and object, essence and appearance,
thought and being) were reconciled. Connected
with this idea was the conviction that what
exists is not immediately and already rational
but must rather be brought to reason. Reason
represents the highest potentiality of man and
of existence; the two belong together."(62)

Reason in this sense epitomizes all the efforts of
previous philosophy to reconcile the aspirations of
man with the reality of a world which was seen as
forever contingent, and yet susceptible to improvements, modifications and changes. It is a reason
with man's wider interests at heart, defined and
grounded in the idea of a community and which sees
its first task as that of promoting, maintaining and
defending this ideal against all odds. Against merely instrumental forms of rationality - economic,
legal, technical or scientific - it argues that ends
must always enter into the idea of what is rational
and efficient (63). The reconciliation of these two
forms of rationality, together with an emphasis upon
the free, liberated and thinking individual is for
Marcuse the mark of nascent bourgeois philosophy,
and characteristic of an early era of expansive
activism with universalistic aims. It is this activist dimension of an earlier bourgeois philosophy,
epitomized by Descartes' then newly-found self-
certain "ego cogito" that Marcuse seeks to recapture:

"Liberated from the bonds and obligations of
the medieval order and empowered to shape his
own world, the autonomous individual saw his
reason presented with the task hypostatized in
the doctrine of essence: realizing the authentic potentialities of beings on the basis of
the discovery that nature can be controlled.
Essence became the object of theoretical and
practical reason." (64)

He adds a little later:

"But in the contemporary form of social organization, the domination of nature through rational methods of production as envisioned by

> Descartes was neither joined to nor directed by
> the sovereign reason of associated invidi-
> duals."(65)

The thrust of Marcuse's analyses in these essays of
the thirties is that the history of philosophy since
Descartes reflects the growing estrangement from
these all-encompassing ideals, leading to a contemplative and passive attitude toward the real human
and social problems.

Marcuse, in contrast to his former colleagues,
never includes Marx in his critique of technological
rationality, and will always be careful to point to
the benefits accruing from a conscious and collectively directed application of such rationality (66).
The point is clearly stated in Reason and Revolution
when Marcuse declares that "Man's struggle with
nature will pursue 'a general plan' formulated by
'freely combined individuals'" (67). In fact, a
common theme for most of the essays of the thirties
is the favourable contrast drawn between Marx and
even the most radical positions of bourgeois philosophy. Marcuse thus argues that idealist philosophy
in particular advocates a concept of reason which
puts a premium upon man's inner freedom, and man's
internal, intellectual and psychological liberation
while at the same time leaves him enslaved in an
environment untouched by such ideals. This he opposes to the conception advanced by the "materialist
theory of society".

> "Western philosophy has established reason as
> authentic reality. In the bourgeois epoch the
> reality of reason became the task that the free
> individual was to fulfil. The subject was the
> locus of reason and the source of the process
> by which objectivity was to become rational.
> The material conditions of life, however, al-
> lotted freedom to reason only in pure thought
> and pure will. But a social situation has come
> about in which the realization of reason no
> longer needs to be restricted to pure thought
> and will. If reason means shaping life accor-
> ding to men's free decision on the basis of
> their knowledge, then the demand for reason
> henceforth means the creation of a social orga-
> nization in which individuals can collectively
> regulate their lives in accordance with their
> needs. With the realization of reason in such a
> society, philosophy would disappear."(68)

This concept is central to <u>Reason and Revolution</u>. It indicates the essential continuity Marcuse sees between the philosophy of the Enlightenment, the ideals promoted by the French Revolution and Hegel's philosophy (69). The concept of reason is presented as a cornerstone of Hegel's philosophy; reason marks the new freedom acquired through the liberalization of the written word, and provides the individual with the first and most basic weapon against all forms of despotism (70). Reason again serves to introduce the comprehensive critique of the positivist movement which restricts all of reason's former claims to truth to the analysis and determination of rigid "natural laws" presumed to be operative even in the society of man (71). Reason also serves to summarize the central features of Marx's debt to Hegel:

"Hegel's system....unfolded and completed 'in thought' all those bourgeois principles (completed 'in reality' in other Western nations) that were not yet part of social reality. It made reason the sole universal standard of society; it recognized the role of abstract labor in integrating divergent individual interests into a unified 'system of wants'; it discovered the revolutionary implications of the liberalist ideas of freedom and equality; it described the history of civil society as the history of the irreconciliable antagonisms inherent in this order."(72)

The importance of this concept of reason for the transition from Marx to Hegel is even more explicit later on, in the discussion of alienated labour. In a few lines Marcuse sketches the central features of the "co-operative society". He adds that "all this has an obvious resemblance to Hegel's idea of reason. Marx goes even as far as to describe the self-realization of man in terms of unity between thought and being" (73). There is one crucial difference and this is that "the whole problem, however, is no longer a philosophical one" (74).

5.4 Happiness, Individuality and Affirmative Materialism

The third major development during this period with respect to Marcuse's "positive philosophy" is the emergence of the idea of happiness. The concept of reason provides the major link between Marx's revolutionary theory and Hegelian philosophy. Happiness, and the idea of an expansive, joyful, "affirmative" materialism, marks in Marcuse's work the most radical disjuncture between the Marxian project and the lofty ideals of classical German philosophy. Related through the prominence in Marcuse's thought of an entirely novel mode of labour and the common framework of the good society, the two notions are in every other way counterposed; they form the mutually opposed poles of a demanding conception of freedom. The resulting tension leads to many fruitful and decisive insights and constitutes one of the most distinctive traits of Marcuse's work.

We find many traces of such a notion of sensual happiness in the 1932 essay, and in tracing Marx's analyses in the Paris Manuscripts back to Feuerbach, Marcuse explicitly emphasises the passive, needy and passionate character of man as a "species-being" (75). Marx himself in this text stresses the idea of a living, sensuous and well-rounded individual, constantly seeking to develop his senses and his sensibility to fully profit from the new material and cultural wealth that capitalism has made possible (76). The idea of happiness furthermore appears in the development from "free labor" to the "abolition of labor" already latent in Marcuse's 1932 essay (77). The intimate relation existing in Marcuse's thought between the latter notion and the idea of happiness is clearly affirmed toward the end of the crucial section entitled "The Abolition of Labor" in Reason and Revolution: "Marx's idea of a rational society implies an order in which it is not the universality of labor but the universal satisfaction of all individual potentialities that constitutes the principle of social organization.... Mankind becomes free only when the material perpetuation of life is a function of the abilities and happiness of associated individuals" (78)

The idea of happiness is crucial to Marcuse's entire argument in Reason and Revolution. The term is only used sparingly, but the idea forms an essential element of the pivotal central sections, where Marcuse presents Marx as at once the true heir of Hegel and the fiercest opponent of the metaphysical character of his philosophy. "The Marxian theory has developed in full contradiction to the basic conception of idealist philosophy. The idea of reason has been superseded by the idea of happiness" (79). An altogether different conception of reason emerges in the process. While the abstract, theoretical and purely philosophical Hegelian reason "could prevail even though the reality shrieked of individual frustration", an idea of reason allied to the demand for individual happiness cannot. The hedonistic strain goes against every aspect of classical German philosophy and culture: "The demand that free individuals attain satisfaction militated against the entire set-up of traditional culture" (80). This radical, uncompromising claim for human happiness and a full life for every individual in society forever divides marxism from a philosophy which "within a framework of social and economic inequalities" upholds the "life of reason (as) a life of higher dignity"; it is opposed to every philosophy that dictates "individual sacrifice for the sake of some higher universal independent of the 'base' impulses and drives of individuals" (81).

Contrary to the 1932 essay, Marcuse now brings to the fore the strong hedonistic element implicit in Marx's treatment of the sensuality of man as a "species-being". Feuerbach's insights are no longer presented as ontological certainties - they show a new potential for happiness. "Nature shapes and determines the ego from without, making it essentially 'passive'. The process of liberation cannot eliminate this passivity, but can transform it from a source of privation and pain to one of abundance and enjoyment" (82).

The happiness that Marcuse envisions is imbued with Feuerbachian humanistic and naturalistic ideals. That the individual and his concrete existence stand at the centre of this conception, is never better illustrated than by the singular inclusion of Kierkegaard as a forerunner to Marx (83) (Heidegger is not mentioned once (84)). Although Marcuse is now highly critical, especially of the antirationalistic thrust of Kierkegaard's philosophy (85), his account brings forth the positive individualistic and radical claim for earthly happiness in this philosophy:

"Salvation could not rely upon external institutions and authorities, nor could it ever be attained by pure thought. Consequently, Kierkegaard now shifts the burden of achieving a life in truth to the concrete individual, the same individual who is the basic concern of Christianity...Kierkegaard returns to the original function of religion, its appeal to the destitute and tormented individual. He thus restores to Christianity its combative and revolutionary force. The appearance of God again assumes the terrifying aspect of a historical event sudden-

> ly breaking in upon a society in decay. Eterni-
> ty takes on a temporal aspect while the reali-
> zation of happiness becomes an immediately
> vital matter of daily life." (86)

Marcuse's insistence upon the concrete and material
happiness of individual men and women is nevertheless not one from which the wider ideals of the "co-
operative society" are absent. Even as far as Kierkegaard is concerned, Marcuse will be quick to point
out that his "individualism turns into the most
emphatic absolutism" (87). As for Feuerbach, not
only does he ignore the crucial role of labour in
human life, but "his 'perceptual materialism' perceives only 'separate individuals in bourgeois society'" (88). Marcuse remains in every way opposed
to methodological individualism (89). It is an issue
that he considered as settled by Hegel (90). The
same point is borne out even more clearly in the re-
interpretation of the idea of "species-being" and
its Feuerbachian roots:

> "The process of alienation affects all strata
> of society, distorting even the 'natural func-
> tions' of man. The sense, the primary source of
> freedom and happiness according to Feuerbach,
> are reduced to one 'sense of possessing'. They
> view their object only as something that can or
> cannot be appropriated. Even pleasure and en-
> joyment change from conditions under which men
> freely develop their 'universal nature' into
> modes of 'egoistic' possession and acquisi-
> tion." (92)

The same opposition to an unreflected, self-centred
and unco-operative materialism is affirmed at the
close of the description of a society characterized
by the "abolition of labor". This is to be replaced
by an "affirmative materialism" which stresses men's
essential sociability and allows a thousand cultural
mediations to turn this materialism into a radical
and novel hedonism:

> "The category of happiness makes manifest the
> positive content of materialism. Historical ma-
> terialism appeared at first as a denunciation
> of the materialism prevalent in bourgeois so-
> ciety, and the materialist principle was in
> this respect a critical instrument of exposé
> directed against a society that enslaved men to
> the blind mechanisms of material production.

The idea of the free and universal realization of individual happiness, 'per contra', denoted an affirmative materialism, that is to say, an affirmation of the material satisfaction of man." (93)

The idea of happiness appears at various other points in Reason and Revolution. Particularly noteworthy is the fact that Hobhouse's insistence upon the happiness of individuals makes his liberalism, for Marcuse, undeniably more attractive than the philosophies of the British neo-idealists (94). And it is this idea which concludes the analysis of the labour process in Marx. "The real possibility of general happiness is negated by the social relationships posited by man himself. The negation of this society and its transformation become the single outlook for liberation" (95).

The idea of happiness appears already in Marcuse's very first essay following the events of 1933. In "The Struggle Against Liberalism in the Totalitarian View of the State", Marcuse explicitly states that when he understands man to be a "rational organism", he means "one that has the potentiality of freely determining and shaping his own existence, directed by the process of knowledge and with regard to his worldly happiness" (96). The same concern for man's happiness, broadly defined in relation to the "co-operative society", also appears in "the Concept of Essence" (97). It is, however, in Marcuse's last three major essays from the thirties - "The Affirmative Character of Culture" (1937), "Philosophy and Critical Theory" (1937) and "On Hedonism" (1938) - that happiness becomes a major category for his vision of the good society. From those essays emerges a far more comprehensive account of his idea of happiness than that of Reason and Revolution. The following features deserve to be singled out.

The social and political character of this idea of happiness is affirmed in no uncertain terms. While it is true that some individuals in capitalist societies can attain a measure of happiness, "the highest point which man can attain is a community of free and rational persons in which each has the same opportunity to unfold and fulfil all his powers" (98). Furthermore, in such a society the individual is "no longer isolated in (his) interest against others. His life can be happy beyond the contingency of the moment because his conditions of existence are no longer determined by a labour process which creates wealth only through the perpetuation of poverty and privation" (99).

Only in such a society will full knowledge of the other, what he is and what he has become, no longer constitute a barrier for happiness. Knowledge and happiness will at last become compatible, and understanding of the other will only heighten this happiness. In a society no longer built upon institutionalized social conflict, "mutual understanding will no longer be permeated by unhappiness, since insights and passion will no longer come into conflict with a reified form of human relationships" (100).

The same theme reappears even more vigorously in the following characterization of the social and profoundly human individualism of much of Western culture:

> "Each individual is immediate to himself: without worldly or heavenly mediation. And this immediacy also holds for his relation to others. The clearest representation of this idea of the person is to be found in classical literature since Shakespeare. In its dramas, individuals are so close to one another that between them there is nothing that is in principle ineffable or inexpressible. Verse makes possible what has already become impossible in prosaic reality. In poetry men can transcend all social isolation and distance and speak of the first and last things. They overcome the factual loneliness in the glow of great and beautiful words; they may even let loneliness appear in its metaphysical beauty. Criminal and saint, prince and servant, sage and fool, rich and poor join in discussion whose free flow is supposed to give rise to truth." (101)

The critical edge of this characterization should not mislead us. Only a few lines later Marcuse declares that "the critical and revolutionary force of the ideal.... in its very unreality keeps alive the best desires of men amidst a bad reality" (102).

Marcuse does not embrace the traditional distinction between "higher" and "lower" pleasures (103). Certain pleasures are considered worthless and "false". The primary target for Marcuse's attacks is neither the body, sensuality or sex, but "pleasure in the abasement of another as well as self-abasement under a stronger will, pleasure in the manifold surrogates for sexuality, in meaningless sacrifices, in the heroism of war" (104). These pleasures, and they only, are "false pleasures". As for sensuality, it must be developed far beyond what has been permitted by a narrow bourgeois morality or what has been possible under hitherto existing levels of productive forces. This for Marcuse cannot be stressed strongly enough:

> "The unfolding of the personality must not be merely spiritual. Industrial society has differentiated and intensified the objective world in such a manner that only an extremely differentiated and intensified sensuality can respond adequately to it. Modern technology contains all the means necessary to extract from these things and bodies their mobility, beauty and softness in order to bring them closer and make them available." (105)

Even masochism and sadism are conceivable in such a society: "In their authentic intention as forms of the sexual instinct they can result in augmented pleasure not only for the subject but for the object as well. They are then no longer connected with destruction" (106).

There is an ethical dimension in Marcuse's conception of happiness, but it is different from that of hitherto existing societies. Traditional morality is not meaningless oppression. On the contrary, "the moralization of pleasure has had a progressive function in the development of the social labor process" (107). What is to follow it is not a beyond good and evil attitude, but an altogether different morality: "Amoral rebellion...puts itself beyond the bounds of even that morality which links the established order with a more rational and happy society" (108). What is needed in a more adequate perception of where the true immorality lies at the current stage of development of the productive forces: "For the poor, hiring oneself out to work in a factory became a moral duty, while hiring out one's body as a means to pleasure was depravity and 'prostitution'" (109).

Yet Marcuse's claim for greater happiness in present-day societies is fundamentally a factual claim, based upon and reinforcing a political will. This is clearly expressed in his discussion of "false pleasures", which are deemed to be so "because the drives and needs that fulfil themselves in them make men less free, blinder, and more wretched than they have to be" (110). In all other respects we

should be grateful for any happiness: "That there is
any happiness at all in a society governed by blind
laws is a blessing. Through this happiness, the
individual in this society can feel secure and protected from ultimate desperation"(111).
    Three remaining points should be noted. The
first is the influence of psychoanalytic theory for
Marcuse's discussion of the concept of happiness.
Particularly striking are the almost Reichian overtones of his account of a complete release of sexual
energies:

> "The unpurified, unrationalized release of
> sexual relationships would be the strongest
> release of enjoyment as such and the total
> devaluation of labor for its own sake. No human
> being could tolerate the tension between labor
> as valuable in itself and the freedom of enjoy-
> ment. The dreariness and injustice of work
> conditions would penetrate explosively the
> consciousness of individuals and make impossi-
> ble their peaceful subordination to the social
> system of the bourgeois world."(112)

Secondly, the full development of hitherto shackled
economic forces and far greater "economic efficiency" will promote colossal changes in "human nature".
"When all present subjective and objective potentialities of development have been unbound, the needs
and wants themselves will change. Those based on the
social compulsion of repression, on injustice, and
on filth and poverty would necessarily disappear"
(113). Not all will be beautiful and marvellous.
"There may still be the sick, the insane, and the
criminal. The realm of necessity persists: struggle
with nature and even among men continues" (114).
Nevertheless the changes will be momentous.
    Thirdly, the "co-operative society" will be a
profoundly political society: "the political sphere
becomes to a great extent independent and determines
the development of society. With the disappearance
of the state, political relations will then become,
in a hitherto unknown sense, general human relations: the organization of the administration of
social wealth in the interest of liberated humanity"
(115).
    No account of Marcuse's conception of freedom
in the thirties is complete without a mention of his
understanding of beauty. We may recall that in the
1932 essay Marcuse duly recounts the only reference
Marx makes to beauty in the Paris Manuscripts, the

idea he advances that man can form "object in accordance with the law of beauty" (116). The idea is given a somewhat different twist in the essay on "The Affirmative Character of Culture":

> "The immediate sensuousness of beauty immediately suggests sensual happiness. According to Hume the power to stimulate pleasure belongs to the essential character of beauty. Pleasure is not merely a by-product of beauty, but constitutes its very essence. And for Nietzsche beauty reawakens "aphrodisiac bliss". He polemizes against Kant's definition of the beautiful as the object of completely disinterested pleasure and opposes to it Stendhal's assertion that beauty is 'une promesse de bonheur'. Therein lies its danger in a society that must rationalize and regulate happiness. Beauty is fundamentally shameless. It displays what may not be promised openly and what is denied the majority."(117)

Here again, as in the discussion of the positive character of the body conceived as a mere object, beauty appears as a mysterious link between the aspirations of the present and the society of the future.

At the end of the same essay, Marcuse briefly expands upon another theme:

> "Every attempt to sketch out the counter-image of an affirmative culture comes up against the ineradicable cliché about the fool's paradise. It would be better to accept this cliché rather than the one about the transformation of the earth into a gigantic community centre, which seems to be at the root of some theories of culture". (118)

Culture will not disappear in the new society - it will simply be transformed.

> "As long as there is a realm of necessity, there will be enough need. Even a non-affirmative culture will be burdened with mutability and necessity: dancing on the volcano, laughter in sorrow; flirtation with death. As long as this is true, the reproduction of life will still involve the reproduction of culture: the moulding of unfulfilled longing and the purification of unfulfilled instinct... by elimina-

> ting affirmative culture, the abolition of (an
> irrational) social organization will not elimi-
> nate individuality, but realize it. And 'if we
> are ever happy at all, we can do nothing other
> than promote culture'". (119)

These considerations on culture, which will be
greatly expanded in postwar years, complete the
picture of Marcuse's "positive philosophy" in the
thirties and forties. Most of the themes will reappear in his later writings, occasionally in modified
form. It now remains to consider briefly a number of
other changes during those years which contributed
further to the movement from "concrete philosophy"
toward the political stance adopted from 1932 onward.

5.5 "Critical Theory" is a Political Theory

Marcuse's work during this period reveals a new
orientation to marxism as a political theory founded
upon the philosophical insights of classical idealist philosophy, but drawing upon the social sciences for the substance of its arguments and overall
perspective. It has been pointed out that among the
leading figures of the Institute, it was undoubtedly
Marcuse who emphasized the political dimension of
"critical Theory" (120). For Horkheimer, for instance, "the critical theory of society .... remains
philosophical even as a critique of economics"
(121). Not so for Marcuse:

> "Philosophy.... appears within the economic
> concepts of materialist theory, each of which
> is more than an economic concept of the sort
> employed by the academic discipline of econo-
> mics....It would be false on that account to
> reduce these concepts to philosophical ones. To
> the contrary, the philosophical contents rele-
> vant to the theory are to be deduced from the
> economic structures. They refer to conditions
> that, when forgotten, threaten the theory as a
> whole." (122)

The same perspective is again reaffirmed in Reason
and Revolution, in the passage introducing the new
"social theory" discovered and elaborated by Marx:

> "The transition from Hegel to Marx is, in all
> respects, a transition to an essentially diffe-
> rent order of truth, not to be interpreted in

terms of philosophy. We shall see that all the historical concepts of Marxian theory are social and economic categories, whereas Hegel's social and economic categories are all philosophical concepts." (123)

The political emphasis in Marcuse's writings also appears in the following passage where he describes the revolution to come:

"The revolution depends indeed upon a totality of objective conditions: it requires a certain attained level of material and intellectual culture, a self-conscious and organized working class on an international scale, acute class struggle. These become revolutionary conditions, however, only if seized upon and directed by a conscious activity that has in mind the socialist goal."

He adds:

"Not the slightest natural necessity or automatic inevitability gurantees the transition from capitalism to socialism." (124)

The idea of "a conscious activity that has in mind the socialist goal" is crucial. We have already seen that Marcuse retains the wider epistemological aims of marxist theory. He does not see marxism as "scientific", but he nevertheless considers marxism to have a higher claim to truth than philosophical reflection and certainly than the findings based upon traditional social science criteria of validity (125). Ultimately the theory rests upon the marxist "praxis" and the new type of society to which it will lead. Yet events may fail to confirm the theory. The short-term trends may even run counter to the whole pattern of events predicted by the theory, however loosely. What then? Marcuse's answer is that "theory will preserve the truth even if revolutionary praxis deviates from its proper path. Practice follows the truth not vice versa" (126). On which grounds does Marcuse base this extraordinary claim? All the signs point in one direction. The "Marxian" theory's claim to truth rests upon the distinctive re-interpretation Marcuse has given it. It is neither a philosophical, nor an economic theory; it is a common project of human liberation for mankind to carry through.
 Marxism is a two-dimensional theory which can

point to the future and indicate ways by which this unrealized future can become a reality: "All the Marxian concepts extend, as it were, in these two dimensions, the first of which is the complex of given social relationships, and the second, the complex of elements inherent in the social reality that make for its transformation into a free social order" (127).

There appear to be three grounds upon which Marcuse rests his case for the validity of this project of human liberation. Firstly, his claim for the truth of marxism thus re-interpreted finds support in the theory's intellectual appeal, its ability to generate ideas and interpret findings, as well as its reliance upon logical coherence and methodological rigour. Marxism generally, and Marcuse's brand of marxism no less so, is a rational political theory and wants itself to be so. Secondly, and nowhere does it come across more strongly than in these writings of the thirties. Marcuse's project for the good society is founded upon important elements of German and Western philosophy and culture, in that order. He has himself characterized this whole period as a return to the sources of marxism (128). The third important foundation stone for this project Marcuse himself describes in detail in his treatment of "The Concept of Essence". He argues there that the "materialist concept of essence" shares with the traditional interpretation the idea that the distance between essence and appearance is to be "measured" by an 'a priori' knowledge of essence. But this is not one based upon intuition. On the contrary:

"It leads back into history rather than out of it. The immemorially acquired image of essence was formed in mankind's historical experience, which is preserved in the present form of reality so it can be 'remembered' and 'refined' to the status of essence. All historical struggles for a better organization of the impoverished conditions of existence, as well as all of suffering mankind's religious and ethical ideal conceptions of a more just order of things, are preserved in the dialectical concept of the essence of man, where they have become elements of the historical praxis linked to dialectical theory. There can also be experience of potentialities that have never been realized....In idealist philosophy the timeless past dominates the concept of essence. But when theory asso-

ciates itself with the progressive forces in
history, the recollection of what can authenti-
cally be becomes a power that shapes the future. The demonstration and preservation of
essence become the motive idea of practice
aimed at transformation." (129)

We shall return to these issues in chapter 7.

NOTES

1. Martin Jay, The Dialectic Imagination, op.
cit., passim.
2. See respectively "A Study on Authority",
Studies in Critical Philosophy, London: New Left
Books, 1972. First published as "Theoretische Entwurfe über Autorität und Familie: (ideengeschichtlicher Teil)", Studien über Autorität und Familie:
Forschungsberichte aus dem Institut für Sozialforschung, Paris: Felix Alcan, 1936, pp. 136-228; "The
Struggle against Liberalism in the Totalitarian View
of the State", Negations, Boston: Beacon Press,
1968. First published as "Der Kampf gegen den Liberalismus in der totalitäen Staatsauffassung". Zeitschrift für Sozialforschung, Vol. III, 1934, pp.
161-195; and "The Concept of Essence", Negations,
Boston: Beacon Press, 1968. First published as "Zum
Begriff des Wesens", Zeitschrift für Sozialforschung, Vol. V, 1936, pp. 1-39.
3. "The Affirmative Character of Culture",
Negations, Boston: Beacon Press, 1968. First published as "Über den affirmativen Charakter der Kul-
tur", Zeitschrift für Sozialforschung, Vol. VI,
1937, pp. 54-59.
4. "On Hedonism", Negations, Boston: Beacon
Press, 1968. First published as "Zur Kritik des
Hedonismus", Zeitschrift für Sozialforschung, Vol.
VII, 1938, pp. 55-89.
5. "Philosophy and Critical Theory", Negations, Boston Press, 1968. First published as "Philosophie und kritische Theorie", Zeitschrift für
Sozialforschung, Vol. VI, 1938, pp. 631-647.
6. That Marcuse never sketches a full picture,
but always proceeds by intimation and suggestion is
a point which is constantly stressed by his commentators. See for instance Kellner, "Herbert Marcuse:
The critique of Bourgeois Civilization and its tran-
scendency", op. cit., p. 23, see also Jay, "How
Utopian is Marcuse", op. cit.
7. "Contributions to Phenomenology of Historical Materialism", op. cit.; see chapter 2, passim.

8. Ibid., pp. 27-28, pp. 63-64.

9. See Lichtheim, G., _The Concept of Ideology and other Essays_, USA - New York: Random House, 1967.

10. See Jay, _The Dialectical Imagination_, op. cit., for a discussion of the problem of truth in Horkheimer.

11. "On Concrete Philosophy", op. cit.; see the analysis in section 3.2 above.

12. "Philosophy and Critical Theory", op. cit., pp. 147-148, pp. 115-116.

13. See Introduction, section 1.5

14. See Jay, _The Dialectical Imagination_, op. cit. p. 29 and chapter 1, passim.

15. _Reason and Revolution_ op. cit., p. 258; the term "Marxian" in Marcuse's writings refers to Marx's original texts, as opposed to the wider body of marxism. The same terminology will be adopted here.

16. Ibid., pp. 398-401.

17. See "The Struggle Against Liberalism in the Totalitarian View of the State", op. cit., passim.

18. See below section 5.5.

19. "Heidegger's Politics: An Interview with Herbert Marcuse by Frederick Olafson", op. cit., p. 7.

20. See for instance Valentino Gerratana, "Heidegger and Marx" in _New Left review_, No. 106, November-December 1977, pp. 51-58 for a somewhat less than serious discussion of the issue which nevertheless indicates the dimentions of the problem for many Heideggerians.

21. "The Struggle Against Liberalism in the Totalitarian View of the State", op. cit., pp. 31-42, pp. 44-45.

22. A whole section of _Reason and Revolution_ is devoted to this question; it also appears in several of the essays; see _Reason and Revolution_, op. cit., and in particular "The Concept of Essence", op. cit., pp. 60-66, pp. 15-20.

23. See "The Affirmative Character of Culture", op. cit. and "On Hedonism", op. cit.

24. See the vivid description of this aspect of the Institute's work in the 30s and 40s in Jay, _The Dialectical Imagination_, op. cit., p. 141.

25. _Reason and Revolution_, op. cit., p. 277.

26. Marx, _Economic and Philosophical Manuscripts_, op. cit.; Marcuse, ibid., p. 275.

27. It is noteworthy that _Reason and Revolution_ even found its way, as a significant interpre-

tation of Hegel in English, in Jean Touchard's comprehensive, but summary Histoire des idées politiques, op. cit., p. 150. This unexpected reference is
given in a work first published in 1959, long before
Marcuse became a household name in France (his major
works were first translated after 1968).
28. Reason and Revolution, op. cit. p. xii and
pp. 409-419; also pp. 180 and 216; Martin Jay, The
Dialectical Imagination, op. cit., p. 78.
29. Ibid., in particular pp. 5-15 and pp. 251
and 257 on the first; introduction, especially pp.
3-4 on the second.
30. See for instance Taylor, Hegel, op. cit.,
passi, or Kojeve, A.,Introduction à la lecture de
Hegel, Paris: Gallimard, 1947.
31. Reason and Revolution, op. cit., p. 78.
32. Ibid., p. 115.
33. Ibid., p. 272, my emphasis.
34. Ibid., p. 271 and pp. 271-272, also p.
275.
35. The most important innovations are to be
found in his treatment of Hegel's early works, especially in chapter 2, and in the above-mentioned discussion of Hegel's "first system", pp. 73-90; see
also on the Hegel-Marx relation pp. 268-272, and on
the Feuerbach-Marx relation pp. 267-273.
36. Ibid., p. 263.
37. Ibid., p. 292.
38. Ibid., p. 292; Marx, Capital, op. cit.,
vol. 1, pp. 667-724; on Weber, see for instance
MacRae, Weber, op. cit., pp. 73-84.
39. Reason and Revolution, op. cit., p. 293.
40. Ibid., Marx, Theories of Surplus Values,
German edition 1905, vol. 1, pp. 258, 260 ff.
41. Reason and Revolution, op. cit., p. 293.
42. "On the Philosophical Foundation of the
Concept of Labor in Economics", translated by Douglas Kellner, Telos, No. 16, Summer 1973, pp. 9-37.
First published as Über die philosophischen Grundla-
gen des wirtschaftswissenschaftlichen Arbeitsbe-
griffs", Archiv für Sozialwissenschaft und Sozialpo-
litik, vol. 69, 1933, pp. 257-292.
43. Marcuse includes in his description of
labour "'intellectual labor'", political activity,
social service work (such as the activity of doc-
tors, teachers, etc..)", see "On the Philosophical
Foundation of the Concept of Labor in Economics",
op. cit., pp. 23-24; the probable, but by no means
certain superiority of intellectual work is discussed in ibid., p. 31.
44. Ibid., p. 29, p. 37.

45. Ibid., p. 32, pp. 41-42.
46. Ibid., p. 34, p. 44.
47. Ibid., p. 35, p. 45.
48. Ibid., p. 35, p. 46, translation modified.
49. Marx, Capital, op. cit., vol. 3, p. 820;
Marcuse, ibid., pp. 36-37, p. 48.
50. Marx, ibid.; Marcuse, "A Study on Authority", op. cit., p. 130, pp. 131-132.
51. Reason and Revolution, op. cit., p. 288.
52. Ibid., p. 292.
53. Ibid., p. 289.
54. See for instance the formulations of the
Critique of the Gotha Programme, op. cit., passim,
as contrasted with the earlier cited passages from
Capital or the Grundrisse.
55. On these points see above, section 1.4 and
below, chapter 8.
56. See for instance Adorno and Horkheimer,
Dialectic of Enlightenment, London: Allen Lane,
1972. First published as Dialektik der Aufklärung,
Amsterdam, 1947, passim; Horkheimer, Eclipse of
Reason, New York: Seabury Press, 1947, (plus new
material, 1974): and in particular the lecture on
"Means and Ends", pp. 3-57; see also Horkheimer's
programmatic essay on "Traditional and Critical
Theory", first published in Zeitschrift für Sozialforschung, Vol. VI, no. 2, 1937, reprinted in Horkheimer, Critical Theory: Selected Essays (with special reference to 'traditional and Critical Theory',
pp. 188-243), New York: Herder & Herder, 1972. First
published in Kritische Theorie, Vols. I & II, Frankfurt: S. Fischer Verlag, 1968, pp. 188-243; see also
the collection of essays by Horkheimer entitled
Critique of Instrumental Reason, New York: Seabury
Press, 1974. First published as Zur Kritik der in-
strumentellen Vernunft, Frankfurt, S. Fischer Verlag, 1967.
57. Jay, The Dialectical Imagination, p. 60.
58. "The Struggle Against Liberalism in the
Totalitarian View of the State", op. cit., p. 14,
pp. 27,28, emphasis in the text.
59. On these points see for instance Jay's
account in The Dialectical Imagination, op. cit.,
pp. 60-61.
60. "The Foundation of Historical Materialism", op. cit., p. 34, p. 162; see also above,
section 4.6.
61. "The Foundation of Historical Materialism", op. cit., p. 35, p. 163.
62. "Philosophy and Critical Theory", op.
cit., pp. 135-136, p. 103.

63. The dichotomy is not as sharp as this may indicate. Rather, as Horkheimer argues at a later date, "the two concepts of reason do not represent two separate and independent ways of mind, although their opposition expresses a real antimony. The task of philosophy is not stubbornly to play the one against the other, but to foster a mutual critique and thus, if possible, to prepare in the intellectual realm the reconciliation of the two in reality"; see Horkheimer, Eclipse of Reason, op. cit., p. 174.

64. "The Concept of Essence", op. cit., p. 47, pp. 4-5.

65. Ibid., p. 49, p. 6.

66. William Leiss, in his persuasive article on "Technological Rationality: Marcuse and his critics", argues that throughout Marcuse's work the following ambivalence prevails on the question: "1. The continuum of domination in the social relations among men shapes the way in which technological rationality develops - and in part the latter determines the evolution of the former; 2. scientific and technological progress in themselves do not undermine the social foundation of domination - on the contrary, the 'technological veil' can serve to support them; 3. scientific and technological rationality constitute one of the essential preconditions for freedom, and in a liberated society they are among the indispensable requisites for the enjoyment of freedom". Leiss furthermore argues that the contradiction between the two latter statements reflects a fundmental contradiction in present day societies. Leiss' last point in particular deserves our attention, as it is all too often neglected in the literature on Marcuse; see for instance Ahlers, R., "Is technology repressive?" in Tijdschrift voor Filosofie, Holland: Vol. 32, 1970, pp. 651-700; see Leiss "Technological Rationality: Marcuse and his Critics", in Canadian Journal of Political Science, Canada: Vol. IV, No. 3, September 1971, pp. 31-42.

67. Reason and Revolution, op. cit., p. 289.

68. "Philosophy and Critical Theory", pp. 141-142, p. 109.

69. "Hegel's idea of reason has retained, though in an idealistic form, the material strivings for a free and rational order of life. Robespierre's deification of reason as the 'Etre suprême' is the counterpart to the glorification of reason in Hegel's system. The core of Hegel's philosophy is a structure the concepts of which - freedom, subject, mind, notion - are derived from the idea of reason".

A little later he states: "The philosophies of the
French Enlightenment and their revolutionary succes-
sors all posited reason as an objective historical
force which, once freed from the fetters of despotism, would make the world a place of progress and
happiness... By virtue is its own power, reason
would triumph over social irrationality and overthrow the oppressors of mankind"; to which Marcuse
hastens to add: "the implication, however, that
reason wil immediately show itself in practice is a
dogma unsupported by the course of history". (Reason and Revolution, op. cit., pp. 5 and 7.

70. "The mark of this essential freedom is the
fact that the thinking subject is not chained to the
immediately given form of being, but is capable of
transcending them and changing them in line with his
concepts. The freedom of the thinking subject, in
turn, involves his moral and practical freedom. For,
the truth he envisions is not an object for passive
contemplation, but an objective potentiality calling
for realisation. The idea of reason implies the
freedom to act according to reason (ibid., p. 255).

71. "Men believed their relations to each
other to result from objective laws that operate
with the necessity of physical laws, and their freedom to consist in adapting their private existence
to this necessity. A strikingly conformist skepti-
cism thus accompanied the development of modern
rationalism. The more reason triumphed in technology
and natural science, the more reluctantly did it
call for freedom in man's social life", ibid., p.
256.

72. Reason and Revolution, op. cit., p. 259.
73. Ibid., p. 275.
74. Ibid.
75. See above, section 3.4.
76. See Marx, Economic and Philosophical Manuscripts of 1844, op. cit., passim; see also for
instance Maguire, Marx's Paris Writings, op. cit.,
pp. 125-127.
77. See above, section 5.2.
78. Reason and Revolution, op. cit., p. 293.
79. Ibid.
80. Ibid., p. 294.
81. Ibid.
82. Ibid., pp. 270-271.
83. Kierkegaard is placed at the very beginning of the section on Marx; he is the only other
author alongside Feuerbach to be included in that
whole section; the insights drawn from the discussion are then transferred to the analysis of Feuer-

bach, and then to the interpretation of Marx, even if the connection is never presented as a direct influence (see ibid., pp. 262-267).

84. A measure of the distance travelled since the Freiburg years is the fact that while Hegel's Ontology and the Theory of Historicity was dedicated to Heidegger, as an acknowledged major influence upon its overall conception, the only implicit reference to the latter in the whole of Reason and Revolution is to be found a few pages later. Marcuse briefly dismisses a broadly characterized "existentialism" on the ground that it rejects "the dignity and reality of the universal... and any universally valid norms for state and society", to replace these by a misplaced exaltation of "certain particularities (such as the race and the folk) to the rank of the highest values" (see Reason and Revolution, op. cit., pp. 262-267).

85. Marcuse's previous treatment in 1929 of the Danish philosopher was surprisingly favorable, see "On Concrete Philosophy", op. cit., pp 146-150, pp. 123-125.

86. Ibid., p. 265.

87. Ibid., p. 264.

88. Ibid., p. 272.

89. See Lukes, S., "Methodological Individualism Reconsidered" in Ryan, A. (Ed) The Philosophy of Social Explanation, England: Oxford University press, 1973; first published in The British Journal of Sociology: No. XIX, 1968.

90. "Hegel has demonstrated that the fullest existence of the individual is consummated in his social life. Critical employment of the dialectic method tended to disclose that individual freedom presupposes a free society, and that the true liberation of the individual therefore requires the liberation of society. Fixation on the individual alone would just amount to adopting an abstract approach, such as Hegel himself sets aside" (Reason and Revolution, pp. 262-263).

92. Ibid., p. 278.

93. Ibid., p. 294, emphasis in the text.

94. "Insistence on man's claim to universal happiness, which is always happiness for each, so frequently found in the pages of Hobhouse's book, renders it one of the great documents of liberalist philosophy"; and a little later, "Hobhouse is of course right against the neo-idealists, just as liberalism is right against any irrational hypostasis of the state that disregards the fate of the individual" (Reason and Revolution, op. cit., pp.

396-397).

95. Ibid., p. 312.

96. "The Struggle Against Liberalism in the Totalitarian View of the State", op. cit., p. 15, p. 28.

97. "The Concept of Essence", op. cit., p. 72, p. 25.

98. "The Affirmative Character of Culture", op. cit., p. 101, p. 70.

99. "On Hedonism", p. 194, p. 163.

100. Ibid., pp. 194-195, p. 163.

101. "The Affirmative Character of Culture", op. cit., p. 102, pp. 70-71.

102. Ibid., p. 102, p. 71.

103. Martin Jay's assertions notwithstanding, the dividing line Marcuse draws is distinct from ancient hedonistic philosophies as well as from the utilitarian version of a modern opponent such as John Stuart Mill (see Martin Jay, The Dialectical Imagination, op. cit. p. 59).

104. "On Hedonism", op. cit., p. 190, p. 138.

105. Ibid., p. 184, p. 152.

106. "On Hedonism", op. cit., p. 189, p. 157.

107. Ibid., p. 178, p. 156.

108. Ibid., pp. 178-179, p. 147.

109. "The Affirmative Character of Culture", op. cit., p. 116, p. 84.

110. "On Hedonism", op. cit., p.116, p.84.

111. He also insists that "rigoristic morality sins against the cheerless form in which humanity has survived. All hedonism is right in opposing it". Ibid., p. 1971, p. 159.

112. Ibid., p. 187, p. 156.

113. Ibid., p. 193, p. 161.

114. Ibid.

115. "Philosophy and Critical Theory", op. cit., p. 157, p. 125.

116. Marx, Economic and Philosophical Manuscripts of 1844, op. cit., p. 68; Marcuse, "The Foundation of Historical Materialism", op. cit., p. 17, p. 148.

117. "The Affirmative Character of Culture", op. cit., p. 115, p. 83.

118. Ibid., pp. 131-132, pp. 99-100.

119. Ibid., pp. 132-133, pp. 100-101; Nietzsche, Werke, 11, p. 241.

120. See Therborn's excellent discussion in his "The Frankfurt School", op. cit., passim.

121. Ibid., p. 110.

122. "Philosophy and Critical Theory", op. cit., pp. 134-135, p. 102.

123. <u>Reason and Revolution</u>, op. cit., p. 258.
124. Ibid., p. 318.
124. Ibid., p.318.
125. See for instance the following statement in "Philosophy and Critical Theory", "Scientific objectivity as such is never a sufficient guarantee of truth, especially in a situation where the truth speaks as strongly against the facts and is as well hidden behind them as today. Scientific predictabi-lity does not coincide with the futuristic mode in which the truth exists"; op. cit., p. 156, pp. 124-125.
126. <u>Reason and Revolution</u>, op. cit., p. 322.
127. Ibid., p. 296.
128. See Marcuse's own introduction to the collection of his essays in <u>Negations</u>, USA, Boston: Beacon Press 1968, translated from <u>Kultur und Ge-sell-chaft</u> I and II, Frankfurt am Main: Suhrkamp Verlag, 1965.
129. "The Concept of Essence", op. cit., pp. 75-76, p. 28.

Chapter Six

THE IDEA OF THE CO-OPERATIVE SOCIETY IN THE LATE
AMERICAN PERIOD

6.1 Marcuse and Post-War America

Not only is 1941 the year when Marcuse published
Reason and Revolution, it also marks the end of his
collaboration with the members of the "Institut für
Sozialforschung" and with it the end of his identification with the "Frankfurt School". The Institute
itself was in a process of disintegration, with
Horkheimer in California and many of the older members involved either in other scholarly activities
or engaged in the war effort (the Institute did not
reassemble an equivalent array of scholars until its
second start in Frankfurt in 1950). Marcuse himself
joined the East European section of OSS (the American Secret Service) and served until shortly before
the outbreak of the Korean war in 1950, only then
resuming his academic career. His next book Eros
and Civilization (1955) appeared nearly fourteen
years after Reason and Revolution.

The period to which we now turn differs from the
preceding one in almost every respect. Marcuse is no
longer a German scholar working closely with other
German exiles, fully engaged in a very political and
committed antifascist struggle; he no longer writes
in German for a German public with a view to retrie-
ving from past German philosophical traditions those
elements which can revitalise Marxist theory. Marcuse is now an American scholar in an American
university, and virtually all of his writings from
now are in English. The social world in which he
lives is also very different. Instead of the last
years of the Great Depression, the USA is experiencing an unprecedented period of economic expansion,
with all the social changes this entails. The working class is no longer the obvious, or even plausible, spearhead of a socialist revolution. The egalitarian, dynamic, democratic society of post-war

America is almost at the opposite pole of the society created by the National Socialist Party in Germany. Marcuse is now an American citizen, living in
the USA, writing for American audiences and teaching
American students.

Evidence of this new environment can be seen
clearly in most of the writings of this period. Eros
and Civilization is concerned with Freud, a thinker
whose influence is arguably greater in the USA than
in Europe itself. Soviet Marxism is in many ways an
indictment of Soviet society reflecting and situated
in American thinking of the fifties, even if it is
strikingly different from the standard textbooks of
that period. One Dimensional Man, Marcuse's most
famous book, is probably also his most American
book. The variety of issues treated in his articles
and essays from this period, the most famous of
which is An Essay on Liberation, reflect in a similar way the context and aspirations of the 1960's
American generation. With the exception of his latest work, Counterrevolution and Revolt, virtually
all the writings from 1955 onwards are profoundly
marked by Marcuse's experience of living in the USA.
There is, nevertheless, a striking continuity between the conception of freedom advocated in these
works and that of the thirties and forties.

All the features of this vision of the co-operative society, as first outlined in 1932, reappear
in the work of this period. Even in Eros and Civilization, overtly dedicated to exploring the philosophical implications of Freud's work, we can find the
following description of the good society. It is a
society which is first and foremost characterised by
a:

> "rational organization of fully developed in-
> dustrial society after the conquest of scarci-
> ty. It is a society which is marked by an
> extensive "satisfaction of the basic human
> needs", which are "vastly extended and refined"
> and are both "sexual as weel as social", inclu-
> ding such things as "food, housing, clothing,
> leisure". Moreover, "this satisfaction will be
> (and this is the important point) without toil
> - that is, without the rule of alienated labor
> over human existence".

Marcuse then emphasizes the importance of a reduction of the realm of necessity - a reduction of the
necessary labour time. "Under the "ideal" conditions
of major industrial civilization, alienation would

be completed by general automatisation of labor, reduction of labor time to a minimum, and exchangeability of functions"(1). The same ideas reappear, in slightly differenty terms, in Soviet Marxism.

> "Marxian theory made an essential distinction betweem work as a realization of human potentiality and work as a "alienated laboour"; the entire sphere of material production, of mechanised and standardized performances is considered one of alienation. By virtue of this distinction, the realization of freedom is attributed to a social organization of labor fundamentally different from the prevailing one, to a society where work as the free play of human faculties have become a "necessity", a "vital need" for society, while work for procuring the necessities of life no longer constitutes the working day and the occupation of the individual"(2).

Again in his last major work, Counterrevolution and Revolt, Marcuse defines the good society in essentially the same terms. He states that "human nature would be different under socialism to the degree to which men and women would, for the first time in history, develop and fulfil their own needs and faculties in association with each other"; elsewhere in the text, he argues:

> "The revolution involves a radical transformation of the needs and aspirations themselves... this transformation appears in the fight against the fragmentation of work, the necessity and productivity of stupid performances and stupid merchandise, against the acquisitive bourgeois individual, against servitude in the guise of technology, deprivation in the guise of the good life, against pollution as a way of life. Moral and aestetic needs become basic, vital needs, and drive towards new relationships between the sexes, between the generations, between men and women and nature. Freedom is understood as rooted in the fulfilment of these needs, which are sensuous, ethical, and rational in one"(3).

Despite variations in terminology, it is not difficult to recognise in these extracts the themes which we have examined in previous sections. Freedom must first of all be understood in social terms,

Table 6

Assumptions and logical implications of Marcuse's conception of a free society as developed between 1948 and 1972.

The co-operative society (3rd version)

ASS 1   Genuine human freedom is only to be found outside of necessary labour, in whatever form. Genuine human freedom is primarily obtained in and through work as the free play of faculties.

ASS 2   a) Work as the free play of faculties is the positive "abolition" of alienated labour as it exists in advanced capitalistic societies. A reasonable approximation would be to describe it as a more or less sustained deliberate and well understood activity whereby the individual or collectivity seek to enhance, develop or merely exercise man's faculties and sensibilities, with no other aim than human joy, happiness and pleasure. It takes place in the realm of freedom.
b) Necessary labour is any purposeful and disciplined activity directly aiming at the transformation of the environment with a view to promote the best conditions for all to be able to engage in work as the free play of faculties. This only takes place within the realm of necessity.

ASS 3   The extent of human freedom is the extent to which work as the free play of faculties becomes possible for all. Complete freedom is a society which allows for the possibility of such work to the full. The cooperative society is such a society. It is des cribed by the assumptions that follows.

ASS 4   The cooperative society is a society where the individual both:
a) participates on a full and equal basis in the necessary rational labour aiming to establish the best conditions for human happiness in the realm of freedom.
b) participates on a full and equal basis in work as the free play of faculties, where he fully dominates the object of his work, plays with the possibilities of any object and is able to shape it in accordance with the most rewarding combination of the constraints imposed by the object's "inner laws" and the needs he feels most expressive of his personality. He understands himself through such work and others through work of the same kind.

181

ASS 5   In the co-operative society, this relation holds true
not only for the individually created or shaped objects, or for those "worked upon" in collaboration with
a few others; it is equally valid for all the achievements of that society at large, be it in terms of the
wider material production, the world of culture or the
social institutions. In all these areas it will be
possible to see not only the mark of the "co-operative"
man, but also that of each individual. The world will
thus be a testimony of all of man's powers and needs,
and of those of all the individuals composing that
society.

ASS 6   The individual's self-growth and capacity for enjoyment
takes place primarily through the direct impact upon
his being of the work as the free play of faculties
which he performs. It also takes place via the collective transformation of the world into a human and life-
enhancing civilisation where aesthetic considerations
and playfulness are the dominant features.

ASS 7   a) Necessary labour is determined in terms of the
indirect and "objective" impact it has upon the development of the "co-operative society" and thereby of
"co-operative man". It is rational in the sense that
generalised automation and exchangeability of functions
will tend to reduce the necessary labour time and its
impact upon daily life to a minimum.
      b) Work as the free play of faculties is almost
wholly determined in function of the direct, immediate
and "subjective" impact it has upon the individual
performing it; this impact is wholly different from
anything conceivable in contemporary capitalistic societies. Work as the free play of faculties is the sum
of these activities which directly promotes the full
and all round development of the individual's powers
and faculties, sharpens his aesthetic sensibilities and
allows him to express a rich variety of social and
individual needs. A whole range of modern techniques
can help to further these aims.

ASS 8   The extent of necessary labour in the co-operative
society is limited to those few clear instances where
the long term benefits of such activities are indisputably greater than the provisional harm caused by the
deviation from the definition of work as the free play
of faculties in assumption 7 b).

ASS 9   When necessary labour is to be performed, and how it is
to be organized, is decided by the "associated producers" participating fully and equally in joint planning

182

decisions. The overriding concern is always the best possible satisfaction of the individual's needs and powers.

ASS 10 The individual himself alone chooses to engage in work as the free play of faculties, be it individual or collective. He determines, alone or in co-operation with others, the character and conditions of this form of work. Only necessary labour, under the conditions that assumptions 8 and 9 fully describe, can be enforced in the co-operative society. This, however, is not incompatible with mild social pressure directly following from the ethical ends described below.

ASS 11 Given that human nature is essentially a social creation, the human needs and powers to be found in the co-operative society are not ascertainable from within the present order of things, but for the following exceptions:

a) The whole range of human emotions, senses and powers will be developed.

b) Wholly new needs and sensibilities are likely to appear.

c) These needs and sensibilities are likely to be linked to a sense of aesthetics vastly more developed and more widespread through this society than in any other society up to this point in history.

d) Sexuality will enter as a binding force in human relations throughout the whole of society to a hitherto unknown degree, and contribute to reinforce the bonds and mutual knowledge between the members of the co-operative society.

e) Concurrently, traditional genital sexuality will possibly lose much of its dominant position, while other forms and facets of human libidinal relations become more prominent and socially acceptable. Homosexuality, polygamy, sexual masochism and sadism can be cited as examples.

f) Generally, material and bodily needs, and their relations to human emotions and the capacity for mutual understanding will receive a far more central place in ordinary human intercourse than it has been the case in many societies up to the present point in history.

g) Submission to the will of another, outside of sexual masochism/sadism between consenting adults, or submission to abstractions divorced from material and bodily realities, will not take place.

h) Similarly there will be no submission to the idea of death in itself, or to any similar socially sanctioned sacrifice based upon the fear of death, which will be considered as nothing but the biological termination of life.

ASS 12 Happiness and knowledge will no longer be incompatible: love and affection for others will be able to rest on the full knowledge of the other.

ASS 13 Culture and aesthetic sensibilities will play an all together more central role in the daily life of the "co-operative" man than has ever been possible in human civilisation up to the present point in history. The whole of reality will become an object of culture; an integral culture, encompassing all areas of life and including memories of a past long before the advent of present day restrictive civilisation will be able to flourish; the transformation of nature and of man will possibly be governed by a new reality principle, based upon sensuality, sexuality and aesthetic judgement.

ASS 14 The rationality guiding the activities of the men and women in the co-operative society is never simply the cold instrumental rationality implied by economic theory or the physical sciences. Such forms of rationality are applied to the organisation of necessary labour and within the confines of the realm of necessity. Even there, it is a rationality which is informed by and supportive of the overriding goal of the co-operative, namely the development and best possible satisfaction of all the individual's needs and powers.

ASS 15 The co-operative society is guided by ethical ends. These ends are fully described in the overriding concern for the full development and best possible satisfaction of all the individuals ocnstituting that society. No other moral value or ethical end can be invoked against this goal, and the freedom of all is as unrestained as possible within the limits set by this goal.

ASS 16 Those aspects of human relations not falling under the limited sphere of necessary labour or the sphere of work as the free play of faculties as defined above are similarly solely governed by the above ethical ends.

(*) Table 6 should be seen in relation to tables 4 and 5. The main differences between 5 and 6 concern labour, the centrality of happiness, a new priority of needs and a distinct role for culture and aesthetic criteria. "labor as the free play of faculties" now overall replace "labor in its true form", while the distinction with "necessary labor" remains unchanged. Changes occur in assumptions 1-8, 10 and 16. The concept of happiness and the related ideas of enjoyment, pleasure, satisfaction or "rich variety of needs" replace or complement the earlier exclusive emphasis upon the development of powers and needs. This applies to assumptions 2, 6, 7, 9 and 14 and 15. The idea of "wholly new needs" is novel, as is the centrality of sexuality as a binding force in human relations. The pre-eminence of non-genital sexuality is equally new, as is the explicit linking of social forms of masochism with the fear of death. Aesthetic sensibilities play in assumptions 6, 7, 9, 13. Together with a new role for culture, these aesthetic sensibilities also play in with sexuality in a new reality principle (assumption 11).

with a view to the changed solidarity and sociability of a new society. But freedom is also an individual affair, and the only goal of the good society is to promote and further the full development of the needs, aspirations and talents of the "total man". Freedom necessarily involves rationality, knowledge, and happiness, and the co-operative society can only be built around a complete transformation of labour. The ideas and impulses deriving from these themes will shape Marcus's work as a Lecturer in sociology and Senior Fellow at the Russian Institute of Columbia University in the years 1950 to 1954. It is the development of these ideas which led to his major work of this period, Eros and Civilization (1958), not long after he joined the History of Ideas programme at Brandeis, in Waltham, Massachussets. It is to these same ideas and themes, with individual variations, that he returned shortly after the publication of One Dimensional Man, when he arrived at the university of California at San Diego in 1965. Student unrest and the New Left movement, which was to acclaim Marcuse as one of its "gurus", was also starting then(4). The rest of the story is well known.

6.2 Labour, Work and Play
No aspect of Marcuse's conception of freedom has been more neglected or misunderstood than the relationships between labour, work and play(5). This constitutes the crucial feature of the co-operative society envisaged by Marcuse. It is his continued interest and emphasis upon the centrality of labour in ordinary human existence that most clearly links Marcuse to the marxist tradition. The importance of the concept of labour in his writings also distinguishes his conception of freedom most sharply from

those of his liberal opponents. Yet, for those commentators who at all consider the question, it is
often precisely Marcuse's conception of the socialist man as "homo ludens" which forms the unbridgea-
ble gap between him and Marx, Faced with repeated
failures of the proletariat in advanced industrial
nations to assume their role as mankind's new vanguard, Marcuse dreams up a position cut off from the
roots of marxism in which man, free at last from the
constraints of this life, will playfully wander
through the golden fields of the socialist Eden(6).

At first sight, Marcuse's lack of concern with
the relationship between labour and freedom, and
with the potential for a good life in a society
where labour may be a co-operative venture, seem to
confirm such a reading. After all, <u>Eros and Civili-
zation</u> is devoted to the largely philosophical analysis of the classical Freudian concepts, seeking to
rehabilitate such unpopular notions as the Oedipus
complex or Thanatos, the death instinct, with no
obvious connection to Marcuse's earlier and more
marxist writings. In the second part of the book
which is devoted to his vision of a different society, it is Schiller (rather than Marx or Hegel) who
is the dominant figure. Against the sketchy, but
nevertheless fundamentally political and economic
categories that in Marx evoke the good society, we
are faced with an almost poetic treatment of the
images of Narcissus, Orpheus, and Dionysus as alternatives to the Promethean man who looms so large in
the marxist tradition (7). Instead of labour or work
in a more extended sense, play and the new need for
beauty constitute dominant themes of that vision;
socialism will bring a new sensibility, even at the
cost of a reduced pace of industrial development.
Similarly, in <u>Soviet Marxism</u> Marcuse appears to
reject labour as a feature of the co-operative society which the "first socialist country" still has
to reach. Large parts of the book are devoted to a
meticulous and devastating critique of the absurd
and dehumanizing Soviet work ethic; the mark of the
good society is again play rather than work, together with all round satisfaction of needs. In
<u>One Dimensional Man</u> there are virtually no referen-
ces to labour, save for a few comments in chapter
9(8). In one passage Marcuse even rejects the central theme of <u>Reason and Revolution</u>, the idea of the
"abolition of labour": "Again all 'technological
Eros' and similar misconceptions, 'labor cannot
become play ...'. Marx's statement precludes all
romantic interpretation of the 'abolition of la-

bor'"(9). Nowhere does Marcuse's distance from Marx
and marxism appear more clearly than in this work.
With Marcuse's next two major works, however, the
situation changes; in tone and content An Essay on
Liberation and Counterrevolution and Revolt, (as
well as his last major piece of writing The Aesthetic Dimension)(10), differ in virtually every respect - including the treatment of labour and freedom
- from the writings of the preceding period (11).
An Essay on Liberation reasserts that for Marx labour cannot possibly become play; but Marcuse then
develops, as his own position, the notion that labour can indeed be "abolished"; in the new society
it will be transformed into an activity whose function will be essentially different, and which will
occur under altogether changed conditions(12). The
idea is drawn more fully at the end of the essay
where he stresses that "the construction of the new
society will create new incentives for work"; work
will become a function of Eros, and its goal will be
the creation of a sensuous environment(13). The same
theme reappears in Counterrevolution and Revolt
where Marcuse cites Marx as envisioning a very different need for work in the considerations leading
to Capital, and which are now reassembled in the
famous notebooks of the Grundrisse (14).
    On closer reading, however, Marcuse's position
throughout these years is far more consistent than
the above account suggests. With the notable exception of One Dimensional Man, the writings all develop or reassert positions already implicit in the
1932 essay or the essay on the concept of labour in
the following year. The analyses of labour, play and
work in postwar years can virtually all be retraced
to the following passage of Reason and Revolution:

> "Marx ... envisioned the future mode of labor
> to be so different from the prevailing one that
> he hesitated to use the same term 'labor' to
> designate alike the material process of capita-
> list production and of communist society. He
> used the term 'labor' to mean what capitalism
> actually understands by it in the last analy-
> sis, that activity which creates surplus value
> in commodity production, or which 'produces
> capital'".

He adds that "other kinds of activity are not 'productive labor and hence not labor in the proper sense"(15). This last sentence is crucial. The glorification of play in Marcuse's post-war writings

must be understood against the particular historical context in which labour takes place. The real target for his attacks is not work <u>per se</u>, but "productive labor" under capitalism. This is what in the last analysis determines his particular understanding of "play". "Play" denotes the kind of activities which take place in the "realm of freedom"; the term "play" should be understood as the closest analogy to such essentially novel forms of activity and human interaction with identifiable patterns of behaviour in present-day societies (16). Following the distinction first elaborated in the 1933 essay on the concept of labour, Marcuse sharply distinguishes any such activity from the transformed mode of "productive labor" which even in the co-operative society would remain a "realm of necessity"(17). As long as work is directed toward some external goal and not toward the full development of human faculties (as first sketched in the analysis of "free labor" in 1932), it cannot serve to characterise the "realm of freedom"; only an activity that holds man's individual and communitarian aspirations as its prime goal can properly do so, and this is best approximated by the term "play".

<u>Eros and Civilization</u> is about Freud and the psychoanalytic tradition. It is concerned with Freud's presentation of biologically determined layers of the psyche and attempts to spell out the implications of Freud's work for our understanding of the unconscious drives which shape the individual from the early days of life; it analyses what Freud presents as the subterranean forces still at work in civilized man. This psychological, para-biological and ahistorical model of man becomes the basis for Marcuse's most unconventional and utopian account of the Marxian "realm of freedom"; in Freud's conservative and deeply pessimistic depiction of an unchanging human nature Marcuse finds the elements for his extraordinary picture of the new post-economic order to which Marx on rare occasions alludes. In constantly contrasting this picture with the realities of late twentieth century civilisation, he evokes the full potential for a rich and diversified human existence already present in the achievements of that civilisation. But first and foremost it provides the background against which to analyse and attack the last major obstacle on the road to a better society: the anachronistic presence throughout present-day societies of a work ethic which may have been justified in an earlier age but now only serves as the mindless repression mechanisme of the

established order. The book's central opposition is between a form of labour which takes up most of man's energies and talents - dominates even his leisure time - and the kind of life that will exist outside the time devoted to "necessary labor" in the co-operative society (and direct even the latter). In this most Freudian of books, the opposition between "free time" and "alienated labor" forms the foundation for every analysis; it forms the starting point and inspiration for Marcuse's original and now famous discussions of "surplus repression", of the "performance principle" and of "libidinous morality"(18).

Marcuse never denounces "productive labor" as such. Douglas Kellner remarks in his commentary on Marcuse's 1933 essay that Marcuse, in contrast to Marx or Hegel, shows little or no concern for the civilisation-building aspect or work, and chooses to focus instead almost exclusively on the direct impact of work upon the worker. As I argued earlier, it would be wrong to conclude from this that Marcuse is unaware of or dismisses the wider social dimensions of work or its repercusssions upon human existence via the mental and physical world it creates (19). Once again it is upon the direct, subjective implications of work that Marcuse's centres his analysis. In Eros and Civilation the social consequences of the sacrosanct "productivity" hold his attention. As the following passage makes clear, the relation he establishes betweeen productivity and civilization is not itself described and civilisation is not itself described in negative terms; the target of his attacks is "productivity" as a way of life:

"The idea expresses perhaps more than any other the existential attitude in industrial civilization; it permeates the philosophical definition of the subject in terms of ever transcending ego. Man is evaluated according to his ability to make, augment, and improve socially useful things. Productivity thus designates the degree of the mastery and transformation of nature: the progressive replacement of an uncontrolled natural environment by a controlled technological environment"(20).

The ethic of productivity itself is not condemned per se. It is the way in which it has developed, its intensity and all-pervasiveness in late industrial civilization that Marcuse questions; it has become

189

the very negation of the civilisation it is meant to promote and futher, and this in an age whose material advances make it less imperative every day:

> "The very word came to smack of repression or its philistine glorification: it connotes the resentful deformation of rest, indulgence, receptivity - triumph of the 'lower depths' of the mind and body, the taming of the instincts by exploitative reason. Efficiency and repression converge: raising the productivity of labor is a sacrosanct ideal of both capitalist and Stalinist Stakhanovism"(21).

The co-operative society in contrast, will be characterized by the unconditional subordination of these values of efficiency, economic rationality and productivity to the wider goals of the community; these goals are diametrically opposed to those fostered by the constraints of economic scarcity which so prominently figure in the pantheon of late industrial societies:

> "Necessary labor is a system of essentially inhuman, mechanical, and routine activities; in such a system, individuality cannot be a value and an end in itself. Reasonably, the system of societal labor would be organized rather with a view to saving time and space for the development of individuality outside the inevitably repressive work world. Play and display, as principles of civilization, imply not the transformation of labor but its complete subordination to the freely evolving potentialities of man and nature. The ideas of play and display now reveal their full distance from the values of productiveness and performance: play is unproductive and useless precisely because it cancels the repressive and exploitative traits of labor and leisure; it 'just plays' with reality" (22).

Such activity can and will include some form of work; not all forms of work are "repressive and exploitative"; Hegel's insight into work as life-enhancing and self-actualizing will still be valid for many of these activities of good society. But to characterize all work in such terms is to be fatally blind to the realities of "productive labour" as it exists in today's world:

"The physical sources and resources of work,
and its relation to sublimation, constitue one
of the most neglected areas of psychoanalytic
theory. Perhaps nowhere else has psycho-analy-
sis so consistently succumbed to the official
ideology of the blessings of 'productivity'.
Small wonder then, that in the Neo-Freudian
schools, where the ideological trend in psychoanalysis triumphs over its theory, the tenor of
work morality is all-permissive. The 'orthodox'
discussion is almost in its entirety focused on
'creative' work, while work in the realm of
necessity - labor - is relegated to the background. To be sure, there is a mode of work
which offers a high degree of libidinal satisfaction, which is pleasurable in its execution.
And artistic work, where it is genuine, seems
to grow out of a non-repressive instinctual
constellation and to envisage non-repressive
aims - so much so that the term <u>sublimation</u>
seems to require considerable modification if
applied to this kind of work. But the bulk of
the work relations on which civilization rests
is of a very different kind ... The work that
created and enlarged the material basis of
civilization was chiefly labor alienated labor,
painful and miserable - and still is. The performance of that work hardly gratifies <u>indi-
vidual</u> needs and inclinations. It was imposed
upon man by brute necessity and brute force"
(23).

In this passage Marcuse reaffirms the distinction
central to the 1933 essay on labor: there is a form
of work which can provide great personal satisfactions, then there is the work that the majority
performs, which more often feels more like toil and
drudgery than a self-confirming activity. The neglect of this all important dimension of ordinary
daily existence vitiates many otherwise praiseworthy
liberal conceptions of freedom (24). It is in reaction to the vague humanism of many liberals that
Marcuse now is opposed to any notion of work as an
avenue for human liberation: only work that can be
likened to playful activity will now characterise
the "realm of freedom".
    It is in the light of this fundamental dis-
tinction that we must understand Marcuse's fierce
attacks on Hendrick's proposed introduction to the
Freudian model of a "mastery instinct", whose aim
would be to "control", or alter a piece of the

environment ... by the skilful use of perceptual,
intellectual, and motor techniques". Hendrick further describes this potential third fundamental
instinct as a drive for "integration and skilful
performance" which is "mentally and emotionally
experienced as the need to perform work efficiently"(25). What is depicted is none other than the
contented "homo faber" that Marcuse clearly wanted
to dissociate himself from in 1932 (26). It is the
very opposite to the notion of "free labor" that
Marcuse entertains then. And this is why in 1955 he
felt obliged to seek an altogether different foundation for his conception of individually meaningful
work. He does not argue, as he could reasonably have
done, that this proposed self-gratifying work instinct is singularly culture-bound (27). His major
argument is that such an approach plays havoc with
conceptual apparatus elaborated by Freud, a claim
far more difficult to sustain (28). This, however,
is consistent with a demarche which seeks to found
the idea of non-alienated labour upon a broadly
understood, culturally evolved and yet biologically
founded Eros. Rather than a break with earlier positions, Marcuse's approach in Eros and Civilization
indicates a shift from Feuerbachian sensuality to
Freudian sexuality within an essentially unaltered
reading of Marx.

The notion of play which opposes labour in
Eros and Civilization goes far beyond the usual
boundaries of play: it incorporates the earlier
ideas of "free labor" and of the "abolition of
labor", where "abolition" must comprehended in the
Hegelian sense of "Aufhebung" (29). Play for Marcuse
is first of all the conceptual opposite of alienated
labour, which still describes the vast majority of
these activities habitually understood as work.
Therefore the prototype of work in the "realm of
freedom" can only be found in minor features of
modern industrial and post-industrial civilisation:
"In a reality governed by the performance principle,
such libidinal work is a rare exception and can
occur only outside or at the margin of the work
world - as a 'hobby', play, or in a directly erotic
situation" (30). The same intransigeant conception
of non-alienated work leads Marcuse to reject even
Fourier's utopian socialism: "Work as free play
cannot be subject to administration" (31). The distinction between the two forms of work is, however,
never more clearly stated than in relation to his
discussion of the goal of labour. The following
passage furthermore highlights the implicit transi-

tion from Feuerbach's naturalist humanism to Freud's para-biological psychology. "It is the purpose and not the content which marks an activity as play or work. A transformation of the instinctual structure of the human activity regardless of its content ... (In the good society) the altered social conditions would therefore create an instinctual basis for the transformation of work into play" (32)

The preceding analyses make clear just how extraordinary an interpretation of Freud Marcuse presents in Eros and Civilization. Building from Freud's insights and arguing within the context of psychoanalytical theory, Marcuse recreates the grand picture of the "realm of freedom" echoing througout Marx's ambitious project of human liberation. The early vision of a co-operative society where work would have become a "means of life" guides Marcuse's imaginative treatment of Freud's difficult and elusive notion of Eros:

"In the light of the idea of non-repressive sublimation, Freud's definition of Eros as striving to 'form living substance into ever greater unities, so that life may be prolonged and brought to higher development' takes on added significance. The biological drive becomes a cultural drive. The pleasure principle reveals its own dialectic. The erotic aim of sustaining the entire body as subject-object of pleasure calls for the continual refinement of the organism, the intensification or its receptivity, the growth of its sensuousness. The aim generates its own projects of realization: the abolition of toil, the amelioration of the environment, the conquest of disease and decay, the creation of luxury. All these activities flow directly from the pleasure principle, and, at the same time, they constitute work which associates individuals through 'greater unities'; no longer confined within the mutilating dominion of the performance principle, they modify the impulse without deflecting it from its aim. There is sublimation and, consequently, culture; but this sublimation proceeds in a system of expanding and enduring libidinal relations, which are in themselves work relations" (33)

This passage is crucial for the transition from "free labor" to erotic labor". It is also characteristic of Marcuse's whole demarche in Eros and Ci-

vilization. Marcuse starts from what after all is
Freud's most important clinical discovery, the importance of sexuality in human personality formation. He immediately proceeds to extract the wider
philosophical implications that Freud himself drew
from the discovery, which are summarised in the idea
of Eros as a general unifying principle. He neatly
transforms the problem from a purely biological one
to a question of the cultural and historical consequences of such a philosophical insight. He then
proceeds to develop the implications for individual
self-development of an instinct which is erotic,
sexual and sensual and at the same time "syntheti-
zing" and creative. Eros thus defined becomes the
dynamic force in the development and refinement of
man's values, needs and sensibilities; it is this
force, rather than the secularized Feuerbachian God,
which is to promote the ideals of man as a "species-
being". It is now Eros that demands the satisfaction
of such needs and sensibilities through association
with partners with the same capacities for enjoyment
and unadulterated hedonism. Eros, furthermore, demands more than immediate sensuality, but also the
progressive transformation of the whole environment
through a new form of work; it epitomizes a "free
labour whose goal is self-fulfilment as well as the
creation of a world with a humane dimension; only
the creation of an environment conducive to new
forms of libidinal relations along with the development of new needs can provide lasting gratifications
for work now entirely under the domination of
Freud's most pervasive instinctual force.

The analysis of labour in Eros and Civilization
shows that Marcuse's original insights into the
implications of Marx's early writings for an extended theory of freedom revolving around non-alienated
labour guides his powerful reinterpretation of
Freud. The new distinction between labour and play
remains squarely within the bounds first outlined at
the end of the Freiburg period.

There were several reasons for Marcuse adopting
this terminology. I have already mentioned the clear
intention to dissociate a basically marxist conception from vague liberal humanism. The perspective
afforded by his new reading of Freud undoubtedly
also played a part. More important perhaps is the
internal development of a series of positions so
radically different from common understanding of
what work entails and signifies for the individual.
Yet another factor is the transformation of the work
world in the last decades and especially the in-

creased free time and economic resources that have
become accepted rewards for socially useful work,
even in societies where the capitalistic ethos is
still predominant. The question of the reduction of
the working hours, one of the major themes of Soviet
Marxism, is also discussed in Eros and Civilization.
Marcuse's argument on this point proceeds in a characteristic two-way movement. First he insists that
technological progress, rationalization and economic
efficiency have not made labour any less alienated,
He then adds that:

> "However, progressive alienation itself in-
> creases the potential of freedom: the more
> external to the individual the necessary labor
> becomes, the less does it involve him in the
> realm of necessity. Relieved from the require-
> ments of domination, the quantitative reduction
> in labor time and energy leads to a qualitative
> change in the human existence: the free rather
> than the labor time determines its content. The
> expanding realm of freedom becomes truly a
> realm of play - of the free play of individual
> faculties. Thus liberated, they will generate
> new forms of realization and of discovering the
> world, which in return will reshape the world
> of necessity, the struggle for existence" (34)

The new promises of a post-economic society form the
most powerful theme of Eros and Civilization. The
depiction of such a society, taking into account the
transformation of the daily existence of the population by virtue of the changed role of labour, constitutes the book's most important message. This
message, however utopian, fabulous and incredible,
does catch the imagination of the yet inchoate New
Left. The booming prosperity of the fifties has left
the young middle class with little taste for the
puritanical values of their fathers; against the
work ethic and ruthless work world Marcuse opposes a
vision of a liberated society whose material abundance has as its goal the full satisfaction of man's
co-operative spirit and individual talents. But he
also retains the vital connection with the wider
marxist tradition in which his own work originates.
This marxist foundation provides the firm and original anchor for his critique of the soviet experiment
in marxist socialism.
    The distinction between the "realm of freedom"
and the "realm of necessity" is also crucial to Marcuse's discussion of Soviet Marxism. The key passage

states that:

> "It is in the last analysis the abolition of
> alienation which, for Marx, defines and justi-
> fies socialism as a 'higher stage' of civiliza-
> tion. And socialism in turn defines a new human
> existence: its content and value are to be
> determined by free time rather than labor time,
> that is to say man coming into his own only
> outside and 'beyond' the entire realm of mate-
> rial production for the mere necessities of
> life. Socialization of production is to reduce
> the time and energy spent in this realm to a
> minimum, and to maximise time and energy for
> the development and satisfaction of individual
> needs in the realm of freedom" (35)

It is on the basis of this distinction between
labour as actually performed and truly liberated
work that the whole argument revolves (36). The
vision of the co-operative society serves equally
for the denunciation of Western work ethics and for
the indictment of the Soviet version, with the pro-
viso that the the Soviet ethic nevertheless points
to a different future. Marcuse, in this sober and
scholarly account of central features of the Soviet
world, nevertheless introduces a notion of play more
utopian and radical than that of Eros and Civilization. The passage which concludes the book's penultimate chapter runs as follows:

> "The technological rationality also contains an
> element of playfulness which is constrained and
> distorted by the repressive usage of techno-
> logy: playing with the possibilities of things,
> with their combination, order, form, and so
> forth. If no longer under the pressure of ne-
> cessity, this activity will have no other aim
> than growth in the consciousness and enjoyment
> of freedom, Indeed, technical productivity
> might then be the very opposite of specializa-
> tion and pertain to the emergence of that 'all-
> round individual' who looms so large in Marxian
> theory - a theory which, in its inner logic, is
> based on the idea of the completed rationali-
> zation of necessary labor, under the truly
> technical administration of things. Needless to
> say, the present reality is so far removed from
> this possibility that the latter appears as
> idle speculation." (37)

The pessimistic note struck at the end of this passage almost becomes the recurrent theme of Marcuse's work between 1959 and 1966-67. It comes across in a variety of articles and essays, of which the best known are probably "Socialism in the Developed Countries", "Socialist Humanism?" and the essay on "Repressive Tolerance" (38). During this period not only does Marcuse do very little to develop his idea of the co-operative society, but he furthermore question the validity of the vision which guided his writing since his second encounter with Marx, the vision that so dramatically transformed his nascent theory of freedom. There are no such questions in One Dimensional Man, nor does this work reflect the robust optimism of his other writings. The central feature of the co-operative society, a form of work essentially different from the alienating work conditions of late capitalism, is also conspicuously absent. As mentioned above, save for a few sparse references, there is nothing on labour whatsoever in what was to become Marcuse's most famous book. Instead what seems to pervade this book of the early sixties is a vague and uncertain humanism. Only by reference to other pieces from this period is it possible to ascertain that even during this period Marcuse still refused to subscribe to the neo-liberal and neo-marxist humanism expounded by Fromm and like-minded colleagues (39)

As indicated earlier, the picture changes towards the end of the sixties. The new trend is nowhere more evident than in the 1967 Berlin lecture on "The End of Utopia" in which Marcuse develops the idea of free play with productive force first sketched at the very end of Soviet Marxism:

"In the Grundrisse Marx showed that complete automation of socially necessary labor is incompatible with the preservation of capitalism. Automation is only a catchword for this tendency, through which necessary physical labor, alienated labor, is withdrawn to an ever greater extent from the material process of production. This tendency, if freed the fetters of capitalist production, would lead to a creative experimentation with the productive forces. With the abolition of poverty this tendency would mean that play with the potentialities of human and non-human nature would become the content of social labor. The productive imagination would become the concretely structured productive force that freely sketches out the

197

> possibilities for a free human existence on the
> basis of the corresponding development of mate-
> rial productive forces. In order for these
> technical possibilities not to become possibi-
> lities for repression, however, in order for
> them to be able to fulfil their liberating
> functions, they must be sustained and directed
> by liberating and gratifying needs" (40)

These new needs, Marcuse then describes in the following terms. There will be a ...

> "vital biological need for peace, which today
> is not a vital need of the majority, the need
> for calm, the need to be alone, with oneself or
> with the other whom one has chosen oneself, the
> need for the beautiful, the need for 'undeser-
> ved' happiness - all this not simply in the
> form of individual needs but as a social pro-
> ductive force, as social needs that can be
> activated through the direction and disposition
> of productive forces" (41)

6.3 A Hedonist Marxism

Most commentators have focused on Marcuse's treatment of the founder of the psycho-analytical tradition or on the use of Freudian or quasi-Freudian
terms such as "polymorphous sexuality" or the later
"repressive de-sublimation" (42). Yet it is surely
not Marcuse as the classical exegete of Freud which
makes the book's force. On the contrary, as has been
pointed out, Marcuse shows a disquieting disregard
for not only the more recent evolution within psycho-analytical tradition; his treatment of the classical Freudian heritage shows important logical
short-comings (43). Marcuse's use of concepts such
as "genitally" or "repression" is often at odds with
the orthodox canons of psycho-analytical theory;
moreover, Marcuse on occasion compresses into a
single notion several distinct concepts of psycho-
analytical theory and practice (44). Marcuse's noto-
rious lack of concern for either the clinical findings of orthodox psychotherapy, or for the empirical
evidence concerning these clinical insights makes
him a most unlikely candidate for the title (45).
     The importance of play versus labour in this
work points in another direction altogether. As Paul
Robinson remarks, Marx is "clearly the unacknow-
ledged hero of Eros and Civilization. That Marcuse
never mentions Marx's name in the book was an ex-

traordinary feat of legerdemain" (46). Rather than
the analysis of Freud, it is the incorporation of
his psychological insights and his basic psychological model into a wider framework which gives the
book its force (47). But it is Marx as interpreted
and developed by Marcuse that gives character to
this study of Freud (48).

Freud provides Marcuse with the invaluable
"mediation" at the individual level of the wider
process of "reification" which according to Lukács
characterizes advanced capitalism. A crucial distinction is that between the necessary "repression"
demanded by any form of civilization and "surplus-
repression", a characteristic of late capitalism.
The original foundation for repression is the justified fear of the unconscious and of the complete
release of instincts leading only to Nirvana, or
death. Yet different civilizations can provide different outlets for the instincts, in terms of both
quantity and diversity, thus reducing the pressure
exerted by the instincts and in turn the measure of
"repression" required. Advanced industrial societies
which have such fantastic resources at their dispo-
sal have gone the other way and maintained, if not
intensified, a level of repression once justified by
the "take off" of industrial civilization. Moreover,
the increase of gratifications that has taken place
enslave men to the existing system of competitive
and self-destructive performance rather than enhance
their capacity to let their instincts flow.

Marcuse most importantly finds and develops
from Freud both a strong materialism and the idea of
a radical, social, shameless hedonism (49). In the
Epilogue (which appeared as a separate essay prior
to the book's publication) Marcuse asserts that
"identifying the energy of the life instincts meant
defining their gratification in contradiction to
spiritual transcendentalism: Freud's notion of happiness and freedom is eminently critical in so far
as it is materialistic - protesting against the
spiritualization of want" (50). This radical hedonism leads him to oppose all forms of socially
sanctioned masochism: "Whether death is feared as
constant threat, or glorified as supreme sacrifice,
or accepted as fate, the education for consent to
death introduces an element of surrender into life
from the beginning - surrender and submission" (51).
The more thorough acquaintance with Freud's work, or
as Robinson suggests, an atmosphere of either reaction (McCarthyism) or inertia (the Eisenhower administration), resulted in an affirmative hedonism

even more radical than that of the thirties (52).
This finds expression in the famous advocacy of
"polymorphous sexuality", the legitimation of all
forms of "sexual deviations", from homosexuality to
sexual sadism (but not, as MacIntyre suggests, co-
prophilia) and the rejection of "mere" genital sexuality (53). This is also clearly stated at a more
general level:

> "Happiness is almost by definition unreasonable
> if it is unrepressed and uncontrollable ... the
> striving for _lasting_ gratification makes not
> only for an enlarged order of libidinal rela-
> tions (community) but also for the perpetuation
> of this order on a higher level" (54)

This depiction of the co-operative society as one of
unbridled licence is to be understood in a "metaphorical" rather than a literal sense. Marcuse's feeling at the time that the liberated society depicted
in the second part of _Eros and Civilization_ ventured
on uncertain ground is perhaps best illustrated by
the fact that nowhere in his writings up to 1959
does he return to the themes developed in that
section of the study. It is thus not without significance, when compared with other equally utopian
elements of his thought, that in _Soviet Marxism_,
written almost concurrently, there is no allusion to
"polymorphous sexuality"; yet the same work contains
radical positions on art and an indictment of the
retrogression of Soviet sexual morality to Victorian
standards (55). More telling is perhaps the fact
that in those essays directly concerned with Freud
and his legacy, Marcuse chooses not to develop the
wider image of a liberated civilization which takes
so important a place in _Eros and Civilization_ (56).
the same applies to Marcuse's major essay on "The
ideology of Death" and the day-to-day attitude this
philosophy reflects (57). Marcuse nonetheless in
these various articles and essays lays great stress
upon the idea of happiness, understood in very direct and material terms, as developed in the analyses of the thirties (58).

6.4 Art, Culture and "La promesse de bonheur"

The character and function of art in modern society,
and the relationship between artistic works and a
"liberated" society belong to the more neglected
areas of Marcuse's thought (59). He never developed

a fully-fledged critique of art in the way that his former colleagues at the institute, such as Adorno or Benjamin, have done (60). Yet much of what Marcuse has to say about art deserves attention, especially in relation to his picture of the co-operative society.

Marcuse's critique of art and the images of the future conveyed through this critique help explain the general appeal of his work. By indicating how his own conception of the good society is assessed in relation to a wider body of literature, theatre or paintings, Marcuse offers an accessible background for often complex or paradoxical arguments. This appeal also rests on more substantial grounds. Marcuse belongs to a generation of Western marxists who, contrary to their predecessors, do not reject en bloc the realm of traditional culture as irrelevant to the goals of marxism. Like Lukács or Goldmann, Marcuse anchors his critique of art and culture in a marxist perspective where day-to-day concerns and the shadow of alienated labour are predominant; philosophical acumen and a sensitivity to those aspects of capitalist reality lead him to raise fundamental questions about the role and even the values of art in contemporary societies (61). It also leads him to visualize art as no longer a dimension of human existence divorced from the realm of ordinary affairs. In particular, Marcuse's various discussions of art and freedom bring into the political arena concerns whose realization is habitually left entirely to the domain of private life or to the artist's personal values. Bronner, for instance, asserts that Marcuse thereby reintroduces into the political vocabulary such concepts as "beauty, softness and sensuality" (62). Moreover, we find in Marcuse's discussions of art and culture his most explicit and intuitively appealing intimations of a different order of things, one in which human feelings, senses and passions finally come into their own. In these analyses of "great bourgeois art" Marcuse succeeds most convincingly in conveying his central notion that in contemporary societies it is possible to visualize a "second dimension" containing the promises of a genuinely co-operative society.

It would, however, be a profound misinterpretation of Marcuse's relation to traditional culture to argue that he simply upholds the values of the artist or of higher culture against the ills of capitalist societies. This for instance is the impression created by Bronner's otherwise perceptive

discussion of Marcuse's treatment of art and freedom
(63). Again with the exception of <u>One Dimensional
Man</u>, Marcuse, while sensitive to the ideals of traditional culture, is nonetheless deeply committed to
values best described as antithetical to many goals
of traditional culture; he will again and again uphold as good, proper and legitimate aspirations of
mankind the notion of unabashed sensuality, the
importance of the body and the idea of joyful sexuality (64). Moreover, Marcuse's judgement of what is
good and valuable in art will always be philosophical; even his most radical postures toward art remain informed by the imperatives of a political
revolution leading to some version of the co-operative society.

This applies fully to <u>Eros and Civilization</u>, in
which literary images and references play an important role in relation to the idea of a different
reality principle; Marcuse emphasizes more than once
that it is precisely in contemporay art that the
most damning indictment of capitalist societies can
be found. Yet the examples he cites and the demarche
he adopts reveal that no such simple dichotomy is
envisaged.

It is significant in this context that Marcuse
early on evokes the work of Baudelaire. Pursuing a
theme already presented in "Philosophy and Critical
Theory", Marcuse argues forcefully for the contribution of fantasy in helping to bridge the gap between
the present and what our "reality principle" declares must remain impossible (65). He adds that:

> "Phantasy not only plays a constitutive role in
> the perverse manifestions of sexuality; as
> artistic imagination, it also links the perver-
> sions with the images of integral freedom and
> gratification. In a repressive order, which
> enforces the equation between normal, socially
> useful, and good, the manifestations of plea-
> sure for its own sake appear as 'fleurs du
> mal'. Against a society which employs sexuality
> as a means for a useful end, the perversions
> uphold sexuality as an end in itself; they thus
> place themelves outside the domination of the
> performance principle and challenge its very
> foundation" (66).

Baudelaire's major work is evoked only, not actually
cited. This reflects a deliberate intention to keep
such images in the background of the main argument.
Art has something to offer that capitalist reality

cannot provide. Yet the content is more elusive and radical than in the thirties. Rather than images of the good and the beautiful, art offers artistic imagination and unconscious wishes and memories.

The idea is fully developed in the second part of Eros and Civilization. In the chapter on "Phantasy and Utopia" Marcuse asserts that

> Art is perhaps the most visible 'return of the repressed', not only on the individual but also on the genetic-historical level. The artistic imagination shapes the 'unconscious memory' of the liberation that failed, of the promise that was betrayed. Under the rule of the performance principle, art opposes to institutionalized repression the 'image of man as a free subject'" (67).

As opposed to the values "affirmed" by traditional culture, Marcuse brings forth the feelings, fears and passions uncovered by Freud's analyses and present in so many great works of art - in the paintings of Goya, the novels of Andre Gide, Fellini's films or even the verses of Ovid (68). These forces of the unconscious appeared not only in isolated works, but in virtually every major work of art; it is one of the greatest merits of the Freudian tradition to have brought to light the latent symbolic content of many classical works (69). There lies the great power of art and its liberating potential. As Marcuse argues a few years later in Soviet Marxism, "Art reveals and at the same time consecrates the (subjectivly and objectively) unmastered forces in man and his world, the 'dangerous zones' beneath and beyond social control" (70). It is this unconscious material that Marcuse now advances to support his claim that "the erotic element goes beyond the perverted expressions. It aims at an 'erotic reality' where the life instincts would come to rest in fulfilment without repression" (71).

In his treatment of art, Marcuse appears to have reached the same impasse as in his discussion of sexual perversions. In both cases he asserts the need to go beyond the bounds of traditional morality. This attempt seems at first both convincing and praiseworthy. He reassembles under one umbrella a broad array of needs, demands and aspirations which are stifled, when not suppressed, in the 'normal' forms of interactions in advanced industrial societies. To argue for the moral and political legitimacy of open homosexuality, the need for more warmth

203

and sensuality in day-to-day interactions, or even the acceptability of sexual masochism under certain conditions would appear to many as courageous and meritorious; so would the advocacy for the intrinsic importance of the many hidden themes in great works of art, music, literature or painting. To argue further that there and only there can genuine freedom be found, and only in secondary forms of sexuality or in the imagination of the artistic is there any hope for mankind is less convincing. The vision that Marcuse evokes is that of an anarchy even more catastrophic than the one invoked by Hobbes. In his insistence upon complete release of the unconscious and upon the integral freedom echoing in works of art, as opposed to any variation upon the prevailing "reality principle", Marcuse appears to advocate nothing but barbarism and irrationality.

The move is deliberate. Marcuse meets head-on Freud's warning against the release of the unconscious. He indicates the full measure of total liberation that Freud's work uncovers (and which Freud immediately rejected); he sharply portrays the opposition between this integral freedom and the long term goals of civilization, an opposition which psychoanalytic practice seeks to conceal. He furthermore points out that to ignore Freud's diagnosis is to undo the long cultural and historical evolution which led to the (relatively) civilized man of modern times. In Marcuse's reading of Freud the image of total freedom:

> "conjures only the <u>subhistorical past</u> of the genus (and of the individual) prior to all civilization. Because the latter can develop only through the destruction of the sub-historical unity between pleasure principle and reality principle, the image must remain buried in the unconscious, and imagination must become mere fantasy, child's play, daydreaming. The long road of consciousness which led from the primal horde to ever higher forms of civilization cannot be reversed" (72).

On the basis of this radical opposition, Marcuse develops his own utopian concept of a different future world. This is not to be a return to a state of nature, but a higher form of civilization. The requirements for instinctual repression would be radically different in a society where economic scarcity has at last been conquered, where competition no longer reigns supreme and where human rela-

tions would be co-operative, communitarian and individually self-confirming. It is to this future state
of mankind rather than to it archaic past that art
is pointed.

The analyses of art and aesthetics in the fifties reflect an overall political position made more
radical by post-war capitalism and its Soviet counterpart. In 1955 Marcuse had ceased to believe in
the (relative) imminence of the revolution. The
defeat of Fascism had not brought such a prospect
any nearer. On the contrary, from the final victory
emerged McCarthyism and the Cold War, with little
prospect for a proletarian upheaval anywhere in the
West, and consolidated Stalinism in the East. Both
Eros and Civilization and Soviet Marxism are in
response to this situation, and they reflect the
changed function that Marcuse attributes to art.
Marcuse now asserts that:

> "Within the limits of the aesthetic form, art
> expressed, although in a highly ambivalent
> manner, the return of the repressed image of
> liberation; art was opposition. At the present
> stage, in the period of total mobilization,
> even this highly ambivalent opposition seems no
> longer viable. Art survived only where it can-
> cels itself, when it saves its substance by
> denying its traditional form and thereby de-
> nying reconciliation; where it becomes surrea-
> listic and atonal. Otherwise, art shares the
> fate of all genuine human communication, it
> dies off" (73).

Marcuse now turns to the Surrealist movement as
the most potent and articulate expression of this
new political position (74). Only within such a
medium can the hopes of earlier days find refuge,
and only then in connection with a stance of absolute opposition to capitalist realities:

> "This great refusal is the protest against
> unnecessary repression, the struggle for the
> ultimate form of freedom - 'to live without
> anxiety'. But this idea could be formulated
> without punishment only in the language of art.
> In the more realistic context of political
> theory and even philosophy, it was almost uni-
> versally defined as utopia" (75).

One Dimensional Man presents a very different
picture than any of Marcuse's previous discussions

of art and freedom. The idea of the co-operative
society, which guides his writings from 1932 onward,
suddenly appears to collapse; we have instead an
ill-defined humanism which he nevertheless presents
as different from "capitalist humanism" (76). In
many respects One Dimensional Man is quite atypical.
Even his links with the marxist tradition appears to
have been cut off. Marcuse, instead of using marxist
analyses of modern monopoly capitalism, refers in
general terms to a strange admixture of traditional
American academic sociology and writings best described as inspired journalism (77)., Therborn argues, moreover, that "One Dimensional Man represents
a step backward for Marcuse vis-a-vis many of his
attitudes to technology, to philosophy and to classical bourgeois culture" (78). The evidence is interpreted by Therborn in terms of a belated return
to the positions advanced by Marcuse's former colleagues Horkheimer and Adorno in the fifties and
early sixties; he asserts that their philosophical
hyper-radicalism, to which Marcuse would now subscribe, precludes a serious commitment to marxism.
This interpretation suffers from various flaws (79).
More convincing is the case presented by Piccone and
Delfini who see in this book a return to Heidegger
(80). The hypothesis, while hardly serious as a
total perspective on Marcuse's work, provides many
useful clues for a reading of One Dimensional Man;
it also appears plausible in what is obviously a
period of disarray. The overall theme of the book is
that of man totally conditioned and imprisoned in a
technological world in which the only escape is an
existentially conceived "Great Refusal" - no longer
the hidden promise of Eros and civilization. Even
sexuality, the grand hope of the fifties, appears
now as no more that "repressive desublimation".
Philosophy is re-affirmed as the only medium for
truth; this truth cannot be conveyed except by personal conviction and the intuition of a different
destiny. Alongside philosophy, only culture remains
a repository for forgotten truths (81).
    Marcuse's treatment of culture in particular
appears to owe everything to Heidegger and nothing
to Marx (82). The 'second dimension' of Marx's concepts is no longer central to the analysis. Instead
looms some Heideggerian notion that somehow, somewhere out there, there is a truth which can be found
by the intuition of an open mind or the searching
eye of the philosopher. The higher culture of a now
dead past provides Marcuse with truths for which
Heidegger searched in the ancient Greek texts:

"The higher culture of the West - whose moral
aesthetic, and intellectual values industrial
society still professes was a pretechnological
culture in a functional as well as chronological sense. Its validity was derived from
the experience of a world which no longer e-
xists and cannot be recaptured because it is in
a strict sense invalidated by technological
society" (83).

Even the concepts which formerly indicated the
distinctive nature of his relation to the classical
marxist texts now appear within a recognisable Heideggerian context: alienation now serves to describe
Brechts's notion of the "estrangement effect" under
the formula of "artistic alienation"; the ideas of
the "Great Refusal" and of an alternative dimension
are relegated to a high culture which is itself
past:

"Now this essential gap between the arts and
the order of the day, kept open in the artistic
alienation, is progressively closed by the
advancing technological society. And with its
closing, the Great Refusal is in turn refused;
the 'other dimension' is absorbed into the
prevailing state of affairs". (84)

The final answer, then, predictably, must be the
poetic verb which occupies so large a place in
Heidegger's philosophy: "creating and moving in a
medium which presents the absent, the poetic language of cognition - but a cognition which subverts
the positive. In its cognitive function, poetry
performs the great task of thought" (85).
    Both the underlying tone and content of these
reflections on art change radically in Marcuse's
next two major works, An Essay on Liberation and
Counterrevolution and Revolt. The question of art
and freedom now appears in relation to two central
themes. The first of these, to which Marcuse devotes
only a short and somewhat contradictory paragraph in
One Dimensional Man (86), is the idea of an alliance
of technology with a new 'aesthetic essence'. This
theme is most fully developed in An Essay on Liberation. There Marcuse returns to his discussion of
Kant and Schiller in Eros and Civilization and to an
idea first advanced in Soviet Marxism, the utopian
notion of a play with techniques.

> The liberated consciousness would promote the
> development of science and technology free to
> discover and realise the possibilities of
> things and men in the protection and gratifi-
> cation of life, playing with the potentialities
> of forms and matter for the attainment of this
> goal ... The term 'aesthetic', in its dual
> connotation of 'pertaining to the senses' and
> 'pertaining to art', may serve to designate the
> quality of the productive-creative process in
> an environment of freedom. Technique, assuming
> the feature of art, would translate subjective
> sensibility into objective form, into reality"
> (87).

The same theme is again affirmed in Marcuse's discussion of <u>Economic and Philosophical Manuscripts
of 1844</u> in his <u>Counterrevolution and Revolt</u>. The
theme of the 1932 essay reappears unchanged, even if
the style and structure are different. The two novel
features are precisely the greater emphasis upon the
senses, upon sensuality as a defining characteristic
of a liberated humanity, and the far more central
role given to the idea of a world shaped "in accordance with the laws of beauty" (88).

The second major aspect of Marcuse's discussion
of art in these works concerns the question of form
and beauty. For Marcuse the essence of beauty resides in precisely the 'estrangement effet' discussed by Brecht (89). Brecht's argument, in short, is
that the total character and interrelatedness of
established institutions, norms and ideas makes it
impossible for the artist to force his public to see
this world as a relative one, which can be judged by
standards other than the prevailing ones; only in
imposing upon familiar images a new strangeness and
sustaining the obtained sharp dissociation from
their usual appearances is it possible for him to
force his public or readership to seriously question
a society or a world which is otherwise only too
self-evident; the "estrangement effect" is a necessary ploy for any artistic message whose content
points beyond the existing society and its institutions. For Marcuse the power of all true art lies in
this effect. In <u>One Dimensional Man</u> he placed much
of his hopes for the continuing presence of the
"second dimension" in the quality of strangeness
shared in his view by radical as well as "great"
bourgeois art. Now, however, the way in which Marcuse chooses to define this effect places art in a
dimension totally absent from his treatment of art

in <u>One Dimensional Man</u>. While beauty may provide the
impulses and principles for a new structuring of the
environment, Marcuse now stresses as essential to a
true work of art its distance from reality - all
reality, including that of the co-operative society.
Thus, for Marcuse, in art "true and false, right and
wrong, pain and pleasure, calm and violent become
aesthetic categories within the framework of the
<u>oeuvre</u>. Thus deprived of their (immediate) reality,
they enter a different context in which even the
ugly, cruel, sick become parts of the aesthetic
harmony governing the whole. They are thereby not
'cancelled': "the horror in Goya's etching remains
horror, but at the same time 'eternalises' the horror of horror" (90). Throughout the whole of his
discussion of art and freedom in the two works in
question, Marcuse now emphasises that the liberating
potential of art is ambiguous in at least two senses. First, pursuing his earlier argument, art is
limited by virtue of the very qualities which make
it art: that of being an illusion, that of being
beautiful, and that of being unreal.

Next, Marcuse points out that it is possible to
find in art a double transcendence from the present
reality. The crucial transcendence from the given
reality is the artistic one. Art has always and will
always attempt to picture what cannot be expressed.
Art is thereby also removed from good and evil and
from the wider ideals of the co-operative society.
The second transcendence is much more limited; it
refers to art's ability to express nevertheless
ideals and images, not only of the past (as argued
in <u>One Dimensional Man</u>) but mainly of a future yet
to come. It is by virtue of this second transcendence only that art can contribute to the wider political struggle; it can do this only insofar as it
enhances our understanding of a particular historical or political situation, or by keeping alive,
through a constant process of artistic creation,
certain hopes and ideals which cannot otherwise be
conveyed (91). The real struggles must be left to
political theory and ultimately political action
(92).

6.5   The rational society
The underlying idea guiding Marcuse's post-war writings, with the notable exception of <u>One Dimensional
Man</u>, is a very definite conception of human freedom
and a conception of the good society carried over,
virtually unchanged, from his more explicitly poli-

tical essays of the 1930s. His conception of freedom, the 'idea', in the platonic sense, of what man
ought to strive for, is built directly upon Marx.
But it is done through a specific and highly personal interpretation of the marxist tradition. Marcuse
developed the idea in the thirties and forties, and
it gave Reason and Revolution the inner unity which
is so striking even on first reading. It is this
idea which links the latter to Eros and Civilization
and Soviet Marxism. The virtual abandonment of this
idea in One Dimensional Man helps explain this
work's lack of inner coherence and vision. The return to a partial elaboration of central themes
within that idea provides the otherwise fairly minor
pieces of the late sixties and early seventies with
much of what they contain in terms of appeal and
overall interest.

One aspect of this idea has not yet been mentioned in the context of the post-war writings. This
is the profoundly rationalist character of his vision of the good society. There is, obviously, little need to dwell upon the importance of ideas such
as reason, rationality, knowledge or education for
marxism. Marcuse himself, in Reason and Revolution,
does much to stress the inner connection between
this intellectual and political tradition and the
rationalist movement of the Enlightment. Eros and
Civilization is, in contrast, explicitly committed
to a defence of those values and instinctual forces
that are threatened or repressed in Western societies in the very name of rationality. Nevertheless
the main thrust in the second part of the book is
the attempt to establish that reason can be reconciled with a far greater latitude for precisely
those needs and values. The discussion takes as its
starting point the "reality principle" that Freud
saw as so central to our conception of the world and
our ability to deal with it. The Freudian category
leads to a stress on causality, on the independent
existence of objects and on the power of disciplined, co-ordinated physical actions as opposed to
simple reflex actions or a reliance on magic; it
argues for a reliance on only what exists. Marcuse
asserts the idea of a different rationality, which
should ally to such demands the further requirement
that the existing reality itself should submit to
rational judgement. Marcuse's whole demarche is that
a rationality in which instinctual needs are given a
far greater influence should allow us to judge, not
so much our physical environment, but the social and
political institutions which contribute to its pre-

sent form. Similarly, the argument in <u>Soviet Marxism</u> is very much an argument against what Marcuse considers distorted rationality. He repeatedly points to those aspects of Soviet society which appear to conform to the standards of rationality Marx saw as essential for a successful transition to "true communism". His final judgement of the achievements of this society also depends upon a rational calculation of the contribution of various aspects of Soviet reality with respect to the goals of the cooperative society. The importance of rationality is far less in evidence in <u>One Dimensional Man</u>. Nevertheless, it should be noted that Marcuse from the outset describes contemporary American society as an "irrational society". Throughout the book there are various references to the idea of a rationality distinct from the prevailing ones, as the discussions of operationalism and behaviourism make only too clear. Yet at the same time the book lacks that sense of inner coherence which is characteristic of the previous works. As noted above Marcuse here exhibits a marked tendency to proceed via a series of anecdotes and vague, unsystematic case studies (93). Some of the same tendencies can be seen in <u>An Essay on Liberation</u>, although the commitment to rationality is more vigorously spelled out. There is no longer the same intransigent opposition to technical progress as opposed to other values of Western society. The positive features of the educational system are clearly brought out. Marcuse also insists at one point that subjectivity can be transcended by a rational analysis based upon independent information and self-reflection (94). The general trend is further confirmed in <u>Counterrevolution and Revolt</u> where rationality is stressed as the essential factor in the revolutionary process. He condemns the anti-rationalist trend of much of the New Left and even asserts against Reich that the choice for the present form of society must be seen as rational, insofar as in the absence of clear alternatives the system at least delivers the goods for the many rather than the few (95).

The goal remains a rational society in which the "realm of necessity" is organized in such a way as to maximize the full development of all individuals in the "realm of freedom".

NOTES

1. <u>Eros and Civilization: A Philosophical En</u>-

quiry into Freud, New York: Oxford University Press, 1941 (Edition used: Routledge and Kegan Paul, 1973), pp. 114-155.

2. Soviet Marxism: A Critical Analysis, New York, Columbia University Press, 1968 (Edition used: Pelican, 1971), p. 192.

3. Counterrevolution and Revolt, Boston: Beacon Press, 1972 (Edition used: Allen Lane, The Penguin Press, 1972), p. 62 and pp. 16-17.

4. See Jay, The Dialectical Imagination, op. cit., p. 284, for biographical details.

5. See above, section 5.1.

6. See Andrew, "Work and Freedom in Marcuse and Marx", op. cit., passim. for a particularly forceful discussion to that effect; see also Schoolman, "Further reflections on Work, Alienation, and Freedom in Marcuse and Marx", op. cit., p. 181.

7. See Eros and Civilization, op. cit., pp. 127-142 and pp. 119-127.

8. See One Dimensional Man: Studies in the Ideology of Advanced Industrial Societies, Boston: Beacon Press, 1965 (Edition used: Abacus, 1972), p. 181.

9. Ibid., p. 188; no reference for Marx.

10. The Aesthetic Dimension, USA, Boston: Beacon Press, 1978.

11. The following only applies to the first two above-mentioned works, not to The Aesthetic Dimension, USA, Boston: Beacon Press, 1978.

12. An Essay on Liberation, USA, Boston: Beacon Press, 1968 (Edition used: Penguin, 1973), pp. 92-93.

13. See the further description in An Essay on Liberation, op. cit., pp. 92-93.

14. Counterrevolution and Revolt, op. cit., pp. 17-18.

15. Reason and Revolution: Hegel and the Rise of Social Theory, New York: Oxford University Press, 1941 1941 (Edition used: Routledge and Kegan Paul, 1973), p. 293.

16. Marcuse never elaborates on the exact meaning of "play" as understood in his post-war writings. Nevertheless, as we shall see, it is best understood as something between play and work, a mode of activity that can only become possible in an altogether different economic, social and political order. In that sense it is closest to the extented sense of labour given in the 1933 essay, which stresses the opportunities for personal self-development and co-operative behaviour above all things. It should not be understood according to the early

analyses of "play" given in that essay and "On the Philosophical Foundation of the Concept of Labor in Economics", op. cit., passim.

17. See above section 5.2.

18. On these points see Eros and Civilization, passim and below; see also Paul Robinson, The Sexual Radicals, op. cit.

19. See above section 4.3 and Kellner's "Introduction to Marcuse's 'On the Foundation of the Concept of Labor in Economics'", op. cit., passim; on Marcuse see in particular "The Foundation of Historical Materialism", op. cit.

20. Eros and Civilization, op. cit., p. 118.

21. Ibid.

22. Ibid., p. 140, emphasis in the original.

23. Ibid., p. 72, emphasis in the original.

24. This is a point where he is at one with Marx, for instance in the following passage in the Paris Manuscripts, cited in part in Reason and Revolution: "The worker ... does not affirm himself but denies himself, does not feel content but unhappy, does not develop his physical and mental energy but mortifies his body and ruins his mind ... (Labour's) alien character emerges clearly in the fact that as soon as no physical or modes of compulsion exist, labour in shunned like the plague", (Economics and Philosophical Manuscripts of 1844, op. cit., p. 66).

25. Hendrick, I., "Work and the Pleasure Principle", Psychoanalytic Quarterly, Vol. XII, No. 9, 1943, p. 314; as cited in Eros and Civilization, op, cit., p. 154.

26. See above section 35.

27. It is perhaps in positions such as those advanced by Hendrick that his claim of a transformation of the "reality principle" into a "performance principle" finds its best support; while it may be characteristic of all advanced industrial societies, it is difficult not to think of such a conception as peculiarly American.

28. There has been much interesting work in recent American psycho-analytic theory to suggest the possibility of reconciling Freud's basic model with, if not exactly Hendrick's notion of a "mastery instinct", so then a need to be active and utilize one's resources in skilful play or efficient work; see in particular the literature reviewed and the arguments presented in R. W. White's excellent attempt to reeoncile Freud and Piaget in White, R. W., Ego and Reality in Psychoanalytic Theory, USA - New York: Psychological Issues Vl. III, No. 3, Monograph II, International University Press, 1963.

29. See <u>Reason and Revolution</u>, op. cit., p. 293.

30. <u>Eros and Civilization</u>, op. cit., p. 155.

31. Ibid., p. 134.

32. Ibid., p. 152, emphasis in the original.

33. Ibid., pp.150-151, emphasis in the original.

34. Ibid., p. 158.

35. <u>Soviet Marxism</u>, op. cit., p. 192.

36. See below, chapter 8 and section 9.2.

37. <u>Soviet Marxism</u>, op. cit. p. 210.

38. See Marcuse, H., "Socialism in the Developed Countries", <u>International Socialist Journal</u>, Vol. II, No. 8, april 1965, pp. 139-152. "Socialist Humanism?", in <u>Socialist Humanism</u>, edited by Erich Fromm, op. cit.; "Repressive Tolerance", <u>A Critique of Pure Tolerance</u>, by H. Marcuse, R. P. Wollf and Barrington Moore, Jr., Boston: Beacon Press, 1965, pp. 81-117 (With 1969 postscript, London: Jonathan Cape Ltd., 1969). Reprinted in <u>Critical Sociology</u>, edited by P. Connerton, London: Penguin, 1976.

39. The essay on "Socialist Humanism?" shows how far Marcuse is willing to push his self-interrogation on the nature of the good society and its foundation in the present one; he insists that "it is the work world, the technical world that (men) must first make their own". He also makes clear that it is by virtue of its ability to demonstrate present potentialities that marxist theory can provide a comprehensive critique of society; as opposed to other forms of humanism or utopianism, "socialist theory has no right to denounce, in the name of other historical possibilities, growing social productivity which allows a better life for more sections of the population" (See "Socialist Humanism?", op. cit. pp 115-116).

40. "The End of Utopia", <u>Five Lectures</u>, London: Allen Lane, The Penguin Press 1970, pp. 66. First published as "Das Ende der Utopie", lecture delivered at the Free University of Berlin in July, 1967.

41. Ibid., p. 67. The same theme is developed in "An Essay on Liberation", op. cit., p. 29.

42. See Paul Robinson, <u>The Sexual Radicals</u>, op. cit.; Lipshires, <u>Herbert Marcuse: From Marx to Freud and Beyond</u>, op. cit.; Rhodes, <u>Pleasure and Reason: Marcuse's Idea of Freedom</u>, op. cit.: Nicholas, <u>Marcuse ou la quête d'un univers transpromothéen</u>, op. cit.: MacIntyre, <u>Marcuse</u>, op. cit., and Jay, <u>The Dialectical Imagination</u>, op. cit.; see also

the thoughtful comments by an English socialist in Peter Sedgwick, "Natural Science and Human Theory - A Critique of Herbert Marcuse", in <u>Socialist Register</u>, 1966, pp. 163-192.

43. MacIntyre's argument is particularly telling on two points. The first is that the metaphorical use of Freud's discussion of the primal horde presents several logical difficulties that Marcuse treats only in the most cursory manner; secondly he correctly points out that instances of aggressiveness cannot themselves constitute sufficient ground within the framework adopted by Marcuse for the existence of an 'a priori' death instinct (Thanatos). His discussion of sexuality, however, is sketchy and superficial, and he fails to show convincingly why Marcuse's parallel between the phylogenetic development of the race and the ontogenetic development of the individual is invalid in relation to either psycho-analytic theory or Marcuse's own framework of analysis.

44. Lipshires, <u>Herbert Marcuse: From Marx to Freud and Beyond</u>, op. Cit., pp. 57-67.

45. Such a work can be found in Jones, Ernest, <u>Sigmund Freud: Life and Work</u>, London, 1953-57.

46. Robinson, <u>The Sexual Radicals</u>, op. cit., p. 201; while giving due credit to Marcuse's careful reading of the classic texts, he also stresses the profoundly marxist and historical character of this interpretation of Freud's legacy.

47. It should be noted that Marcuse in his 1955 preface to the study emphasises social and political events has made it necessary to develop the political and sociological substance of Freud's psychological concepts. Both the Freudian material of the book, i.e. Freud's most speculative work, <u>Civilization and its discontents</u>, and the organisation of the book, whereby Freud's work constantly is replaced within the wider body of Western philosophy, indicate that Marcuse retain this position throughout, a position compatible with that of the famous <u>Authoritarian Personality</u>, published by Adorno et al. a few years before, of whose German forerunners Marcuse was weel acquainted. That Marcuse later in 1966 and 1967 was to speak of "biological" needs, and this even in the new political preface to the book, must thus be understood either as a figure of speech, or as Lipshires suggests, a temporary aberration not unrelated to his sudden fame, and which he later retracted (Se Lipshires, <u>Herbert Marcuse From Marx to Freud and Beyond</u>, op.cit., p. 68 and Marcuse, <u>Eros and Civilisation</u>, op.cit., p. 13,

An Essay on Liberation, pp. 17, 20, 25, 27, 30, 33
and 90, "The End of Utopia", op. cit. p. 67, Marxism
and the New Humanity: An Unfinished Revolution" in
Marxism and Radical Religion: Essays Toward a Revolutionary Humanism, by J.C. Raines and T. Dean,
Philadelphia: Temple University Press, 1970, p.9,
Counterrevolution and Revolt, op. cit., pp. 63-66).
    48. Paul Robinson, for instance, stresses the
degree to which Marcuse remains in the realm of pure
theory (Paul Robinson, The Sexual Radicals, op.
cit., p. 223). Sidney Lipshires similarly emphasises
the extent to which Marcuse himself conceived of
Eros and Civilization as primarily a philosophical
investigation (Sidney Lipshires, Herbert Marcuse:
From Marx to Freud and Beyond, op. cit., p. 85).
James M. Rhodes, in his sensitive treatment of Marcuse's idea of freedom since Reason and Revolution,
also lays great stress upon the fact that Marcuse's
treatment of happiness and freedom in Eros and Civilization does not admit of empirical resolution. He
explicitly refers to Marcuse's approach to Freud as
one which emphasises the long neglected "metapsychology" and is primarily concerned with the philosophical foundation of that theory, offering solutions
and hypotheses which should largely be taken into
account by virtue of their 'symbolic value rather
than as statements about Freudian theory' (James M.
Rhodes, "Pleasure and Reason: Marcuse's Idea of
Freedom", op. cit., p. 82).
    49. Marcuse once more counters the isolated,
monadic individual of bourgeois theory and practice
with the idea of the "whole individual" no longer at
war with others in the good society; even sadism is
only to be condemned when the social context makes
it an "inhuman, compulsive and destructive force";
see Eros and Civilization, op. cit., pp. 108-110 and
p. 146.
    50. Eros and Civilization, op. cit., p. 187.
    51. Ibid., p. 165.
    52. Robinson, The Sexual Radicals, op. cit.,
pp. 234-235.
    53. For this whole discussions see Marcuse,
Eros and Civilization, op. cit., pp. 144-146; see
also MacIntyre, Marcuse, op. cit., p. 47.
    54. Eros and Civilization, op. cit., p. 158.
    55. See soviet Marxism, op. cit., pp. 108-113.
    56. See "Freedom and Freud's Theory of Ins-
tincts" and "Progress and Freud's Theory of Instincts", both from 1957, reprinted in Five Lectures,
USA, Boston: Beacon Press, 1970.
    57. See "The Ideology of Death", in The Mea-

ning of Death, edited by Hermann Feifel, New York: McGraw Hill, 1959, pp. 66-76.

58. See for instance his Preface to Raya Dunayevskaya's Marxism and Freedom, London: Pluto Press, 1971 (first published 1958), p. 11. Similarly, in "The Ideology of Death" he opposes to the notion of death as a moral or ontological sanction the idea of the good life, which he defines as that in which individuals "have the possibility to develop and satisfy human needs and faculties (and where) their life is an end in itself rather than a means for sustaining themselves" ("The Ideology of Death", op. cit., p. 69 and passim).

59. See however Bronner, S. E., "Art and Utopia: The Marcusian Perspective", in Politics and Society, vol. III, No. 2, Winter 1973, pp. 129-161; Jameson, Marxism and Form, Princeton, 1971, pp. 83-116, especially the section on "Marcuse and Schiller"; and Martin Jay's occasional remarks in his The Dialectical Imagination, op. cit., passim.

60. See Martin Jay, ibid., chapter 6, for further comments.

61. See in particular his essay on "The Affirmative Character of Culture", op. cit., passim.

62. Bronner, "Art and Utopia: the Marcusian Perspective", op. cit., p. 129.

63. Ibid., pp. 133-134.

64. In the following, Marcuse's characterization of traditional culture in terms of "higher needs" and "higher values" will be adopted as a reasonable basis for discussion (see his "The affirmative Character of Culture", op. cit., passim).

65. See "Philosophy and Critical Theory", op. cit., pp. 154-156, pp. 122-125.

66. Eros and Civilization, op. cit., p. 50.

67. Ibid., p. 110.

68. On the latter, see later in the text, ibid., p. 125.

69. Ibid., p. 134.

70. Soviet Marxism, op. cit., p. 111.

71. Eros and Civilization, pp. 111-112.

72. Eros and Civilizaton, pp. 111-112.

73. Eros and Civilization, op. cit., p. 111.

74. A similar position can also be seen in Soviet Marxism. For Marcuse whatever the merits of the Soviet case, the insistence upon realistic art can only serve to close off a whole possible medium of ideas and communication, a channel whose importance increases in direct proportion to the degree to which the Soviet version of socialism falls short of the idea of communism advanced by Marx. This

leads him to express again his support for surrea-
lism: "Art as a political force is art only insofar
as it preserves the image of liberation; in a society which is in its totality the negation of these
images, art can preserve them only by total refusal,
that is, by not succumbing to the standard of the
unfree reality, either in style, or in form, or in
substance ... The works of the great 'bourgeois'
anti-realists and 'formalists' are far deeper committed to the idea of freedom than is socialist and
soviet realism" (Soviet Marxism, op., cit., p. 111).
    75. Eros and Civilization, op. cit., p. 113.
    76. See "Socialist Humanism?", op. cit., pas-
sim.
    77. Therborn, "The Frankfurt School", op.
cit., p. 112.
    78. Ibid.
    79. That philosophy rather than marxism is
ultimately the Archimedean point for both Horkheimer
and Adorno, rather than the marxist tradition, political commitment or the classical marxist tests, is
highly probable; this however does not deny that
even in their latest work the original marxist imprint constantly reappears. See for instance the
difficult discussion of "objectivity and reification" in Adorno's Negative Dialectics, London: Routledge and Kegan Paul, 1973, pp. 189-192. First published as Negative Dialektik, Frankfurt: Suhrkamp
Verlag, 1966; or Horkheimer's latter essays in Critical Theory, op. cit., passim. The marxist origins
also show forth in their attitude to technology,
which retains throughout a measure of ambivalence
which is not even evident in One Dimensional Man;
the same applies, although to a lesser degree, to
their relation to traditional culture; Adorno's
utter rejection of jazz does not exclude a profound
interest in the resolutely modern atonal music of
Schönberg,, which he defends on similar grounds to
Marcuse in Eros and Civilization: see Jay, The Dialectical Imagination, op. cit., for further discussion of these points.
    80. Piccone and Delfini, "Marcuse's Heidegge-
rian Marxism", op. cit., pp. 44-47.
    81. See One Dimensional Man, op. cit., Intro-
duction and chapters 3, 6 and 8; see also the argument presented by Therborn, "The Frankfurt School",
op. cit. On Heidegger, see his Being and Time, op.
cit. and chapters 2 and 3 above: see also Beimel,
Martin Heidegger: An illustrated Study, op. cit.,
passim and Metha, Martin Heidegger: The Way and
the Vision, op. cit., passim.

82. Marcuse does not entirely relinguish his earlier positions. His discussion of culture in One Dimensional Man develops an earlier position from the essay on the "Affirmative Character of Culture" in that he asserts that the transition to a new age itself has invalidated much of what traditional culture stood for, and that this is only for the best in some respects: "The assimilation of the ideal with reality testifies to the extent to which the ideal has been surpassed. It is right down from the sublimated realm of the soul or the spirit of the inner man, and translated into operational terms and problems. Here are the progressive elements of mass culture" (One Dimensional Man, op. cit., p. 58).

83. Ibid. The following passage is perhaps even more telling: "With its code of forms and manners, with the style and vocabulary of its literature and philosophy, this past expressed the rhythm and content of a universe in which valleys and forests, villages and inns, nobles and villains, salons and courts were a part of the experienced reality. In the verse and prose of this pre-technological culture is the rhythm of those who wander or ride in carriages, who have the time and the pleasure to think, contemplate, feel and narrate" (Ibid., p. 59).

84. Ibid., p. 62.
85. Ibid., p. 65, emphasis in the original.
86. Ibid., p. 188.
87. An essay on Liberation, op. cit., p. 32.
88. Counterrevolution and Revolt, op. cit., pp. 63-74.
89. See One Dimensional Man, op. cit., p. 64.
90. Counterrevolution and Revolt, op. cit., p. 99.

91. See again on these points and especially with regard to a discussion of the function of art in differing contexts, Bronner. "Art and Utopia: The Marcusean Perspective", op. cit., passim.

92. Counterrevolution and Revolt, op. cit., pp. 108-109.

93. See for instance also Rhodes, "Pleasure and Reason: Marcuse's Idea of Freedom", op. cit., or Therborn, "The Frankfurt School", op. cit.

94. At one point Marcuse attacks the existing liberal democratic representative systems as unrepresentative - arguing that "the representation is representative of the will shaped by the ruling minorities". If there is no alternative than rule by an elite, he furthermore argues that "the dreaded

intellectual elite" may perhaps not be the worse choice. To this he adds the following, however: "The revolution would be liberating only if it were car- ried by the non-repressive forces stirring in the existing society.... Prior to its realization, it is ... only the individual, the indivduals, who can judge, with no other legitimation than their con- sciousness and conscience.... Their judgement tran- scends their subjectivity to the degree to which it is based on independent thought and information, on a rational analysis and evaluation of their society. The existence of a majority of individuals capable of such rationality has been the assumption on which democratic theory has been based", <u>An Essay on Libe- ration</u>, op. cit., p. 74.

95. See <u>Counterrevolution and Revolt</u>, op. cit., pp. 129 and 131.

Chapter Seven

FREEDOM AND THE DIALECTIC OF LIBERATION

7.1 Freedom in Historical Perspective

The emphasis Marcuse gives to a positive idea of
freedom, as opposed to alienation or exploitation,
is unusual for a marxist author. Marcuse's work is
largely of a critical nature, yet the vision of the
co-operative society appears constantly in his writings as a distinctive background against which he
contrasts existing social and political institutions; it is also a thread of continuity throughout
most of his analyses. Freedom is mentioned in virtually every one of his works. It generally plays a
central role in the exposition of his thought; it is
the key term in <u>Eros and Civilization</u>, <u>Reason and
Revolution</u> and the essays of the thirties. Nevertheless, the Marxian taboo on any detailed description
of the good society still holds: there is very
little in Marcuse with freedom as the main theme for
discussion (1). In fact, of a dozen books and essay
collections, a hundred or so articles and book reviews, only three texts - and minor ones at that -
have freedom as their major subject. One of these,
"The Realm of Freedom and the Realm of Necessity" is
a brief and somewhat superficial discussion of
Marx's classical formula (2). The second, "Freedom
and Freud's Theory of Instincts", given in 1957 as a
lecture to commemorate the hundreth anniversary of
Freud's birth, consists of a short restatement of
the now familiar themes of <u>Eros and Civilization</u>,
but without the bold utopian forays of the latter (3).

Originally delivered as a lecture at Geneva in
1969, the third essay, "Freedom and the Historical
Imperative", is an ambitious sketch of a broad theory of human liberation building upon Hegel, Marx and
Kant. Central themes from previous works are interwoven into this theory and the relationships between

Table 7

Asumptions and logical implications underlying Marcuse's theory of human liberation, from Reason and Revolution up to 1972.

The Theory of Liberation (2nd version)

ASS 1   a)   The Hegelian notion of "Historical Imperative" is an integral part of a conception of history as entirely determined by a pre-established, ontological and all-encompassing series of dialectical processes.

b)   Hegel's notion of "Historical Imperatives" implies that there is both an ineluctable historical movement toward an ever increasing human mastery over nature and a likewise ineluctable historical movement toward an increased freedom for all men to enjoy and develop all their faculties; these two trends may not co-incide at all times, but they inevitably move in the same direction.

c)   The culmination of these two movements, and of the entire dialectic of history, is for Hegel the Absolute Spirit, alternatively the Prussian state.

d)   The development of this dialectic in history is extraordinarily complex; it means to encompass all areas of human culture and the whole of man's natural environment; it operates at many levels and involves many different aspects, a large part of which remains inaccessible from within the time horizon in which they are effective; the Hegelian notions of the subject-object identity, of the unity of oppositions, of the negation of the negation and of the "abolition" (Aufhebung) of a previous state of affairs are central for all dialectical processes.

ASS 2   Marx has shown conclusively that:

a)   There is no logical necessity for greater freedom to follow from an increased mastery of nature.

b)   That economic forces and men's material conditions in general must be the primary determinants of any such dialectic of history.

c)   That there are no logical or ethical necessity for it to culminate in the Absolute Spirit, and that there are good logical and ethical grounds for such a dialectic in history to lead to a society based on full and equal access to the means of production, where all will have full freedom to develop and enjoy all their faculties, needs and sensibilities.

ASS 3   The Marxian dialectic - as opposed to later marxist

views - should be understood as follows:

a) The Marxian dialectic is not ontological, but social and historical.

b) The Marxian dialectic is not all-encompassing, but applies only to social processes, and to nature only insofar as it becomes part of these social processes.

c) The Marxian dialectic is neither pre-established, nor ineluctable; it always involves an element of active human will.

d) The Marxian dialectic will not be applicable to a free society such as the co-operative society.

e) The Marxian dialectic is not fully applicable to the transition to a free society such as the co-operative society.

f) The Hegelian notion of the subject-object identity, as described below, is fundamental for the Marxian dialectic, as opposed to many later marxist and non-marxist conceptions of the dialectic.

ASS 4   The Marxian conception of the notion of the subject-object identity implies that:

a) No subject and no (social) object exists in isolation from other subjects and objects.

b) This applies to all objects within the sphere of human activities.

c) The relations and interactions that take place between subject and object are determining for both, and far more so than their actual or potential make-up.

d) The interactions which take place in labour are the most potent and most fundamental of all subject-object relations.

e) In labour the subject establishes with the object a pattern of continuous, purposive and effective interactions, which eventually results in the related transformation of both object and subject; a temporary, imperfect and everchanging identity is thereby established between subject and object.

f) Similarly if less potent subject-object identities will follow from other forms of human activities.

g) Any reasonably comprehensive set of such interactions between one or more subjects (individual or collective) and one or more objects, will constitute a dialectical totality.

h) Any dialectical totality can be analysed in terms of Hegel's notions of the unity of oppositons, of the negation of the negation and of the "abolition" (Aufhebung) of a previous state of affairs.

i) The founding totality is always the dialectical totality of society.

ASS 5   a) Labour is any purposeful and disciplined activity
         aimed at the transformation of the environment with a
         view to enhance the fulfilment of human needs.
            b) Work as the free play of faculties is a yet
         unknown form of labour which has as its prime aim the
         worker's enjoyment in exercising and developing all
         manners of talents, powers and sensibilities.
            c) Necessary rational labour is that labour which in
         a free society cannot be performed as described above
         and is nevertheless clearly essential for the mainte-
         nance and development of that society.
            d) Alienated labour is a form of labour where the
         worker has virtually no direct or indirect control over
         the process of labour, the objects created or the use
         of the means of production; its aims are other than the
         needs of the worker, and most often other than those of
         humanity at large.

ASS 6   Society is the totality of human activities and rela-
         tions as they stand at a particular point in history.

ASS 7   The overall setting for these activities is given at
         any particular point in history by:
            a) The natural environment in which the society is
         situated.
            b) The transformation of that environment by human
         labour up to that point of history.
            c) The mode of production of society.

ASS 8   a) All societies up to the present in history have
         been class societies.
            b) The Marxian dialectic applies fully to these
         societies.

Implication 1: a) All different kinds of activities influen-
            ce all the others.
            b) No one set of activities fully determines all the
         others.
            c) Labour activities are nevertheless decisive for
         the maintenance and/or evolution of these societies.
            d) The form and conditions of labour activities are
         crucial for the development of these societies (Ass. 4,
         6, & 7).

Implication 2: a) Hence class societies can only be changed
            totally, not incrementally.
            b) To change the form and conditions of labour is
         crucial for any radical change in class societies (Ass.
         8 and imp. 1).

Implication 3: a) The historical dynamic of these societies is constituted by a complex interplay of economic, social, political and ideological forces.

b) The fact of classes, class struggles, the relations to the means of production and the development of productive forces are constant and all-important aspects of this interplay of forces; intensive class struggles have often proved decisive for the transition from one society to another.

c) The character, position and impact of alienated labour is nevertheless the most crucial element of this whole dynamic (Ass. 4, 5, 6, 7, 8 and Imp. 1).

ASS 9 This dynamic is blocked in advanced capitalism for the following reasons:

a) The alienation of labour is more complete and more pervasive than at any other point in history.

b) The alienation of labour now affects all areas of life.

c) The social products of alienated labour, such as commodities and social institutions, appear more alien and more inaccessible to human control than ever.

d) The alienation of labour and its consequences is made more tolerable by the partial fulfilment of a number of human needs outside of labour, and by the denial of others.

e) The alienation of labour is also made more supportable by the partial fulfilment of acquired needs which diminish rather than enhance the free development of human faculties.

f) To the extent these needs are maintained, and at least partially fulfilled, a whole series of interrelated ideologies in the field of politics, of economics, of sciences and even in the private sphere, will be able to make advanced capitalism appear as the only possible, realistic and reasonable of all worlds for most people.

g) To the extent these needs are maintained, and at least partially fulfilled, a further factor of cohesion will emerge from the competition between successful advanced capitalistic societies and other less successful societies (advanced capitalistic, state capitalistic, others).

ASS 10 Man is free only if all men can enjoy and develop their diverse powers, talents, skills and sensibilities through work as the free play of faculties.

ASS 11 a) Man is capable of reconciling an ordered civilisation leading to further material and cultural development for all men with a vastly reduced amount of social and instinctual repression.

    b) Specifically, the reduction of social and instinctual repression will make it possible to develop and enjoy altogether different forms of human relations, in which love, sexuality and sensuality, as well as aesthetic sensibilities, will play a dominant and hitherto unprecendented role; a new eroticised and aesthetic rationality will emerge.

ASS 12 To increase or merely maintain the present level of social and instinctual repression will endanger the attained level of civilisation.

ASS 13 The extent of freedom is the extent to which work as the free play of faculties is possible for all. Complete freedom is a society which facilitates this to the full. Real self-determination denotes the capacity for collectively directing the evolution of society as a whole, either directly via each individual's work or indirectly through full and equal participation of all in collective planning decision. The co-operative society is such a society. It is described by the assumptions 14-27.

ASS 14 The co-operative society is a society where the individual both:
    a) participates on a full and equal basis in the necessary rational labour aiming to establish the best conditions for human happiness in the realm of freedom.
    b) participates on a full an equal basis in work as the free play of faculties, where he fully dominates the object of his work, plays with the possibilities of any object and is able to shape it in accordance with the most rewarding combination of the constraints imposed by the object's "inner laws" and the needs he feels most expressive of his personality. He understands himself through such work and others through work of the same kind.

ASS 15 In the co-operative society, this relation holds true not only for the individually created or shaped objects, or for those "worked upon" in collaboration with a few others; it is equally valid for all the achievements of that society at large, be it in terms of the wider material production, the world of culture or the social institutions. In all these areas it will be possible to see not only the mark of the "co-operative" man, but also that of each individual. The world will thus be a testimony of all of man's powers and needs, and of those of all the individuals composing that society.

ASS 16 The individual's self-growth and capacity for enjoyment
takes place primarily through the direct impact upon
his being of the work as the free play of faculties
which he performs. It also takes place via the collective transformation of the world into a human and life-
enhancing civilization where aesthetic considerations
and playfulness are dominant features.

ASS 17   a) Necessary labour is determined in terms of the
indirect and "objective" impact it has upon the development of the "co-operative society" and thereby of
"co-operative man". It is rational in the sense that
generalised automation and exchangeability of functions
will tend to reduce necessary labour time and its
impact upon daily life to a minimum.
  b) Work as the free play of faculties is almost
wholly determined in function of the direct, immediate
and "subjective" impact it has upon the individual
performing it; this impact is wholly different from
anything conceivable in contemporary capitalist societies. Work as the free play of faculties is the sum of
these activities which directly promote the full and
all round development of the individual's powers and
faculties, sharpen his aesthetic sensibilities and
allows him to express a rich variety of social and
individual needs. A whole range of modern techniques
will help to further these aims.

ASS 18 The extent of necessary labour in the co-operative society is limited to those few clear instances where the
long term benefits of such activities are indisputably
greater than the provisional harm caused by the deviation from the definition of work as the free play of
faculties in assumption 7 b).

ASS 19 When necessary labour is to be performed, and how it is
to be organized, is decided by the "associated producers" participating fully and equally in joint planning
decisions. The overriding concern is always the best
possible satisfaction of the individual's needs and
powers.

ASS 20 The individual himself alone chooses to engage in work
as the free play of faculties, be it individual or
collective. He determines, alone or in co-operation
with others, the character and conditions of this form
of work. Only necessary labour, under the conditions
that assumptions 8 and 9 fully describe, can be enforced in the co-operative society. This, however, is not
incompatible with mild social pressure directly following from the ethical ends described below.

ASS 21 Given that human nature is essentially a social creation, the human needs and powers to be found in the co-
operative society are not ascertainable from within the
present order of things, but for the following exceptions:
a) The whole range of human emotions, senses and
powers will be developed.
b) Wholly new needs and sensibilities are likely to
appear.
c) These needs and sensibilities are likely to be
linked to a sense for aesthetics vastly more developed
and more widespread through this society than in any
other society up to this point in history.
d) Sexuality will enter as a binding force in human
relations throughout the whole of society to a hitherto
unknown degree, and contribute to reinforce the bonds
and mutual knowledge between the members of the co-
operative society.
e) Concurrently, traditional genital sexuality will
possibly loose much of its dominant position, while
other forms and facets of human libidinal relations
become more prominent and socially acceptable. Homosexuality, polygamy, sexual masochism or sadism can be
cited as examples.
f) Generally, material and bodily needs, and their
relation to human emotions and the capacity for mutual
understanding will receive a far more central place in
ordinary human intercourse than it has been the case in
many societies up to the present point in history.
g) Submission to the will of another, outside of
sexual masochism/sadism between consenting adults, or
submission to abstractions divorced from material and
bodily realities, will not take place.
h) Similarly there will be no submission to the idea
of death in itself, or to any similar socially sanctioned sacrifice based upon fear of death, which will
be considered as nothing but the biological termination
of life.

ASS 22 Happiness and knowledge will no longer be incompatible:
love and affection for the other will be able to rest
on the full knowledge of the other.

ASS 23 Culture and aesthetic sensibilities will play an altogether more central role in the daily life of the "co-
operative" man than has ever been possible in human
civilization up to the present point in history. The
whole of reality will be able to become an object of
culture; an integral culture, encompassing all areas of
life and including memories of a past long before the
advent of present day restrictive civilization will be

able to flourish; the transformation of nature and of man will possibly be governed by a new reality principle, based upon sensuality, sexuality and aesthetic judgement.

ASS 24 The rationality guiding the activities of the men and women of the co-operative society is never simply the cold instrumental rationality implied by economic theory or the physical sciences. Such forms of rationality are applied to the organization of necessary labour and within the confines of the realm of necessity. Even there, it is a rationality which is informed by and supportive of the overriding goal of the co-operative society, namely the development and best possible satisfaction of all the individual's needs and powers.

ASS 25 The co-operative society is guided by ethical ends. These ends are fully described in the overriding concern for the full development and best possible satisfaction of all the individuals constituting that society. No other moral value or ethical end can be invoked against this goal, and the freedom of all is as unrestrained as possible within the limits set by this goal.

ASS 26 Those aspects of human relations not falling under the limited sphere of necessary labour or the sphere of work as the free play of faculties as defined above are similarly solely governed by the above ethical ends.

ASS 27 Men wish greater freedom

ASS 28   a)   Men have within them the potential to see through the complexity, alienation and reification of advanced capitalist societies and to envision a society which is radically different, and yet able to maintain and develop all the achievements of an advanced technological civilization.
       b)   The various ideologies of advanced capitalist societies can all be affected and ultimately be defeated through rational political argumentation, given that the basic objective conditions for a transition to a free society have long been fulfilled.

ASS 29 Men are able collectively to carry out this transition and to collectively realise a free society such as the co-operative society.

ASS 30 The term "historical choice" is used to describe the particular character of the transition to a free society, a transition which will differ from previous ones insofar that:

a) The extent of alienated labour in late capitalism and its pervasive role in the society as a whole in it-self prevents a clear consciousness of a free society to emerge.

b) The nature of a free society governed through real self-determination instead of dialectical forces requires a conscious collective decision to engage in this last transition.

c) The modalities of this transition as well as the realisation of a free society likewise demands a series of collective decisions.

d) The detailed construction of a free society, the historical choice leading to it and the vey possibility for such a choice requires a whole series of histori-cal, economic and political analyses to support or al-low rational argumentation.

e) The concept of historical essence can be used to suggest the broad outlines of such a free society and to indicate the ethical and political goals such a society should seek to achieve.

Implication 4: Most individuals, if made aware that advanced capitalistic societies frustrate the full development and enjoyment of their faculties, needs and sensibili-ties, that there is no constraining logic in human terms for such a social organisation and that a free society such as the co-operative society is a realistic possibility, will either engage in or support a radical collective action to change society.

Implication 5: For those who wish to change society, the most promising strategy is to contribute to such an aware-ness, by increasing the knowledge of the preceeding propositions, by carrying out the ncessary historical, economic and political analyses, and by, everywhere, laying bare the ideological mechanisms at work in ad-vanced capitalistic societies.

(*) Table 7 should be seen in relation to tables 2 and 3. A number of changes have taken place in relation to 3, but they affect nothing essential. The references to Hegel serve mainly to sharpen Marcuse's interpretation of the Marxian dialectic. The description of the subject-object relation is essentially a systematisation of the relation man-labour-nature, described in assumptions 5, 7 and 8 on table 3 and in 4 on table 7. The four definitions of labour summarise the changes since 1932, namely the explicit division of the original concept of labour into "necessary labor" and "work as the free play of facul-ties", to which is added the initial "alienated labor" (as-sumption 5, t. 7). The analysis of alienation is now more complex (assumption 9, t. 7 vs assumption 11, t. 3). Assumptions 11, 28 and 30 (table 7) are new. Assumption 11 states explicitly the major contention underlying <u>Eros and Civilization</u>, namely that an ordered civilisation can be reconciled with a vastly reduced level of social and instinctual repression. Assumption 28 spells out Marcuse's implicit belief in man's ultimate capacity to see through all capitalist ideologies. Assumption 30 specify the broad outlines of a transition to the co-operative society. Assumptions 14 to 27 as a whole serve to precise the idea of the co-operative society first described in table 3.

his own theory of liberation - of which the idea of the co-operative society forms the crucial part - and other interpretations of freedom are summarily indicated(4). The logical structure underlying this late essay is presented in table 7. It offers a convenient summary of Marcuse's theory of liberation in the post-war period. It also makes it possible to present Marcuse's interpretation of the Marxian dialectic in relation to that of Hegel. This dialectic is central to Marcuse's theory.

7.2 The Identity of The Subject and The Object
The nature of the Marcusian dialectic emerges more clearly by comparing it to the conception advanced by Franklin and Bykhovskii (5). The latter, a Soviet philosopher, appears to base his interpretation of Hegel and Marx squarely upon Engel's extraordinary "dialectic of nature" and on the entire system of "dialectic materialism" expounded in <u>Anti Dühring</u> and <u>Ludwig Feuerbach</u> (6). The dialectic that Bykhovskii presents is little more than a thinly disguised displacement of Hegel's idealist system to the monist philosophical materialism so dear to Lenin. Moreover, all nuances, ambiguities or equivocation in Hegel is squared out into dogmatic truths of a closed scholastic system. Instead of the derterminism of "Reason" shaping history into a coherent pattern, we have the still more implausible hyperdeterminism of matter, which, in some unexplained manner, directs all actions of mankind toward a materialist version of the "Absolute Spirit" postulated by Hegel. For Bykhovskii the dialectic is everywhere, affecting all beings, stones and bushes, the molecules of the ocean and the space between the stars; it furthermore wisely directs helpless humanity towards its better future. The busy "materialist" dialectic has in fact quite a say in the in-

THE DIALECTIC OF LIBERATION

teraction between human beings and the way in which
ideas, politics, and institutions function; and if
we listen to Bykhovskii it appears that it is now
quietly preparing behind our backs yet another "negation of the negation" that we need only to wait
upon.
Bykhovskii has read Reason and Revolution. He
points out - and vehemently attacks - what Marcuse
sees as significant distinctions between Hegel's and
Marx's dialectic. In particular, he states that for
Marcuse it is essential to understand "that Marx
'detached dialectic from its ontological base'; that
in him it lost its 'metaphysical' (i.e. universal
philosophical) character; that he refrained from
'generalising' dialectics, from extending it to 'a
movement of all being'; that for Marx the dialectical principle is not a general principle equally
applicable to any subject matter" (7). The same
theme is further developed in a passage which ends
with what is clearly meant as the most damning
attack on the heretic Marcuse: "When Marcuse says
that 'the Marxian dialectic is a historical method',
he is not aiming at historicity as the principle of
all motion and development, but he is denying the
dialectic of nature. For Marcuse, where there is no
society, there is no dialectic" (8). He also reports
(and castigates) Marcuse for stating that the dialectic will cease to apply in a society no longer
dominated by capitalist or pre-capitalist laws of
development and that the use of the dialectic is
restricted to what Marx described as the 'pre-histo-
ry' of mankind (9). These points are correct, and
they are all important. They fail, however, to account for a crucial characteristic of Marcuse's
dialectic, namely the "identity of the subject and
the object", which he sees as common to Marx and
Hegel, as opposed to many later marxist interpretations (10).
This phrase implies that there is no radical
ontological discontinuity between the subject and
the object; the world of man and the world of nature
is in constant and mutual interaction; social reality can only properly be apprehended as the fusion of
objective natural laws and subjective desires, perspectives and projects (11). We meet the world as a
meaningful world, only through this meaning do we
see it, understand it and act upon it; inversely,
the meaning we attach to the world, the wishes we
possess and the projects we devise are themelves
products of natural forces as well as of our interaction with them. It is this whole process that

Marcuse after 1932 describes in relation to the all-pervasive role of labour in human life. Through labour we learn to know the world, in labour we develop our potentialities and through labour we impart to the natural world the shape of our desires and passions. The formula of "the identity of the subject and the object" demands that the starting point for the analysis is no longer either the object in itself or the subject isolated from the world, but the total pattern formed by their mutual interrelation. This notion Hegel expresses in the postulate of "Absolute Reason", Marx in the idea of society as a social whole, Lukács by the primacy of the totality, and Heidegger in terms of the concepts of "Being" ("Sein") and "Being There" (Dasein). Marcuse expresses this notion by "negative totality" or "dialectical totality" (12).

An important consequence of this whole approach is that all the familiar dichotomies which help structure our world, such as the subject-object dualism, the radical separation of knowledge and action, theory and praxis, and the sharp dividing line between facts and values, prove themselves upon reflection to be part of a larger whole, a totality. The dialectical method therefore seeks to re-establish the underlying connections between apparently disjointed or opposite facets of reality, replacing them within a larger whole, which in turn is related to another similar "totality" so as to show a yet more global totality, and so on. What appears to the untrained observer as a single aspect of reality, a given fact, an "immediate" concrete thing or phenomenon, must be replaced into successive and progressively larger totalities - by establishing the relevant "mediations" - to obtain its full and really concrete significance (13).

There are further corollaries of practical or methodological character. Goldmann for instance points out that the distinction a child finds so difficult to establish between thought and action (an obvious reference to Piaget's work), whilst in itself essential for the growth of the individual adult, may well severely handicap his ability to see the two as part of a same movement (14). Similarly, the distinction between theory and practice appears as the logical concomitant of a division of labour which itself has proven highly effective in promoting co-operation and instrumental efficiency; yet, it also conceals the intimate unity of the two, and the possibilities this implies. it should be noted that it is quite possible to conceive of a dialecti-

cal method - proceeding to reconstruct the individual fact or aspect of reality from the totality,
through a whole series of mediations - that is not
necessarily grounded in a dialectical ontology. Such
an approach can be used as a powerful overall method
in social sciences, and would not need to be justified by more than the usual criteria of parsimony,
range, scope and explanatory power. There is also
another possibility: the dialectical method may be
adopted as the structure for a broad theory of action aiming toward reliable knowledge as well as
concrete political goals.

This is Marcuse's own approach. The analyses of
"The Foundation of Historical Materialism" are
clearly reminiscent of Heidegger's own conception of
"Being" as the totality of all existing, and Marcuse
himself expressed his conclusions in ontological
terms. Yet the thrust of the essay is non-Heidegge-
rian and, as we saw in chapter 3, there is in this
essay a definite break with Hegel's own dialectic, a
break whose significance is only fully spelled out
in Reason and Revolution. Marcuse's dialectic is not
all-inclusive, as Bykhovskii correctly perceives: it
is a dialectic only valid within the realm of human
existence. Only within the broad limits of human
society - a society developed and constantly maintained through historical and therefore in principle
alterable human actions - does the Marxian dialectic
(as opposed to that of the marxist tradition) operate. It is not an ontological given; it is simply
the most adequate method for comprehending and at
the same time transcending the existing reality. It
is a dialectic where human action and human praxis
have all-important functions. Finally, while history
can be shown through reflection to have been governed by a set of broad economic and social laws best
ascertained by the dialectical method, this is no
reason to presume that this "historical dialectic"
could not disappear once the conditions for its
existence have been abolished. The particular dialectic Marcuse identifies will therefore come to an
end once "history" - the "real" history of mankind
Marx envisioned - comes into being.

The essence of his argument can be summarised
as such. Marcuse regards the transition from the
Hegelian to the Marxian dialectic as consisting essentially in a transposition of the combined ontological and epistemological framework in Hegel to a
broad para-sociological theory of historical development. This process is already enunciated by Hegel
himself; it includes the transfer of several ele-

ments of Hegel's theory, in particular the subject-object identity and the role of labour within it, to the new historical dialectic; it is only schematically indicated by Marx in the Economic and Philosophical Manuscripts of 1844; yet it appears implicitly in many of his other writings (15). The Kantian distinction between noumena and phenomena applies more or less fully to those aspects of the real world which have not been affected by human intercourse. This dialectic is no longer absolute; its status depends upon its capacity to relate and explain the elements which the theory considers as most significant. Similarly, and more importantly, there is always an element of "free will" or pure consciousness escaping the closed dialectic of the social and human world. The Kantian distinction applies more or less fully to those aspects of reality which have not been affected by human intercourse. As for the others, depending upon their social content and signification, Marcuse appear to suggest that they are best considered, in a figurative way perhaps, as "pure" phenomena; at the limit, they have no other reality than accorded by society, or more precisely by a well structured fabric of society, which, if predictable, nonetheless can be transformed by radical collective action.

To help clarify Marcuse's position it may be useful to sketch out the respective positions of the authors we have mentioned with respect to the dialectic. The following five writers all share the perspective given by the identity of the subject and the object, yet they will differ greatly with respect to their conception of the dialectic, its mode of operation and its area of application:

1) Hegel operates with a dialectic which is pre-established, ontological and all-encompassing. At least in some of his works the presumed factual development of Western civilisation plays a decisive role for the way in which this dialectic is seen to unfold. Language, labour and property all constitute fundamental nexi of the subject-object interactions, although their importance vary at different points of the reconstructed historical development.

2) Marx operates with a dialectic which he certainly does not consider as ontological, nor is it all-encompassing in the same sense, as its primary field of action is society. The development of Western civilisation, as reasonably can be ascertained by more advanced impirical researches, constitutes the main terrain for this dialectic, with occasional excursions in other areas of the world.

Productive labour, but also the development of productive forces in general, together with other facets of the economy, become the determinant factors in this new historical dialectic. The fundamental subject-object interactions, mainly in the form of a long struggle against a reticent nature, virtually all take place at the economic level, with the vast framework of class struggles as its powerful reflection at the social and political levels.

3) Lukács, for his part, follows upon a period marked by an extensive popularisation of Marx's main works through Engels, Kautsky, Luxembourg and Plekhanov and dominated by neo-Kantian and positivistic thinking. His reaction against one-sided economism and this whole ethos is to emphasise once more the numerous ideological, institutional, social and economic factors in a full blown Hegelian reading of Marx's historical dialectic. The consciousness of the proletariat becomes the decisive subject in a series of battles conducted primarily at the level of ideas, of science and of competing ideologies. Man's consciousness regains a place, and a fairly dominant one at that, even if the economic level retains its determining role in relation to the epic struggle with nature.

4) Heidegger returns further afield in the search for the lost unity of man and his universe, first of all to the prestigious Greek thinkers. The dialectic once more becomes ontological and epistemological, and exclusively so. The problem of history becomes one of historicity, philosophy the primary object of historical inquiries and, with it, the "destruction" of the history of ontology a major goal. While the Hegelian dialectic as a whole only plays a minor role, the identity of the subject and the object is all dominant. Language, mental habits and customary ways of looking upon the world are the significant nexi of a series of interactions which virtually all take place at the level of all powerful ideas and of the meaning we accord to the various facets of our daily environment.

5) Marcuse, for a time attracted by this perspective, although always in relation to an overall marxist framework, rediscovers the grand historical framework of Hegel's dialectic as first re-interpreted and transformed by Marx in the manuscripts. He develops through this encounter a view upon Marx's dialectic in which the interactions between man and nature through labour are all determining for human civilisation. The dialectic is primarily social and serves as the short hand description for

the factual history of modern civilisation; it is a
history in which ideas, human will and class struggles also play their role. The play of ideological
and institutional forces so forcefully depicted by
Lukács now further enter as a useful and necessary
complement to the fundamental economic determinations, where again it is labour in its various forms
which remains decisive for social evolution. The
last transition to a free society will nevertheless,
given the nature of that society and given an unpre-
dicted stalemate of dialectical forces, rest with
the awareness, will and decisiveness of the collective subject.

7.3   The Historical Choice for the Co-operative So-ciety

It remains to sketch a full picture of Marcuse's
theory of liberation. At its centre is the tremendous force of human labour, changing (and learning
to know) human nature and human nature. This process
has the dual consequence of transforming man's natural environment into a human environment and of
transforming man's nature itself through successive
alienated forms toward growing self-consciousness
and more developed historical human needs.

The dialectic moves through the familiar marxist stages, from primitive community to antiquity,
and from feudalism to capitalism. These vast and
complex processes span centuries and cannot be precisely delimited (16). The last stage is the well-
known picture of "true communism". The transition to
that last stage, however, will proceed differently.
So far mankind has increased its power and knowledge
at the expense of one or more oppressed classes,
whose eventual liberation was due to the combination
of circumstances and the action of particularly
determined sections of the new ruling class. The new
society, however, is to be one of freedom, and no
such automatism will and can prevail. While it can
only become a reality on the basis of the development of productive forces and the right strategic
conditions, it also has to evolve through the conscious action of a collective subject striving to
create a co-operative society of free individuals,
The last "negation of the negation" is by necessity
different, since "there can be no blind necessity in
tendencies that terminate in a free and self-conscious society" (17).

The task of the new extended theory of liberation can be defined as follows. The objective pre-

conditions for a transition to the next stage of the dialectic must be precisely ascertained. These objective conditions include a high level of material wealth, and the necessary potential in human and natural resources for a high material and cultural standard of living; they also demand that such resources are to an extent translated into new needs and talents for a large section of the population; the theory furthermore should be able to point to the objective social and economic contradictions which undermine the continued existence of the capitalist order; it should also investigate the objective parameters for action, the possibilities for a translation of such contradictions into an organized revolutionay movement capable of coherent and coordinated action. On all these points classical marxist theory is quite adequate (18). It needs to be broadened, however, on the following three points. Firstly, the theory must specify the range and effectiveness of the human element in the transition to the co-operative society. There is an essential human freedom to be reasserted in the light of the task which lies ahead. Secondly, the very existence of such a freedom and the reality of the goal it makes possible must both be reaffirmed against the forces that make it appear unreal and utopian. It must fight as effectively as possible the ideological forces that militate against this idea and its possible realisation. The way to do so is through a series of "critiques" aiming to reconstruct the historical development of ideologies and of central political and social institutions and to demonstrate their function in relation to the prevailing social totality; they must also bring forth those elements pointing to a different order or things. Thirdly, this task itself, together with the changing material and cultural circumstances, necessitates a reconsideration of the future socialist society. The new theory denotes an idea of freedom sufficiently flexible not to preempt the freedom of action of the "associated producers" and yet precise enough to be able to point to essential features of the proposed good society. This idea of freedom is the co-operative society.

The essential freedom to opt for the co-operative society, described by Marcuse as the "historical choice", presupposes a great range of freedoms. It demands and postulates a great measure of "free will". Marcuse's entire work is marked by a pronounced voluntarism, opposing fatalistic notion of ever lasting class societies or of automatic revolution, as well as any compromises which may endanger the goal. It demands a large measure of "freedom of thought", whereby it becomes possible to see through the relative and historically conditioned veil of ignorance which follows from alienation, reification and the imperatives of a class ridden society dominated by the "performance principle". It demands and seeks to promote "internal freedom" in the sense of a belief in one's judgement, capacities and ideals. In all these respects it is reminiscent of Sartre's "transcendental freedom" for the free subject to opt for "authentic existence" through a self-chosen project (19). Marcuse has on several occasions referred with sympathy to Sartre's work, and uses himself the term "project" to describe the "historical choice". Yet, as we shall see in the following chapter, Marcuse is also profoundly critical of the conception of freedom that Sartre expounds in Being and Nothingness. Marcuse's project is historical and embedded in a marxist conception of the world. It demands a "free will" which can translate itself into action upon the world. The "freedom of thought" it presupposes must build upon detailed economic, social and political analyses of society and require further freedom of expression in a material sense, through speech, writings and other media. It naturally must require freedom from starvation, want and toil. The "internal freedom" of the individual must find support, accept and co-operation from others. There must also be some measure of "political freedoms", if a nascent movement is not to be crushed by all out repression. In many respect it is thus more akin to T.H. Green's "positive freedom" than to many other positions, and the formula "collective positive freedom", while inequate, may perhaps best express the nature of the essential freedom to make the "historical choice" for the co-operative society. Marcuse says little or nothing as to how this freedom is to be realised, outside of the famous but vague references to the lumpeproletariat or the student vanguard, what also may be a reflection on his assessment of the revolutionary potential of American society. Yet even at the period of One Dimensional Man, his relation to the marxist theory upon which his work builds was never severed, and Marcuse's collective project for the good society could perhaps also be compared to Gramsci's conception of the "Modern Prince", whereby a collectively re-created independent communist party should work co-operatively to define and realise the society of the future (20).

7.4 Criticisms and Concluding Remarks

The exposition and discussion of Marcuse's theory of liberation is now completed. A summary of the entire theory, re-inserting the idea of the co-operative society (last version, as on table 6) within the theory of liberation can be found on table 7. The next chapter will focus on Marcuse's critique of freedom in contemporay societies, and the last will form the conclusions for this research. The present section is devoted to general conclusions and criticisms of Marcuse's theory of liberation, while his critical work will be assessed in section 8.5. Chapter 9 will then focus on the idea of the co-operative society itself.

Neither the theory of liberation, nor the idea of the good society which animates it, is as such explicitly put forward by Marcuse in a single text - the 1969 essay on "Freedom and Historical Imperative" being the only partial exception to this general rule. It has only emerged from a reconstruction of the major assumptions and logical implications underlying his texts, starting with the very first essay on the "Contributions ..." to about 1972 - the few texts which appeared between this date up to Marcuse's death do not to my knowledge affect any of the leading assumptions. The idea of the co-operative society, together with the general theory surrounding it, rests, it has been argued here, upon Marcuse's original interpretation of Marx's entire legacy on the basis of the Economic and Philosophical-Manuscripts of 1844, re-discovered in 1932 and "reviewed" the same year. This idea was thereafter a constant of his thought, guiding and structuring his most diverse works, with One Dimensional Man as the notable exception. The theory of liberation throughout serves to articulate this idea within a wider framework and to provide the necessary links with Marcuse's critical analyses of fascism, of Hegel or of American society. It may be noted that the overall argument found unexpected support, in a discussion between Marcuse and a few fellow academics (Jürgen Habermas, Heinz Lubasz and Telman Spengler), published in Telos in 1978 (21). Marcuse there returns to the question of his early enthusiasm for Heidegger, whose philosophy at the time appeared as a genuine break with the dominant neo-Kantian Schools and a fresh hope after the failure of the German revolution, Disenchantment began around 1932. Marcuse then adds: "I had read Marx and was continuing to do so. Then the Economic and Philosophical Manuscripts of 1844 appeared. This was, in a certain

sense, a new Marx, who was really concrete and at
the same time went beyond the petrified practical
and theoretical Marxism. After this, Heidegger versus Marx was no longer a problem for me" (22).

Marcuse's theory of liberation, as it has emerged from the present analyses, is not without problems. The most important of these are also immediately apparent when first approaching his work,
namely the question of Marcuse's evidence and the
issue of the general methodology applied. These two
problems were touched upon in the introduction (sec-
tin (1.2), discussed in chapter 2 (section 2.2) and
again in chapter 5 (section 5.5). We saw there that
Marcuse added to an often difficult manner of presentation a general disregard for commonly accepted
methodological procedures in the social sciences and
allied disciplines. Marcuse rarely accounts for the
method employed, the assumptions guiding the research or the criteria by which the findings should
be judged. The evidence is at best sketchy, incidental, illustrative, when it does not directly appear
biased toward a particular interpretaion of the problem at hand, or of the history of philosophy or
again of the nature of liberal capitalist institutions. Possible counterarguments are seldom, if
ever, taken up to provide a balanced assessment, and
a single line of argument is generally impressed
upon the reader, leaving little or no room for
discussion.

These problems are not incidental to Marcuse's
research. They tie in with the particular type of
theory developed by Marcuse. This does not make
these issues less problematical, rather it places
the onus upon the theory itself and the approach
adopted. It is in my view possible to consider Marcuse's reseach in terms of two such approaches,
which can be taken as alternative or complementary
to each others. The first makes this research a
meta-philosophy or meta-sociology. As mentioned in
chapter 3, this implies that the theory's essential
aim is to criticise and to reflect upon the findings, methods and general orientation of one or
more disciplines, considered in isolation or combined in some way. Such a theory could not in principle be bound by any of the norms prevailing in the
discipline(s) in question. It would nevertheless
seem reasonable to expect a good measure of intellectual rigor and honesty, an attempt to present a
balanced account and some efforts to convince others
on the basis of commonly accepted arguments. The
second approach makes this theory first of all a

rational political project for human liberation. The project is rooted in the marxist tradition. It derives it ethical momentum from "immemorially acquired image of essence", itself derived from concrete historical and social struggles and most easily accessible in philosophy, or particular forms or works of art. Its rationale lies in the factual possibility of a free and better society that is present in the human make-up, techniques and resources of contemporary societies. Its force rests with its ability to generate individual and lasting commitment among the greater part of the peoples constituting a given society. Its ultimate proof will be the realisation of a free society such as the co-operative society. Each of these appoaches can account in some measure for the recurrent problems of evidence and methodology. Each of these approaches fits reasonably well with Marcuse's stated or most plausible aims. Both these approaches leave Marcuse's open to a number of criticisms.

The approach in terms of a political project will be taken up in chapter 9. We will here focus upon Marcuse's research in terms of a meta-theory. While its primary objective is to criticise and reflect upon existing scientific or academic disciplines, it derives its impetus and much of its overall plausibility from the idea of an alternative society and the theory leading to such a society, together with the above mentioned criteria. Both Reason and Revolution and Eros and Civilization would fit this perspective very well. Rather than attempt a comprehensive critique, a few points can be taken up. Marcuse's exclusive emphasis upon the ontological character of Hegel's philosophy, the contrast he draws with Marx's theory, and the resulting picture of classical marxism all contribute to create an impression of both Hegel and Marx which is neither fair nor accurate. Hegel's own empirical ambitions, visible in particular in his philosophy of history, disappear entirely from such a perspective. The ambiguous character of the all important Economic and Philosophical Manuscripts of 1844, alternating between ontology, historical research, journalism and economic theory, is equally smoothed out of existence. The later Marx is generally read into the early works, while the philosophical context sketched in the Manuscripts, which undoubtly was retained in a measure by Marx, is now written large in all the major works, under the name of economic theory alone. The often confused, contradictory and indefinite nature of Marx's own writings

disappears totally in the clear and forceful presentation of a unified theory which runs through the
whole of Marx. Moreover, Marx the scholar, for all
his revolutionary ambitions, appears to totally
overshadow the political pamphletist, the organisa-
tor of the First International and the untiring
watchdog of the German, French or European socialist
scene. The detailed empirical researches entering
into so much of Marx's economic or historical analyses likewise disappear into the background.

If we consider <u>Eros and Civilization</u> Marcuse
initially states very clearly the political and
philosophical character of his interpretation. It is
only later that he will try to re-introduce the idea
of some biological interpretation as well, (see
chapter 6, note 47). This later contention is best
understood as a temporary aberration or a provocative ambiguity that a sudden fame made all too tempting. A political or philosophical framework of
explanation alone would justify that clinical or
empirical evidence be so largely disregarded. At
this level, the interpretation has much to offer; it
is bold, imaginative, stimulating, and there is no
doubt that it is not only one of Marcuse's best
works, but also an important work on Freud in its
own right. It seems therefore difficult not to accept what may appear as flights from our common
perception of realities, but for one point. The
assertion that the present level of instinctual
repression could be so very substantially reduced
within a different social world, as argued in the
book, is difficult to accept to the extent advocated
by its author. Marcuse offers mostly the allusive
images of Orpheus and Narcissus, and a very indirect, if suggestive parallel between Freud's analyses of sublimation and Max Weber's ambiguous treatment of the protestant ethic and the "spirit of
capitalism". This largely leaves it to his readers
to follow him or not.

Marcuse's treatment of the marxist dialectic is
in many ways useful and important. It succeeds in
conveying a picture of that dialectic which is more
convincing and interesting than most of the orthodox
marxist expositions on the subject. The identity of
the subject and the object is undoubtedly an important facet of both Hegel's and Marx's conceptions of
the dialectic, and it is one which appears plausible
in the light of what psychologists or sociologists
tell us about self-perception, social meanings or
our selective structuring of the world. In many circumstances it is the meaning we invest into the

243

given object or even subject which is decisive for its ultimate reality in our lives. Similarly the central role that Marcuse accords to "labor" fits plausibly with its central position in Marxian theory, and appears reasonable in view of its probable role for our self-esteem and self-maintenance. The major weakness of Marcuse's dialectic, however, is that Marcuse is vague and generally ambiguous as to the area and mode of operation of this dialectic - the above account is as precise as the texts allow it. This is true at the micro level, where such a dialectic could otherwise be used to analyse a given phenomenon or situation - as Sartre does, although with a different approach to dialectical thinking. It is also true at the grand planetary level at which Marcuse usually moves when speaking of the dialectic - it there serves more of a general mental outlook than a definite mode of explanation. This in turn implies that the global theory of liberation presented in the preceeding is best conceived as a general framework for understanding the world. Marcuse is most convincing when he for instance speaks of the internal unity of capitalist society as opposed to the feudal world, when he points to the combination of ideological forces and economic mechanisms which helps to sustain such a society, when he insists that it has emerged from processes spanning centuries, or when he emphasises the fact of classes as decisive for both our life chances and our most predictable outlook upon the world. However, attempts to go beyond Marcuse's often elaborately cautious formulations invariably leads to the same host of problems - what are the identifiable issues, how should the concepts be further defined, what are precisely the cause-effects relations, are there any working hypotheses which could be used for research, can any test situations be conceived from this basis?

Marcuse is of course not unusual in this respect. It would not be difficult to retrace a number of these ambiguities in Marx's own texts, for instance. The concept of labour, equally central to the whole of Marx's writings, is also one which fulfills many different functions, seldom clearly distinguished from each other, and the sense that Marx attaches to the concept itself will also vary. Max Weber's analyses of the protestant ethic and the "spirit" of capitalism can be cited in this context as a masterpiece of ambiguity, an ambiguity which as much as its obvious insights and scholarship may have served to ensure the enduring quality of the work (23). The quality of detachment of Marcuse's texts, however, which is for instance <u>not</u> present in Marx, will often make it difficult to establish direct and meaningful relations with other bodies of academic research. The period of <u>One Dimensional Man</u> also suggests that Marcuse for a time himself felt it difficult to relate the hopefulness and unity of his conception of freedom with his experiences of American society or even to envision ways in which this could be done.

This leads us back to the question of ontology. My argument, as stated in chapter 2 and touched upon in section 5.5 is that Marcuse's project should not be considered as ontological and that at no point has this been his prime consideration. Yet the nature of the research and the methodology is reminiscent of ontological enquiries. What in the last instance distinguishes Marcuse's research from any such ontological search is the direction and ultimate goal of this research, as stated by Marcuse and substantiated by the present study, i.e. a conception of the good society as a co-operative society, a conception which in turn animates and gives impetus to a whole theory of human liberation. This ambition and this vision, as well as Marcuse's scrupulous respect for the given authors' most generous impulses or best insights, as he see them, is also what makes his interpretations of Hegel, Marx or Freud often brilliant and always inspiring. Marcuse's bold political project for humankind is what marks and defines his research. His work is not without flaws, and this, as we shall see, is also true for his conception of the good society. Yet there is much in Marcuse well worth reading, and the hope and optimism of his vision, coupled with complex analyses and perceptive insights, should gain him a lasting repute among exegetes of Marx and Hegel, theorists of freedom and all those of us who wishes for a more human world. Marcuse is a <u>political</u> theorist in the best sense of the term. We shall now consider his critique of freedom in contemporary civilisation.

NOTER

1. See above section 1.1.
2. "The Realm of Freedom and the Realm of Necessity: A Reconsideration", <u>Praxis</u>, Zagreb, No. 1/2, 1969, pp. 20-25, passim.
3. "Freedom and Freud's Theory of Instincts", op.

cit., pp 401-424.

4. "Freedom and the Historical Imperative", Studies in Critical Philosophy, London: New Left Books, 1972.

5. Franklin, M.: "The Irony of the Beautiful Soul of Herbert Marcuse", in Telos, No. 6, Fall 1970, pp. 3-35.

6. On the historical impact of these works and their formative influence upon a whole generation of marxists, see Coletti's "Introduction" to Marx Early Works, op. cit., pp. 7-56.

7. Bykhovskii, B., "Marcusism against Marxism: A critique of uncritical criticism", p. 208, in Philosophy and Phemenological Research, Vol. 30, 1969, pp. 203-18; Marcuse, Reason and Revolution, op. cit., pp. 314-15.

8. Bykhovskii, op. cit., p. 209.

9. Bykhovskii, op. cit., p. 209; Marcuse, op. cit., pp. 316-20.

10. Goldmann, Lukács and Heidegger, op. cit., p. 11; Marcuse, H.: Reason and Revolution, op. cit., p. 59.

11. Much of this analysis derives from Goldmann's excellent Lukács and Heidegger, op. cit. His main argument is that Lukács and Heidegger, in very different ways, recaptured the distinctive Hegelian approach to the world as founded upon the constant interaction between man and his environment, an approach summarized in the notion of the identity of the subject and the object, a perspective shared by Marx, but lost in the intervening half-century of Neo-Kantian and positivistic thinking.

12. Marcuse, Reason and Revolution, op. cit., pp. 313-14.

13. See Goldmann, Lukács and Heidegger, op. cit., pp. 15-16 and pp. 101-109. This he illustrated with the following obvious paraphrase of Marx's Wage, Labour and Capital; "A black is a black. It is only under certain social conditions that he becomes a slave, a tribal chief or, one should add today, a minister of an independent state. A machine is a machine. It is only in certain social conditions that it becomes capital and, therefore, a means of human exploitation or, on the contrary, the collective property of the community and thus a means of liberation" Goldmann, Lukács and Heidegger, op. cit., p. 107; compare with Marx, Selected Works, op. cit., Vol. I, p. 159.

14. An insight which is all important for the idea of ideology as reality constituting. Goldman, Lukács and Heidegger, op. cit., p. 104.

15. Marcuse, Reason and Revolution, op. cit., pp. 259-60; "The Foundation of Historical Materialism", op. cit., pp. 40-260.
16. Soviet Marxism, op. cit., introduction.
17. Reason and Revolution, op. cit., p. 318.
18. Reason and Revolution, op. cit., p. 318.
19. All references to Sartre in Marcuse's work are to his Being and Nothingness, op. cit., by far his most lucid and appealing philosophical work. The later Critique of Dialectical Reason is much less central for his existential perspective, and Marcuse himself recently indicated that its difficulty prevented him finishing it despite his admiration for Sartre; see Sartre, Critique de la Raison Dialectique (précédé de Questions de Méthode); Tome I: Théorie des Ensembles Pratiques, Paris: Editions Gallimard, 1960; see Marcuse's interview with Olafson. Heidegger's Politics, op. cit., pp. 36-37.
20. See Gramsci, Selections from the Prison Notebooks, edited by Q. Hoare and G. N. Smith, London: Lawrence and Wishart, 1971.
21. See "Theory and Politics: A discussion with Herbert Marcuse, Jürgen Habermas and Telman Spengler", Telos, No. 38, Winter 1978, pp. 124-153. First published in J. Habermas, S. Bovenschen (eds), Gespräche mit Herbert Marcuse, Frankfurt am Main, pp. 9-62.
22. "Theory and Politics", op. cit., p. 125.
23. Max Weber, The Protestant Ethic and the Spirit of Capitalism, op. cit., passim. See also, D. G. MacRae, Weber, op. cit., and David S. Landes, The Unbound Prometheus: Technological Change and Industrial Development in Western Europe from 1750 to the Present, England: Cambridge University Press, 1972, pp. 21-23.

Chapter Eight

FREEDOM AND CONTEMPORARY CIVILISATION

8.1   Freedom and Politics

The third facet of Marcuse's conception of freedom -
his distinctive brand of "Critical Theory" - is by
far the best known and most widely commented aspect
of his work. It is not necessarily the best understood part. The ambiguous formulations of the later
works - especially One Dimensional Man - accounts
for much of the misapprehensions (1). Only in relation to Marcuse's "second dimension", the idea of
the co-operative society, and in the context provided by his broader theory of liberation, does the
full measure of his critique become immediately apparent. Rather than a dispersed array of unrelated
critical works, what Marcuse offers is a comprehensive critique of freedom in contemporary societies.

This critique can be divided into the following
four areas: 1) Freedom and politics 2) Market freedom 3) Freedom and private life 4) Freedom and culture.

The first of these areas is fundamental to
Marcuse's entire outlook. That Marcuse's re-interpretation of Marx is a political one cannot be over-
emphazied. It is political in a broad sense, at the
level of large social forces rather than in any detailed or tactical sense. Marcuse is no Lenin, and
one would look in vain for a theory of the party,
reflections on the problems of organization, or a
rigorous analysis of the state. Marcuse's interpretation of Marx is political insofar as he is first
and foremost concerned to explore the wider context
for political action: How can we rationally conceive
of the good society? How can we envisage the transition to such a society? What forces can promote this
goal? What are the greatest impediments for rational
political action?

Marcuse's work focuses upon ideologies shaping
social realities, entire societies and the men and

women composing them (2). Ideological forces appear
in his analyses as at once all powerful and yet
easily destroyed. On the one hand, they are all
powerful because they are embodied in specific institutions, long-standing patterns of interaction or
deep-rooted emotional commitments. As such, they are
more than ideas or ideals, and they affect not only
our relation to reality, but reality itself.

On the other hand, Marcuse always sees ideologies as easily affected by the evidence that can be
marshalled against them. The approach implicit in
all his writings is that the distance between alienation and objectification can be overcome by restoring the human dimension of social realities and
human nature (i.e. the product of man's interaction
with nature).

The classical marxist foundation is essential
here. Marx has convincingly demonstrated, at least
to Marcuse's satisfaction, that the objective conditions for a genuine marxist revolution have now
long been fulfilled. The imminent collapse of ideological thinking is based upon the demonstrable
existence of real and constantly aggravating contradictions. Even the apparent foundation in human
nature of such ideological thinking, perhaps nowhere
more elaborately argued than in Freud's Civilization and its Discontents, is in itself no reason for
accepting it as an inescapable human condition. The
dual thrust of Marcuse's argument in Eros and Civilization is that it must firstly be reconsidered in
the broad historical (and therefore not beyond man's
conscious control) context of capitalist or quasica-
pitalist developments, and that it must be contrasted with the real, if still utopian possibility of a
mature technological civilization requiring only a
fraction of present levels of instinctual repression.

There is a profoundly democratic strain in
Marcuse's thought. Underlying all his work is the
belief that a correct assessment of the realities of
late capitalism is potentially available to everyone; all, sooner or later, will see and experience
the unacceptable discrepancy between what is and
what could be; and men will act upon it, if it is
not too late. Marcuse offers insights, ideas and
reflections; only if a vast majority of people
choose to act upon such ideas and notions will their
worth and validity be confirmed. Until then there
can only be an appeal to reason, to good sense, and
trust in man's capacities for creating "a life worth
living" (3). Against Lenin, Marcuse stands for a

continuation of the Luxembourg line.

This is again reflected in his occasional comments upon the liberal "political freedoms". Marcuse follows Marx, and not unreasonably points to the contrasts between the ideals of the French Revolution and the realities of European (and American) liberalism. In the essay on "The Struggle Against Liberalism in the Totalitarian View of the State", he states that:

> "The ideas of 1789 have by no means always been on the banner of liberalism and have even been sharply attacked by it .... Pacificism and internationalism were not always causes it adopted, and it has often enough accepted considerable intervention of the state in the economy.... Despite structural variations in liberalism and its bearer from one country or period to another, a uniform foundation remains: the individual economic subject's free ownership and control of private property and the politically and legally guaranteed security of these rights. Around this stable center, all specific economic and social demands of liberalism can be modified - modified to the point of abolition... Those basic political demands of liberalism, resulting from its economic views, that are so hated today (such as freedom of speech and of the press, complete publicity of political life, the representative system and parliamentarianism, the separation or balance of power) were never, in fact completely realized. Depending on the social situation, they were curbed or dropped" (4).

The same critical assessment of the undoubted achievements of liberal institutions comes across some twenty-five years later in Soviet Marxism. He draws attention to the fact that "it was more than 'politics' when Marx and Engels drew attention to the possibilities of a legal and democratic transition to socialism" (5). He emphasises that "the Marxian notion of socialism implies some form of 'representation' because the proletariat cannot act as a class without organization and division of functions"; and he makes it clear that, as long the representation was by the class itself, "directly delegated by and directly responsible to the 'immediate producer'", the forms may vary (6). Liberal institutions and liberal political freedoms are never condemned per se; they are attacked for fai-

Table 8

Overview over the main propositions, derived from the theory
of liberation and the idea of a co-operative society, which
underlies Marcuse's extended critique of contemporary societies.

A. On Freedom and Politics

Proposition 1: Given the nature of a free society such as the
        co-operative society, only through persuasion and through
        the involvement of large masses of individuals in a given
        society can a free society be realised.

Proposition 2: Such a collective involvement requires cons-
        tant and radical political discussion at all levels and
        in all parts of the given society.

Proposition 3: Radical political discussion in turn requires,
        at the very minimum, that freedom of speech and free ac-
        cess to the media is guaranteed, that political life is
        conducted under full public exposure, and that all indi-
        viduals in the society have a full and equal legal access
        to public functions.

Proposition 4: The legal system necessary to regulate matters
        of common interests should be truly impartial, predicta-
        ble and based upon an extensive rationality taking the
        individual's most essential interests as its basis.

Proposition 5: The system of political representation neces-
        sary for the smooth working of society should be made di-
        rectly and constantly accountable to all members of so-
        ciety.

Proposition 6: Genuine political freedom is nevertheless
        first of all dependent upon the conditions in the society
        as a whole, in particular upon the form and conditions of
        labour activities in the given society.

B. On Market Freedom

Propsition 7: Genuine freedom in any social system is first
        and foremost a measure of the degree to which work as a
        free play of faculties is possible for each of its mem-

bers. The less an economic organization of labour is guided toward this goal and the more it is determined by other aims, the less genuine freedom there is in the given society a a whole.

Proposition 8. The less a social division of labour is directed by the concern for the full development and satisfaction of individual talents and aspirations, the less freedom there will be in the society as a whole.

Proposition 9: The more the production and distribution of economic and social goods are governed by concerns other than the full happiness and development of individuals through work as a free play of faculties the less freedom there is in the society as a whole.

Proposition 10: While the capitalistic institution of "free labour" meant a real emancipation from feudal bonds, it also meant a new enslavement for the vast majority of workers, through insecurity, loss of self-esteem, loss of status and material deprivation, when not poverty, fear and outright starvation. The more the "free worker" of advanced capitalism is forced in such a way to relinquish all personal control over his work and its products, over the disposition of his labour power and over any rights of access to whatever means of production which may help to promote his happiness and his ability to engage in work as a free play of faculties, the less freedom there is in the society as a whole.

Proposition 11: The more the institution of the "free contract" helps to legitimate such a state of affairs, the less freedom is likely to obtain in the society as a whole.

Proposition 12: The more the situation of individual producers resembles that of a random game with unpredictable results, governed by opaque chance alone, the less freedom there is in society as a whole.

Proposition 13: The less the economic system of a society as a whole is directed by rational collective planning governed by a constant concern for individual development and happiness, and the more it is directed by deified, ostensibly nature-given, and blind economic laws, the less freedom there will be in the society as a whole.

Proposition 14: The more profit making, the drive toward economic efficiency, and the all pervasive application of technological rationality operate as goals in themselves, without relations to individual happiness or the wider interest of society, the less genuine fredom is likely to be obtained in the given society in the long run.

C. On Freedom and Private Life

Proposition 15: a) Human relations in general within a
capitalist society are not regulated by the concern for
the happiness and development of individuals, but by the
requirements of the capital and of the production of
commodities. Their typical form is the free labour contract.
   b) This applies not only to relations of labour, but
to all relations within society, including human relations typically considered as belonging strictly to the
private sphere.

Proposition 16: The fact of classes, and relations of classes, which arise from the economic organization of society, likewise pervades all human interactions within society.

Proposition 17: The reification of economic laws serves to
re-inforce the rigidity of such a pattern of relations in
all life situations and gives it the appearance of a
state of nature over and beyond any human control.

Proposition 18: Even in relations of love and friendship, the
ugliness, inconstancy, decay and ephemerality encountered
by uncompromising knowledge will not belong to the individuals in question, as characteristic traits, to be
overcome by understanding concern. They will merely be
the reflection of a whole society founded upon generalised alienation, fear and reification.

Proposition 19: a) The pervasive character of alienated human relations has its first and principal source in the
alienation of labour.
   b) The internalisation of an outdated "protestant
ethic" through socialization at work and outside of work
in the form of a general "performance principle" helps to
maintain this universal alienation.
   c) Another source is the increasing fear of social
chaos and of the demand for radical instinctual liberation, that has become more pressing due to the growing
satisfaction of material needs and to the ever increasing
meaningless of the performance principle.

D. On Freedom and Culture

Proposition 20: With the ascending bourgeoisie an affirmative
     culture has developed, proclaiming as absolute, a set of
     values humanistic in content and universalistic in in-
     tent. This affirmative culture impedes rather than pro-
     motes the realisation of freedom, because:
       a) By virtue of its isolation from surrounding econo-
     mic and social realities, it tends to offer cultural
     compensations for these realities rather than any impe-
     tus to change.
       b) In affirming its values as eternal, absolute and
     beyond ordinary human life, which is presented as belon-
     ging to an essentially different and inferior order of
     things; it denies at the same time that these values
     could, and possibly should be applied to the wider socie-
     ty.
       c) To the extent it succeeds in propounding genuinely
     humane and truly universal values, by virtue of its force
     and position in the social totality, it will severely
     impede the emergence of social and political movements
     tending toward a specific alternative society, as any
     such movement by comparison can only appear narrow, ex-
     treme and sectarian.
       d) The force of its message of understanding, beauty
     and human compassion in the midst of capitalistic, social
     and economic realities can only reinforce the dividing
     line between spiritual satisfaction and material happi-
     ness, thus contributing to the material ascetism and
     self-denial demanded by the "capitalistic spirit".

Proposition 21: More specifically, an affirmative culture
     helps to bridge the gulf between the bourgeois notion of
     the free individual, striving toward self-development and
     self-actualisation, his own wishes and aspirations as his
     sole guides, and the realities of a capitalist order
     dominated by the production of commodities, by the emo-
     tional and material poverty of the vast majority, by
     class divisions, and by the all out capitalistic competi-
     tion between each and everyone.

Proposition 22: In particular the central position which the
     concept of "soul" and (pure) "love" occupies within the
     affirmative culture as the exclusive realm of inner free-
     dom helps to justify and excuse the need for submission,
     the often unnecessary material deprivation and the in-
     constancy of an absurd social order.

Proposition 23: a) Freedom of thought plays a very distinct
     role within affirmative culture. In opposition to "inner

freedom" it requires a mind which is inquisitive and action-oriented, an existence with a minimum of material well being, reasonable access to relevant literature and spare energies, together with a system of social communication which is open, flexible and without too much censorship.

b) Art, by virtue of its isolation can paradoxically offer the ground for much freedom of thought.

c) Any curbing, blunting or outright suppression of this freedom of thought, in social relations, or through art, be it achieved through mindless mass productions, uncritical and streamlined educational systems, the systematic denial of conflicts of interests or sheer terror, will impede the realisation of a free society.

E. On Freedom and Progress

The following propositions are not commented in this chapter but can equally be established through an analysis of Marcuse's works.

Proposition 24: The advances of an ever more streamlined technological rationality, not only through the whole economy, but in all areas of life, is not to be condemned per se, as many truly human needs can be better fulfilled through the material progress of the last few decades. Neither this progress, nor the advances of technological rationality are identical with progress toward genuine human freedom, however:

a) To the extent it differs from a rationality which takes as its basis the full development and happiness of the individual, primarily through work as a free play of faculties, to that extent it will tend to produce less freedom in society as a whole and tend to impede the realisation of a free society.

b) To the extent it contributes to the alienation of labour and to the increasing competitive capitalist ethos, it will produce less freedom and impede the realisation of a free society.

Proposition 25: a) Critical reflection shows philosophy to have gradually relinquished all claims to be a master science, and to retreat into esoteric areas left by other disciplines; the intrinsic connection with individual existence has disappeared and the practical imports of its teachings have more and more receded into the background.

b) Philosophy can be shown to have evolved through a reflection upon specific social and historical struggles;

the values which emerge from that reflection should be
re-captured and re-assessed if philosophy is again to
play a role in society.

c) The concepts and categories of philosophy can and
should be used as tools for an improved reflection upon
society and human existence, and are as such essential
complements or alternative to narrow scientific terminologies.

d) The self-abdication of philosophy is itself a measure of the ever growing reification of society and of
the instrumentalisation of sciences and technique within
advanced capitalist societies.

Proposition 26: a) Against the narrow instrumentalistic
outlook of positivist sciences, a new eroticised rationality, open to all that is human and guided by aesthetic
criteria, should everywhere be promoted.

b) There is no genuine and effective social science
which ignores human self-understanding as an active element of social change.

c) The identification, exploration and development of
alternative visions of society, of human happiness or of
new ways of living is an essential part of any genuine
social science.

d) The positivist all out commitment to adequate methodology and tools of enquiry in itself constitutes a
powerful drive for the transformation of all scientific
activities into purely instrumental activities at the
service of the power holders in society, with narrow
social engineering as the supreme goal for all scientific
efforts.

ling to translate fully the ideals of liberalism
itself (7).

Liberal political institutions are not inheren-
tly unworkable; This applies also to the controversial essay on "Repressive Tolerance" (8). If they
fail to provide genuine democracy or even effective
protection for individuals, the reasons must be
sought in their application by political leaders or
groups in class society rather than in the political
institutions themselves. Marcuse firmly believes political discussion is necessary for the creation of
the good society. Effective action must rest upon a
new political consciousness (9). Yet the roots of
the problem are not in the political arena itself.
They must be located in the wider "civil society".

8.2   Market Freedom

It is important to stress the role of economic institutions in Marcuse's work, for these institutions
and the resulting class organization are fundamental
to Marcuse's perspective. The analysis of this aspect of civil society commands all further discussions of private life, culture and progress in contemporary societies. Yet, partly due to Marcuse's
demanding and ambiguous method of presentation and
partly because of the emphasis usually placed upon
his more esoteric research, this aspect is often
lost.

We have already seen the central role of labour
in Marcuse's theory of freedom, and there are numerous references in his works to the crucial role of
economic institutions in the overall organization of
society. Marcuse himself provides a comprehensive
and coherent account of the economic dimension and
its interrelation with other spheres of society in
Reason and Revolution (10). The lucidity of that
account is all the more remarkable as Marcuse in
three short sections develops his largely unchanged
(in relation to the 1932 essay) interpretation of
the 1844 Manuscripts into a full-blown and fairly
orthodox account of the main lines of Capital (11).
We shall therefore not discuss Marcuse's rendering
of the classical marxist analyses of the labour
process, or of the centrality he accords to concepts
such as surplus value, the falling rate of profit or
the distinction between abstract universal labour
and concrete specific labour in marxist theory as a
whole (12). Nor shall we concern ourselves with the
many aspects of the co-operative society interwoven
into this account (13). A number of points in this
account of Marcuse are particularly relevant to the
idea of market freedom. While Marcuse in 1932 strikingly omits any mention of the actual conditions of
the working class in Victorian England (that Marx
describes at such length and with such vigour in the
manuscripts), the account in Reason and Revolution
starts by placing the problem of poverty squarely at
the centre of Marx's analyses (14). The material
dimension of Marcuse's idea of freedom and of his
critique of contemporary societies is generally
ignored or dismissed; the passage therefore deserves
to be quoted in full:

> "Classical political economy (Marx quotes Adam
> Smith and J.B. Say) admits that even great
> social wealth means nothing but stationary
> poverty for the worker. These economists had

shown that poverty is not at all the result of
adverse external circumstances, but of the
prevailing mode of labor itself. 'In the pro-
gressing condition of society the destruction
and impoverishment of the worker is the product
of his own labor and of the wealth he has
himself produced. Misery thus springs from the
<u>nature</u> of the prevailing mode of labor' and is
rooted in the very essence of modern society"
(15).

It is this problematic that Marcuse extends into a
comprehensive critique of market freedom under capitalism. There is such a freedom, and it is real
enough, althugh very differently so for the various
classes in society. The other side of this freedom,
however, is the denial, repression and negation, on
a hitherto unprecendented scale, of the most vital
and crucial freedoms for the worker (applying, to a
lesser extent, to other strata of society as well).
This multiple alienation affects the worker's material, social, cognitive and psychological needs, "to
the point of starvation" and in complete denial of
all that is human in him/her (16). Its full scale
can only be gauged in relation to the comprehensive
picture of a free society and with a clear apprecia-
tion of the historically developed human nature. The
extent and depth of this total alienation is reflected in all areas of society. The roots of the problem, in a schematic form, can be described as
follows:

"The social division of labor, Marx declares,
is not carried out with any consideration for
the talents of individuals and the interest of
the whole, but rather takes place entirely
according to the laws of capitalist commodity
production. Under these laws, the product of
labor, the commodity, seems to determine the
nature and end of human activity" (17).

The establishment and deification of a particular
set of economic mechanisms, presented as "natural
laws" not to be disturbed if they are to have their
full "beneficial" effect upon the economy constitutes Maruse's prime target (18). They in fact impede, arrest and render less probable a different
historical development, that constituted by the next
step toward the co-operative society (19). The ruthless application of these "blind laws" of the economy and its consequence in a rigid division of labour

results in a universal alienation of man from man.
This furthers the general "process of reification
through which capitalist society makes all personal
relations between men take the form of objective
relations between things" (20). This process is seen
by Marcuse as the fundamental characteristic of
capitalist human interactions: "The system of capitalism relates men to each other through the commodities they exchange. The social status of individuals, their standard of living, the satisfaction of
their needs, their freedom, and their power are all
determined by the value of their commodities (21).
　　Capitalism contains progressive features. "It
has made possible the rational exploitation of all
kinds of material resources, it has constantly increased the productivity of labour and has emanci-
pated a hitherto unknown multitude of human capacities" (22). Marcuse states elsewhere that "free
labor is the achievement of capitalist society"
(23). This idea, with its obvious Weberian overtones, is developed a little later.

> "For labor power to become a commodity, howe-
> ver, there must be 'free' labor: the individual
> must be free to sell his labor-power to him who
> is free and able to buy it. The labor contract
> epitomized this freedom, equality and justice
> for civil society... The labor contract, from
> which Marx derives the essential connection
> between freedom and exploitation, is the funda-
> mental pattern for all relations in civil so-
> ciety. Labor is the way men develop their abi-
> lities and needs in the struggle with nature
> and history, and the social frame impressed on
> labor is the historical form of life mankind
> has bestowed upon itself. The implications of
> the free labor contract lead Marx to see that
> labor produces and perpetuates its own exploi-
> tation" (24).

We shall not go any further into the details of
these implications, which have been treated excel-
lently by others (25). The important point that Marcuse makes is that the freedom of the labourer is a
real freedom, and one he must enjoy if he is to contribute effectively to the development of the capitalist forces - which in the end, without ever quite
suppressing it, make a mockery of this freedom.
　　The universalistic tendencies and the increasing social and economic integration of developing
capitalism are adequately reflected in the <u>mirroring</u>

aspect of bourgeois ideologies. Marx is correct in
pointing out that the scope of the bourgeois ideas
of "freedom, equality and justice" is far greater
than that of the corresponding feudal ideas of "ho-
nour, loyalty and so on" (26). The distorting effect
of these ideologies can be seen in analysing the
actual impact upon individuals and/or classes of the
social institutions which are supposed to embody
them.

But if there is virtually no real freedom for
the labourer to enjoy in effective terms, what about
the producers, those free competitors fostered by
capitalism and in whose name the whole edifice is
justified? This is the economic freedom so vaunted
by ultra-liberal conservatives (Goldwater) and radical libertarians (Novacks) alike. It is in this
freedom that all the virtues of capitalism can be
experienced and realized (27). Here Marcuse's account goes far beyond Marx in sketching the realities of this aspect of capitalism. The crucial passage runs as follows:

> "The individual is 'free'. No authority may
> tell him how he is to maintain himself; every-
> one may choose to work at what he pleases. One
> individual may decide to produce shoes, another
> books, a third rifles, a fourth golden buttons.
> But the goods each produces are commodities,
> that is, use-values not for himself but for
> other individuals. Each must exchange his pro-
> ducts for the other use-values that will satis-
> fy his own needs. In other words, the satis-
> faction of his own needs presupposes that his
> own products fill a social need. But he cannot
> know this in advance. Only when he brings the
> product of his labor to the market will he
> learn whether or not he expended social labor-
> time.... If he can sell them at or above his
> production cost, society was willing to allot a
> quantum of its labor-time to their production;
> otherwise he wasted or did not spend socially
> necessary labor-time" (28).

In the pivotal 1941 essay on "Some Social Implications of Modern Technology", which owes so much to
Weber, Marcuse shows how the impact of reified economic "laws" and institutions now makes itself felt
more directly and "efficiently" upon the individual
(29). The basic social organization is unchanged
with respect to any planning effectively aimed at
promoting the full development of individuals –

Marcuse's constant criterion for a good society.
There simply is none. But there are plenty of other
forms of planning, sharing two common characteristics: 1) the individual has no say in them, 2) they
are not governed by any clearly rational goal for
society. Faced with goals he cannot comprehend (no-
body can) or affect (the "natural" order of society)
the individual is once more prisoner of the modern
version of the "capitalist spirit". As Marcuse puts
it,

> "Individuality, however, has not dissapeared.
> The free economic subject has developed into
> the object of large-scale organization and co-
> ordination, and individual achievemet has been
> transformed into standardized efficiency. The
> latter is characterized by the fact that the
> individual's performance is motivated, guided
> and measured by standards external to him,
> standards pertaining to predetermined tasks and
> functions. The efficient individual is the one
> whose performance is an action only insofar as
> it is the proper reaction to the objective
> requirements of the apparatus, and his liberty
> is confined to the selection of the most ade-
> quate means for reaching a goal which he did
> not set" (30).

The target of Marcuse's analyses in post-war
years is this transformed subjection to reified
institutions and economic rules, internalized into
an ever more reliable and reassuring (updated) "protestant ethic" and administered by an ever better
co-ordinated network of private and public burreau-
cracies. In Eros and Civilization he denounces
"pure", technical and unthinking efficiency (31). In
One Dimen-sional Man it forms the overall theme for
onesided analyses which owe more to Heidegger than
Marx or Weber. In Soviet Marxism it is again the
main target of a long analysis of a Soviet communist
morality all too reminiscent of the "protestant
ethic" or an earlier bourgeois age (32). There is,
however, one important difference.
The goal in itself, whatever the present realities of Soviet socialism, is a rational goal; and it
can be measured by the very standards that the Soviet state endlessly propounds. The last chapter of
Soviet Marxism is concerned to show that the form of
"technological rationality" characteristic of the
regime is not presented as a goal in itself, but as
a means to such goals as the full development of

individual mental and physical faculties or shorter working hours for all. A time will come where the tension between these goals, the achievements in material well-being, scientific knowledge and technical know-how, and the institutions meant to promote the former will become too strong; the freedom to create a co-operative society will be felt as a political and ethical necessity for all to experience.

8.3 Freedom and Private Life

Even where Marcuse shows himself most explicitly marxist in his critique of freedom, Marcuse invariably addresses his conclusions to individual persons in as direct and explicit a manner as possible. The conclusions are neither for humanity as a whole nor for the proletariat alone; they are for everyone who is prepared to listen or read. Furthermore, Marcuse always focuses upon those aspects of life most critical for a person's dignity, sense of selfhood and personal self-direction. The tone and style themselves strive to convey this sense of the personal. They also help to point out the intimate relation between the public domain and any search for personal growth and happiness, and to stress the importance of wider issues in the web of apparently purely individual problems and worries.

To retrace this facet of Marcuse's work in all its complexity would be a fascinating task, but there is not the space to do so here (33). Yet, in view of the fame of Marcuse's least marxist book, One Dimensional Man, it would be useful to extract a few passages from "On Hedonism" where such themes are clearly underpinned by a coherent vision of the co-operative society. A major thesis of the essay concerns the relation between happiness and knowledge. Marcuse asserts that "Any relationship to men and things going beyond their immediacy, any deeper understanding, would immediately come upon their essence, upon that which they could be and are not, and would thus suffer from their appearance" (34). The existentialist and Hegelian echoes of this passage are unmistakeable. The truth is to be discovered by reflection and will be striking with the force of evidence. It would furthermore be, by its very existence, a commitment and, presumably, a motive for action. Yet Marcuse develops these themes directed by the idea of the co-operative society, and in which, characteristically, orthodox marxism, Freud, Lukács and Weber all enter in varying degrees. Witness the following passage.

"In this society all human relationships transcending immediate encounter are not relations
of happiness: especially not relationships in
the labor process, which is regulated with regard not to the needs and capacities of individuals but rather to profit on capital and the
production of commodities. Human relations are
class relations, and their typical form is the
free labor contract. This contractual character
of human relationships has spread from the
sphere of production to all of social life.
Relationships function only in their reified
form mediated through the class distribution,
of the material output of the contractual partners" (35).

This account itself comprises several distinct
theses. One is that society is an interrelated
whole, a historical product and can thus be transcended. The second is that this society is for all
practical purposes governed by economic laws alone.
The third is that a class system arises from this
society which pervades all human interactions. The
fourth is that "the free contract" is the decisive
legal instrument in helping to enshrine this state
of affairs. The fifth is that human relations are
not only governed by economic laws and ensuing class
relations, but that the reification of such laws
"freezes" otherwise fluctuating relationships into
the appearance, and thereby almost the reality, of
conditions beyond man's control. The sixth is that
class relations affect through their influence upon
consumption every activity of life.

The market is all-powerful. The compulsive
"freedom" of the market pervades everything, and the
key element in its hold over men is the process of
reification developing over centuries of bourgeois
rule. It is this mechanism which decisively buttres-
ses the class system of interpersonal relations.
This system itself shapes every man's freedom.

"The class circumscribes the actual range of
individual freedom within the general anarchy,
the area of free play still open to the individual. Each is free to the extent his class is
free, and the development of his individuality
is confined to the limits of his class: he
unfolds himself as a 'class individual'" (36).

The process of reification goes in fact still deeper and forms the very individuality of the person in even those areas most distant from the dictates of the capitalist economic system. Marcuse on this point extends the marxist critique of alienation into every aspect of existence.

> "Society has released a whole dimension of relationships whose value is supposed to consist precisely in their not being determined by contractual achievements and contractual services. These are relationships in which individuals are in the relation of 'persons' to one another and in which they are supposed to realize their personality. Love, friendhsip and companionship are such personal relations, to which Western culture has relegated man's highest happiness. But they cannot sustain happiness, precisely when they are what they are intended to be. If they are really to guarantee an essential and permanent community among individuals, they must be based on comprehending understanding of the other. They must contain uncompromising knowledge. To this knowledge the other reveals himself not merely in the uninterrupted immediacy of sensual appearance that can be desired and enjoyed as beautiful, through satisfaction with appearance, but rather in his essence, as he really is. His image will thus include ugliness, inconstancy, decay and ephemerality not as subjective properties that could be overcome by understanding concern but rather as the effects of social necessities into the personal sphere. These necessities actually constitute the instincts, wants and interests of the person in this society" (37).

Marcuse's relation to existential themes comes clearly across in his critique of Sartre (38). The central themes of this critique include Sartre as the heir of Heidegger and Husserl, the hypostatisation of a specific historical development as a human condition, the role of sexuality, the impossible freedom of the "For itself", and the limitation of the phenomenological approach (39). The major criticism, significantly, is that Sartre does not succeed in breaking through the multiple layers of the pervasive reification he so lucidly describes. He ends up postulating in the midst of an absurd world the essential freedom and dignity of man. Thus:

"Behind the nihilistic language of Existentialism lurks the ideology of free competition,
free initiative, and equal opportunity. Everybody can 'transcend' his situation, carry out
his own projects; everybody has his absolutely
free choice. However adverse the conditions,
man must 'take it' and make compulsion his
self-realization. Everybody is master of his
destiny. But in the face of an 'absurd world'
without meaning and reward, the attributes of
the heroic period of bourgeois society assume
naturally an absurd and illusory character.
Sartre's 'Pour soi' is closer to Stirner's
Einsiger und sein Eigentum than to Descarte's
"Cogito". In spite of Sartre's insistence on
the Ego's "Geworfenheit" (being thrown into a
pregiven contingent situation), the latter
seems to be wholly absorbed by the Ego's ever-
transcending power which posits, as his own
free project, all the obstacles encountered on
its way" (40).

The translation of Heideggerian "Geworfenheit" into
a complex of socio-historical problems, accomplished
years before, is retraced in relation to Sartre's
work (41). The combination of these ideological
forces with the complementary ideologies of market
freedom is again the crucial mechanism that Marcuse
discerns through the "mirroring" ideology of Sartre's doctrine of freedom.
    Marcuse's later research again focuses upon the
impact of capitalist work conditions upon the individual. Max Weber's work plays a central role in
pointing to the historical roots of "surplus repression" and of the maintenance of an outdated "performance principle" (42). The maintenance of a modified
"capitalist spirit" is itself founded upon deep-
rooted psychological mechanisms that Freud brought
into light. Marcuse does not dwell upon the unavoidable time lag entailed by the introjection of pa-
rental values into a Freudian superego relatively
inaccessible to rational arguments. He strives instead to demonstrate the mechanisms by which the
prospects of impending human liberation can themselves, paradoxically, strengthen the hold of such
irrational and unconscious moral injunctions. Better
conditions of living, health, education and the
steady flow of necessary and luxury goods will further the demands for more integral freedom. The
pressure will be exacerbated by the thousand mea-

ningless constraints of a competitive, ruthless and
divisive late capitalist civilization. The demands
for liberation can find no visible outlet in such a
social order, and little comfort in the fate of a
civilization riddled with fundamental contradictions
whose goals are either uncertain or downright irrational. In such a reality, to give in to the "pleasure principle" would be a catastrophe on the social
and the individual level. On the social level it
would mean the final collapse into barbarism. On the
individual level it can only mean an unqualified and
unrestrained search for pleasure, ending up in a
pure Nirvana situation - the end of all pain and all
tension - that is death. Both prospects must then
demand the strengthening of irrational checks: at
the individual level this will translate into an
implacable and intolerant superego ("The Authorita-
rian Personality"); at the social level this must
emerge as more ruthless economic, political and
military institutions (43). These processes will
further be strengthened or modified by the constant
intervention of Thanatos, nurtured by the aggression
and frustration of half-promises and wholesale demands of such a civilization (44).

Marcuse's treatment of Freud remains firmly
committed to the material, sensual and sexual dimension of happiness. It is clear that in this view
there is no adequate analysis of private life which
can justifiably ignore this dimension. It is by
virtue of this fundamental material dimension of
individual private life that the power of the ideological forces of reification and "market freedom"
can be imposed and felt in the least expected areas
of life. The solution of "ontological anxiety" must
therefore ultimately be to transform existing societies into a more rational and sensual civilization.
To do this requires the concerted action of a collective subject willing the creation of the co-
operative society.

8.4 Freedom and Culture

The power of Marcuse's idea of freedom is perhaps
nowhere more evident than in his sensitive and yet
ruthlessly effective critique of culture as the
realm of human freedom. This extraordinary synthesis
of neo-Kantian, Idealist, Freudian and marxist elements provides a thread of continuity for a series
of finely balanced considerations on such themes as
love and death, joy and misery, work and happiness,
as they are presented in the theatre and in literary

works; he discusses the role of beauty in effecting
an impossible reconciliation with the capitalist
world; he also investigates the possible connections
between recurrent motives in classical art and central tenets of the "protestant ethic".

By far the best treatment he gives such questions is found in the essays of the thirties. The
most detailed and comprehensive analyses are presented in the essay on "The Affirmative Character of
Culture". The core argument is familiar enough: the
realm of culture provides only illusory freedom
because it is actually little more than escapism
from an irrational social order. All the same, culture can provide us with important illustrations of
how the world should be and could be. We ought therefore not to reject outright even bourgeois culture
without due process.

It is around these ideas that Marcuse develops
his inquiry (45). In the Greek cities, art was an
integral part of daily existence, an area of human
activity and knowledge which naturally merged with
the pursuit of other activities and pleasures. This
was so because every form of human knowledge was
oriented toward a practical activity and every area
of knowledge, however obscure, was seen to have
implications for the daily business of living. Aristotle, for instance, maintained "the practical
character of every instance of knowledge" (46). Yet,
at the same time, certain forms of knowledge were
considered above others, and were held in higher
esteem, they belonged to the realm of the "beautiful" as opposed to the merely necessary or utilitarian. This break in turn was reflected in the social
hierarchy, and only for a small and privileged minority was art truly a part of daily life. Art was for
free men, not for the slaves, who had other tasks to
perform and other things to worry about. This is
even more true of Plato's radical vision of the good
society (47).

The same again holds true, with modifications,
for the feudal world. The advent of a bourgeoisie
with universalistic values and egalitarian preten-
sions changes all that. The radical break between
art and the necessary, the beautiful and the useful
remains, and is even strengthened; it is now perceived as a fundamental ontological reality. Art is
no longer for the few alone; it is for everyone, and
all may partake in the realm of "the true, the good
and the beautiful". Better still, every individual
in the new social order should and must take upon
himself, as part of his person, the values of a

realm now declared to be his to enjoy or develop.
The individuals of bourgois society, barely emerging
from the multiple ties of the feudal world, "must
absorb (these universal values) into their lives and
let their existence be permeated and inspired by
them. 'Civilization' is animated and inspired by
'culture'" (48). Yet, and this is decisive for Marcuse's argument, these values are not such that the
individual should attempt to live his life by them,
and even less attempt to realise them through a
transformation of the social world. These values,
while universal and in every way superior to those
embodied in the economic institutions do not belong
to the 'real world'. Moreover, these values can be
modified or adapted, but they should not be significantly changed. While Marcuse clearly differentiates
between the two processes of reification in economic
life and deification of values in cultural life, he
nevertheless asserts that "as in material practice
the product separates itself from the producers and
becomes independent as the universal reified form of
the 'commodity', so in cultural practice a work and
its content congeal into universally valid 'values'"
(49).

These views lead him to the following characterization of the essential traits of bourgeois culture as an "affirmative" one.

"By affirmative culture is meant that culture
of the bourgeois epoch which led in the course
of its own development to the segregation from
civilization of the mental and spiritual world
as an independent realm of value that is also
considered superior to civilization. Its decisive characteristic is the assertion of a universally obligatory, eternally better and more
valuable world that must be unconditionally
affirmed: a world essentially different from
the factual world of the daily struggle for
existence, yet realisable by every individual
for himself 'from within' without any transformation of the state of fact. It is only in this
culture that cultural activities and objects
gain that value which elevates them above the
everyday sphere. Their reception becomes an act
of celebration and exaltation" (50).

The passage points to four separate ideological
functions of culture. Firstly, art in all its forms
acts as a safety valve against the frustrations of
daily life. The escape into culture, into the illu-

sory realm of the beautiful and the truly human, is
all the more real and potent as the two realms, that
of culture and of the merely necessary, are separated by an abyss. Secondly, the cultural realm is
itself "affirmative", that is it promotes in every
way the idea of a better humanity, the idea of "true
love" and of a spiritual communion with others. Reality is not only denied, it is decried as "incon-
stant, insecure, unfree - not merely in fact, but in
essence" (51). What is offered instead is a much
more humane vision of tragic passions, supreme vic-
tories and unequal compassion. Thirdly, insofar as
this culture succeeds in promoting what are seen as
genuine and truly universal values, because it affirms so loudly and so convincingly that its world
is the true world of man, it necessarily makes competing visions of the world appear as narrow, extreme or unjust. The very force and validity of much
of what "affirmative culture" propounds as its own
makes it difficult to argue for an alternative society as more true or more humane. Fourthly, because
of its success as an open window upon "a garden of
Eden" in the midst of the social order of liberal
capitalism, "affirmative culture" can fulfil yet
another function - to maintain and uphold as strictly as possible the separation between the soul and
the body which, with its concomitant asceticism, is
at the heart of the "capitalist spirit".

Other themes underlie the extended critique of
"affirmative culture". The first of these is the
bourgeois liberal notion of the free individual, and
of culture and private life as the realm for individual self-development and self-actualization. Marcuse will attack the inegalitarian and ultimately
illusory notion of individual freedom in a society
dominated by marked forces and the fact of classes.
Marcuse likewise attacks the idea of the well-rounded personality, the nice cultured middle class
personality, the ideal of a humanism which has long
lost its teeth in becoming more closely associated
with the values and attitudes of a dominant class.

> "The personality is the bearer of the cultural
> ideal. It is supposed to represent happiness in
> the form in which this culture proclaims to be
> the highest good: private harmony amidst gene-
> ral anarchy, joyful activity admist bitter la-
> bor. The personality has absorbed everything
> good and cast off or refined everything bad. It
> matters not that man lives. What matters only
> is that he lives as well as possible. That is

one of the precepts of affirmative culture. 'Well' here refers essentially to culture: participating in spiritual and mental values, patterning individual existence after the humanity of the soul and the breadth of the mind. The happiness of unrationalized enjoyment has been omitted from this ideal of felicity. The latter may not violate them, for it is to be realized immanently. The personality, which in developed affirmative culture, is supposed to be the 'highest happiness' of man, must respect the foundations of the status quo: deference to given relations of domination belongs to its virtues" (52).

The qustion of "inner freedom" is the second central theme underlying this critique. Marcuse again does not deny that the values embodied in this culture are in themselves worthwhile human ideals. He has furthermore elsewhere underlined the progressive nature of the "inner freedom" proclaimed by affirmative culture as part of the struggle of an ascending bourgeoisie against the grip of the church and other feudal powers (53). The parallel with the "inner freedom" preached by Luther and Calvin is not fortuitous. The central core of "inner freedom" as it appears in "affirmative culture" is the pure freedom of the "soul", as a haven of love, compassion and human dignity. The price for the new absolute "inner freedom" was an equally absolute submission to "conviction", accompanied by an unwavering respect for the laws this "freedom" was supposed to guard against (54).

Nevertheless the "soul" is the only lasting refuge from the all-pervading proces of reification. The gist of Marcuse's argument - and the tone he used to put it across - are best conveyed in the following passage:

"The soul alone has no exchange value. The value of the soul does not enter the body in such a way as to congeal into an object and become a commodity. There can be a beautiful soul in an ugly body, a healthy one in a sick body, a noble one in a common body - and vice versa. There is a kernel of truth in the proposition that what happens to the body cannot affect the soul. But in the established order this truth has taken a terrible form. The freedom of the soul was used to excuse the poverty, martyrdom and bondage of the body" (55).

"Affirmative culture", as described in the
thirties, is not without redeeming features, however. An important facet is that while it remains
forever cut off from the realities of existence, and
is less and less seen as capable of affecting them,
it nevertheless (and in inverse proportion) becomes
a refuge not only for soulful longing, but for au-
dacious explorations of taboos and forgotten possibilities. The truth value that art can acquire
thereby is stressed by Marcuse in the following
terms in the thirties:

"Reification is transpierced in private. In art
one does not have to be 'realistic', for man is
at stake, not his occupation or status. Suffering is suffering and joy is joy. The world
appears as what it is behind the commodity
form: a landscape is really a landscape, a man
really a man, a thing really a thing" (56).

There is another aspect to the (relative) freedom of thought enjoyed in art. It not only conveys
ideas, but projects images and awakens passions,
thus restoring the activist dimension which has been
slowly eroded from philosophy and the sciences. The
beautiful, which allows art to sustain and immorta-
lize illusions and which serves to reconcile and
soothe also gives force to this distinctive form of
freedom of thought. "Beauty has been affirmed with
good conscience only in the ideal of art, for it
contains a dangerous violence that threatens the
given form of existence.... The immediate sensuousness of beauty immediately suggests sensual happiness .... Beauty is fundamentally shameless. It
displays what may not be promised openly and what is
denied the majority" (57).

It is from the analyses of this period that
Marcuse develops his later thoughts on the subject.
We have considered above how his pro-surrealist
stance in Eros and Civilization followed from the
critique of the thirties (58). The wider discussion
of "mass culture", which is a much better known
facet of the "Frankfurt School"'s work shall not be
dealt with here. Suffice it to say that the implied
emphasis upon whatever "freedom of thought" can be
found in classical culture is likely to disappear
when the exigencies of modern book marketing, mass
sales and the striving for "best sellers" enter into
the picture, not to speak of the limitations of
other mass media. Yet even in One Dimensional Man

where Marcuse's stance appears much nearer to Heidegger than it ever was in the thirties, there is
still a sense of proportion: Marcuse makes it quite
clear that cheap paperback editions of classical
works can never be but a blessing (59). The trend of
Marcuse's further comments on culture, the latest
being his The Aesthetic Dimension, appear to waver
between two extremes: 1) art may be the nearest to
genuine freedom of thought in which even the co-
operative society can be evoked, and 2) that art
will always remain a realm apart, whatever the society.

8.5   Criticisms and Concluding Remarks

We have alredy considered some of Marcuse's most
characteristic weaknesses in chapter 7, and will return to similar issues in chapter 9. The following
will therefore merely consist in a few critical
observations.

My first comment, however, is that the propositions listed in table 8 and the corresponding text
do not do full justice to his abilities as a critic
of social institutions at large. These are best seen
in his essays of the thirties and perhaps in a work
such as Eros and Civilization, whose "epilogue" is
still one of the most effective critique of the Neo-
Freudians I have come across. The high level of abstraction remains, but it is combined with a cutting
wit, perceptive insights and an evocative vocabulary
which gives much of its edge to the text. The evocation of an alternative reality often usefully serves
to give force to this critique, even if it always
remains hidden in the background.

The preceding account, however, has made clear
that such an alternative exists in Marcuse, and that
it has been developed in successive traits through
each of the major writings. It makes for the force
of the best works, such as Reason and Revolution or
Eros and Civilization, where a single sweeping perspective serves to impose a new and bold interpretation. It also makes for the weakness of less convincing ones, either because this vision is lacking, or
because Marcuse's lack of consideration for possible
counterarguments makes this vision less tangible
than in the major works - the latter being the case
for an Essay on Liberation or Counterrevolution
and Revolt.

These traits makes also difficult to comment in
detail upon the set of propositions presented in
this chapter. They shall be left to the reader's

judgement, but for two further observations. The
first has already been touched upon. Marcuse's critique of positivism, which I tend to support, is
made less convincing by the fact that the implied
alternative, that of a dialectical approach, is left
in the most general terms. Unless prepared to move
at the same Hegelian heights as Marcuse, this would
leave even the reader to some variation upon the
positivistic theme, even if tempered with a commitment for broader human values and a sense for the
social dimensions of existence. Marcuse's own works,
however, also points to other alternatives. His
analyses and intepretations of classical texts,
whose method he adopted from Heidegger, is scrupulous, inspiring and imaginative. His analyses of
private life and culture points to the potentialities of a phenomenological perspective different
from that of Sartre or his sociological counter-
parts. He also brings up linguistic analyses as a
means of uncovering and countering elitist, reactionary or militaristic usages or developments of the
language. His critique of the social sciences leads
to forms of research where the scholar actively seek
to change as well as uncover the parameters of a
given situation and opens discussion with the subjects of his study. Above all, Marcuse's commitment
to the goal of a rational co-operative society by
the concerted action of a majority offers guidelines
which can be of value in the choice and application
of many methods other than the Hegelian or Marcusian
dialectic.

The second comment concerns the critique of
market freedom, which constitutes a centerpiece of
Marcuse's critical work. Marcuse here lacks critical
distance in relation to Marx's own work. Marcuse is
no economist, and cannot be expected to have evolved
an original contribution to marxist economics. Yet
his lack of concern for newer marxist economic theories, of which many would have fitted his own more
recent concerns better than those of classical marxism, is especially striking in the later works. It
is only with the late <u>Counterrevolution and Revolt</u>
that he does take up the issue, with economists such
as Baran and Sweezy or Magdoff (58). The relation to
the Western marxist tradition, which is essential
for Marcuse's entire project, and which had almost
disappeared in the late fifties and early sixties,
is once more established as the necessary context
for his research.

NOTES

1   See the introduction, section 1.5.
2.   It is significant in this context that the American edition of One Dimensional Man is subtitled "The Ideology of Adavanced Industrial Societies"; mixed with despair and discouragement there is also in the book the hope that its publication may help to counteract the pervasive ideology of contentment and resignation whose most articulate expression was the "end of ideology" thesis; for Marcuse see Piccone and Delfini, "Marcuse's Heideggerian Marxism", op. cit., p. 44; see also Wasman, C. (ed.): "The End of Ideology Debate", USA - New York: Funk and Wagnalls, 1966.
3.   See One Dimensional Man, p. 10.
4.   "The Struggle Against Liberalism in the Totalitarian View of the State", op. cit., pp. 8-9, pp. 21-22.
5.   Soviet Marxism, op. cit., p. 27.
6.   Ibid., p. 28, note 9.
7.   The above remarks would apply equally to the workers' and soldiers' councils Marcuse briefly experienced in 1918 and to a radical liberalism of the never implemented Jacobin constitution of 1791 in France.
8.   In the essay on "Repressive Tolerance", written during the period of One Dimensional Man when Marcuse's hopes for a better society were at their lowest, the argument is hyperdemocratic rather than undemocratic. Tolerance, "laissez faire" attitudes and liberal democratic institutions are attacked because they prevent the realisation of genuine democracy based upon full equality of economic resources, information and knowledge. Against the politics of "muddling through" to the point of shrugging off any form of long-term thinking, Marcuse asserts the political demands for substantive rationality, meaningful equality and fully shared freedom. This last theme reappears in the 1969 postscript where "pure tolerance" is denounced on the basis on substantive tolerance, ("Repressive Tolerance", in Wolff, P.R., Barrington Moore, J. R. and Marcuse, H., A Critique of Pure Tolerance, London: Jonathan Cape, 1969, pp. 93-137, passim).
9.   There is an element of determinism in Marx; it is not all the consequence of later reinterpretations by Engels, Bernstein or Kautsky; on this point see in particular Berlin, Karl Marx, op. cit.
10.   Op. cit., pp. 273-312.
11.   It should be noted that the only reference

in this account outside Marx himself is to the highly technical, mainstream work of Henryk Grossmann,
one of the earliest collaborators of the Institute
and one of the few to retain an unconditionally
supportive attitude towards the Soviet experiment,
Reason and Revolution, op. cit., p. 296, note 78 and
p. 311, note 107; See Jay, The Dialectical Imagination, pp. 16-21, 55 and 151 for an assessment of
Grossman's work, see also Lubasz, op. cit.

   12. Reason and Revolution, op. cit., p. 307,
311 and 298.

   13. See above sections 5.2 and 6.5.

   14. See chapter 5, passim for the discussion
of the 1932 essay, which was a contribution to the
internal marxist debate. Reason and Revolution is
the first major work ever published in English by
any the close collaborators of the Institute, and
this for an American public not expected to be familiar with either Marx or "critical theory".

   15. Marx, Economic and Philosophical Manuscripts of 1844, op. cit., Reason and Revolution,
op. cit, p. 274.

   16. Reason and Revolution, op. cit., p. 277;
Economic and Philosophical Manuscripts of 1844, op.
cit., p. 63.

   17. Reason and Revolution, op. cit., p. 273.

   18. This argument is more fully developed in
"The Struggle Against Liberalism in the Totalitarian
View of the State", op. cit., pp. 6-18 and pp. 23-
31, pp. 20-33 and pp. 36-45; see also Reason and Revolution, op. cit., pp. 278-82.

   19. Marcuse in his 1932 essay speaks of "a
catastrophe of human essence" as a fitting summary
of these processes; see "The Foundation of Historical Materialism", op. cit., p. 29, p. 158.

   20. Reason and Revolution, op. cit., p. 279.

   21. Ibid.

   22. Ibid., pp. 281-282, note 46.

   23. Ibid., p. 292.

   24. Ibid., pp. 308-309.

   25. For a classical and still very readable
introduction to Marxist economics see Lenin's Karl
Marx, Moscow: Progress Publishers, 1972; see also
Desai, M., Marxian Economic Theory, London: Gray
Mills Publishing Ltd., 1974, for a highly technical,
but interesting study of the underlying economic
model, as well as Mandel's Marxist Economic Theory,
London: Merlin Press, 1962, 1968. The relationship
Marx establishes between market ideology and the
underlying realities of capitalism is best shown in
Martin Nicholaus's excellent "Foreword" to the

Grundrisse, op. cit. It can be seen there, and also in Carol Gould's clear, if less detailed presentation in Marx's Social Ontology, op. cit. (especially pp. 119-128), that Marcuse's account in Reason and Revolution prefigures these later reinterpretations of Marx based on the material of the Grundrisse.

26.   Ibid., p. 285.

27.   Friedman, D.: The Machinery of Freedom, Guide to a Radical Capitalism USA - New York: Harper & Row, 1973.

28.   Reason and Revolution, op. cit., pp. 300-301.

29.   Marcuse focuses on Weber's analysis of the "protestant spirit" and of the wide repercussions of the various "rationalization" processes he observed in late Imperial Germany. See "Some Social Implications of Modern Technology", in Studies in Philosophy and Social Sciences, Vol. IX, pp. 414-439. Reprinted in Arato, A., and Gebhart, E., (editors), The Essential Frankfurt School Reader, op. cit.

30.   Ibid., p. 417.

31.   See in particular Eros and Civilization, op. cit., pp. 155-156.

32.   See in particular Soviet Marxism, op. cit., pp. 192-197.

33.   It should also be noted that the more recent work of Henri Lefebvre and Michel Bosquet move along similar lines, with perhaps a better sense for the detail and a more systematic exposition; see Lefebvre, H., Everyday Life in the Modern World, London: Allen Lane, 1971 (first published as La Vie Quotidienne dans le Monde Moderne, Paris: Editions Gallimard, 1968), and Bosquet, M., Capitalism in Crisis and Everyday Life, London: Harvester Press, 1977 (first published as Critique du Capitalisme Quotidien, Paris: Editions Galilée, 1973); see also on Marcuse Bruce Brown's not altogether convincing Marx, Freud and the Critique of Everyday Life, Toward a Permanent Cultural Revolution, New York and London: Monthly Review Press, 1973.

34.   "On Hedonism", op. cit., p. 164, p. 132.

35.   "On Hedonism", op. cit., p. 164, pp. 132-133.

36.   Reason and Revolution, op. cit., pp. 289-290.

37.   "On Hedonism", op. cit., pp. 164-165, pp. 133-134.

38.   In the aforementioned 1948 review of Being and Nothingness in "Existentialism: Remarks on Jean-Paul Sartre's L'Etre et le Néant'", op. cit.

39.   Nevertheless, Marcuse commends Sartre for

retaining the ideal of rationalism and for "the relentless clarity and lucidity of the mind which refuses all shortcuts and escapes" (ibid., p. 160). And this in a world which has become absurd, where there appears to be nothing left but "consciousness and revolt" and where "defiance is (life's) only truth" (ibid., p. 160). Nietzsche is explicitly mentioned in this context, and favourably so.

40. "Existentialism: Remarks on Jean-Paul Sartre's L'Etre et le Néant, op. cit., p. 175.

41. Ibid.

42. See above chapter 6.

43. Marcuse in this interpretation remains close to the Marx of the Paris Manuscripts. Eros and Thanatos are only regarded as two broad psychological-biological forces whose further fate and multiple ramifications are determined by the total material and intellectual culture of society. Capitalism has furthered this "cultural evolution" by opening up a whole range of possibilities, new needs and talents for an increasingly large proportion of the population. There is no return to some imaginary "golden age", and the wealth of the new civilization is truly a blessing. This in no way alters his judgement that unacceptable needs are induced, supported and nurtured by the system and that a thwarted sense of realities helps promote the vicious circle of aggression, repression and further frustration in the light of so much wasted potential (Baran and Sweezy, Monopoly Capitalism, is the classical indictment of organized wastage in the USA; see also M. Nicholaus, "The Crisis of Late Capitalism" in The Revival of American Socialism, op. cit.).

44. In the controversy with Fromm, he attacks not only the facile pseudomarxism of an almost ontological Fear of Freedom (op. cit.) which retraces everything to market mechanisms susceptible to substantial improvements, but also the concomitant assertion that psychoanalysis can "cure" the ills of society in "maladjusted" individuals who are to be better adapted to the realities of "life" (Eros and Civilization, op. cit., Epilogue).

45. "The Affirmative Character of Culture", op. cit., pp. 88-98, pp. 56-67.

46. Ibid., p. 88, p. 56.

47. ibid., p. 92, p. 60.

48. Ibid., p. 94, p. 62.

49. Ibid.

50. "The Affirmative Character of Culture", op. cit., p. 95, p. 63.

51. Ibid., p. 89, p. 57.

52.   "The Affirmative Character of Culture",
op. cit., pp. 122-123, pp. 90-91.
53.   "A Study on Authority", op. cit., pp. 56-
78, pp. 59-80.
54.   Ibid.
55.   Ibid., p. 109, p. 77. A little later he
states the connection between reification and this
aspect of affirmative culture in even more forceful
terms: "The soul appears to escape reification just
as it does the law of value. As a matter of fact, it
can almost be defined by the assertion that through
its means all reified relations are dissolved into
human relations and negated".
56.   "The Affirmative Character of Culture",
op. cit., p. 121, p. 89.
57.   Ibid., p. 115, p. 83. Elsewhere Marcuse
expands upon the same theme in the following terms:
"There is an element of earthly delight in the work
of great bourgeois art, even when they portray hea-
ven. The individual enjoys beauty, goodness, splen-
dor, peace and victorious joy. He even enjoys pain
and suffering, cruelty and crime. He experiences
liberation" (pp. 120-121, p. 88).
58.   See above section 6.4.
59.   Counterrevolution and Revolt, op. cit.,
pp. 1-59.

Chapter Nine

CONCLUSIONS

Marcuse's view of the good society is one of co-
operation, mutual understanding and all round individual development. It is a society where all will
be able to engage in the type of work which most
suits their needs and their aspirations. It is a
society where all share equally in the available
resources; it is a society where all will take part,
on a basis of equality and fairness, in the various
forms of necessary labour which will remain to be
done. This labour will be reduced to a minimum by a
rational use of modern techniques, and made more
attractive through an extensive exchangeability of
functions. All decisions concerning the distribution
of necessary labour will be based on joint planning
decisions in which all members of society participate on as full and equal a basis as possible. The
overriding concern will at all times be the best
satisfaction of each individual's needs and faculties, and all round sexuality, pervasive sensuality
and aesthetic demands will all figure prominently
among these needs. The individual will alone choose
to engage in any given area of activity - with the
exception of necessary rational labour, where mutual
agreement will prevail - and there will be no other
constraints than those following naturally from the
need to let others similarly enjoy their full share
of satisfaction and happiness through their own
freely chosen activities. These are the salient
features of the co-operative society. It is further
described, in the context of the theory of liberation, in table 7.
     Marcuse's idea of the good society is an appea-
ling one. Contrary to the impression conveyed by
many other implicit or explicit utopias appearing in
the literature, it is resolutely future orientated.
It is not a return to the green pastures of the

279

past, to the small, warm, cosy, if oppressive and intolerant rural communities of earlier ages, or to some forgotten land of milk and honey with no pollution and no industry, but also without hospitals, schools or theatres. His vision is that of a large scale society, with an extensive network of communications, a high level of technical competence and well developed artistic skills, combining the advantages of large scale production with a high regard for human happiness. The strong ethical element is also one which is first of all geared to ensure rather than to restrain the development, blossoming and enjoyment of the many facets of human personalities.

Yet this expansive vision of a happy good society is not without problems. My first reservation concerns a key motif in the underlying conception of human nature, summarized in the present assumption 9 on table 7. It states that man is capable of reconciling an ordered civilization leading to further material and cultural development for all men with a vastly reduced amount of social and instinctual repression. Three distinct, if related contentions are at play here. The first is that social institutions more than any other factor account for the observable level of violence in contemporary civilization. The second is that a vastly changed social order will entail major changes in the balance of instinctual forces. The third is that such a reduction in aggresiveness at the social and at the intinctual level is compatible with a dynamic and changing society.

The first of these contentions do not appear to me as very problematical. We are after all typically moving within the realm of ontological statements, i.e. those statements which are necessary for our orientation in the world (whether explicitly or not) as well as for any research. While a continual interchange of ideas and findings between philosophy and the social or biological sciences is desirable on such issues, it is nevertheless prudent to keep an open mind and flexible attitudes on such matters. This is no less true for the issue at hand, namely the impact and characteristics of a distant future society, whose existence should not be precluded on the basis of what may be very relative evidence conditioned by a host of historical accidents. This is true for these three contentions, and also for the greater part of Marcuse's other assumptions. In the present case, the assumption of all powerful institutions is furthermore one which is defensible

and academically respectable. To this can be added
such commonsensical evidence as can be provided from
a cursory comparison between existing social systems. With respect to aggresiveness in particular,
the contrasts between USA and Britain is striking -
football hooligans notwithstanding - and this despite a common cultural background and shared language.

The distance between the available evidence,
scientific or commonsensical, and the second contention is far greater, however. We can all go along
with Marcuse some of the way. Pain, hunger, frustration, lack of attractive prospects, at least up to a
point, will further aggression; the reverse also
holds. Yet, as argued in chapter 7, there is a world
between this and the near total disappearance of
aggression and violence, not only at the social
level, but also as the instinctual level. The resi-
lience of ancestral aggresiveness, for one thing,
cannot merely be a product of some primal guilt, as
Marcuse would have us to believe, but must also have
deeper roots in an age of human evolution where it
was sine qua non for survival. Moreover, it would
seen distinctly unplausible that every form of ag-
gressivity could disappear even in the best of society, what is the third contention underlying the
above mentioned assumption. Marcuse clearly does not
envision a totally non-competitive society, however
much material security, diversity and brotherly love
may have softened its edges. The survival of some
innate aggresiveness seems too probable not to be
taken into account; that it will find some support
in social institutions and human interactions must
in my view be taken for granted; that it will to
some extent be encouraged because of its positive
functions in work situations, in times of personal
crisis or in engaging interpersonal relations must
also follow from the dynamic aspirations of the co-
operative society, if not in terms of sheer individual survival. A potential for conflict will exist
even in the most co-operative of societies.

This lead me to the second reservation. There
is no indication in any of Marcuse's texts, outside
of very broad generalisations, as to how conflicts
of interests, and perhaps more importantly in this
context, how competing visions of the further development of the free society are to find a resolution. What we are presented with are very broad and
very general ethical guidelines, together with a
belief in sociability, companionship and mutual
understanding that will emerge from free co-opera-

tive work and shared duties. Yet anyone concerned
with politics will know how difficult it can be to
reach working solutions even within a little group
of like minded people engaged in voluntary activities for a common cause. They may not be the ideal
conditions of the co-operative society, but the
situation is surely not without parallels. However
brotherly and at peace the co-operative men and
women may be, and I have sympathy for the idea, this
alone will not resolve all problems in establishing
and maintaining working institutions for joint decision-making, for the dissemination of relevant information from and to all parties concerned and for
the administration, when not enforcement, of rules
and decisions affecting the welfare of all. This is
so much more the case as Marcuse obviously does not
envision the co-operative society as small self-
centered communities living solely upon the immediately available natural resources. It is on the
contrary a perspective where all useful scientific
and technological advances will be made to serve the
needs of a complex, highly diversified and individualistic society. The problem of common political
institutions will therefore arise at the very least
at the local, regional and central level. With this
follows all the questions concerning limitations of
power, the (full and equal) access to central or
local planning, co-ordinating and decision-making
functions, and the various guarantees for individuals, groups and regions.

These problems, for being obvious, are nonetheless real, and this however limited the power of
such instances may be in term of scope and depth.
Danger may also lie in too drastic a limitation of
the collective political decision-making bodies. A
minimum of co-ordination will always be necessary,
however plentiful the society of the future, and
however much is left to the individuals themselves
to decide. To the extent such functions are not
performed by the political institutions themselves,
it may be performed through other channels - with
what this may entail in terms of arbitrary and/or
unchecked power. Alternatively, necessary decisions
may be enforced through an appeal to individual or
collective commitment, itself presumably borne out
by a strong sense for ethical and social values.
This may well work for a time, but the long effect
will more likely than not be stifling and intolerant
conformism, enforced through social pressures, socialisation and instinctual repression - whatever
the official emphasis upon individual development

and hedonism. Too severe limitations upon the role
and power of overtly political institutions may
again entail that real conflict of interests or
ideals, which will eventually arise in any dynamic
society, are either played down or ignored all together. This in turn will lead to crisis in one form
or another, with all the uncertainties this can
bring - the alternative again being a completely
static society, where all innovative or controversial impulses must be constantly checked. There are
also other problems, when considering more closely
the idea of the co-operative society. Marcuse for
instance does not touch upon the whole issue of
education in such a world, and whether the principle
of "work as a free play of faculties" will also
apply fully to this area. Whatever the merits of
letting the child alone decide when and what is to
be learned - these merits are real, as the example
of the "Summerhill School" illustrates - it would
seem that the requirements of a complex society, as
well as questions of time and economy, will probably
weigh in favour of collective teaching forms with a
broad general curriculum made obligatory for all; it
is not only the acquisition of basic skills and
fundamental knowledge, necessary for the fulfilment
of common duties and general functions within society which is at stake; it is also the need to acquire
such knowledge as may be necessary for later "work
as a free play of faculties" and for a full access
to the opportunities available in any such society.
This raises all manners of questions about the organization and general orientation of the curriculum
and the educational system necessry to dispense it.
Political decisions are necessary. The socialization
to freedom may well come about in unexpected ways,
and this points to what is perhaps one of Marcuse's
weaknesses in this context. While the contradictory
nature of present capitalist societies is ever present in his work, the images his texts convey of the
co-operative society are always ones of peace and
harmony. These is only a passing reference to "the
sick, the insane and the criminal" in the 1938 essay
on hedonism, but otherwise there is no suggestion
that such a society may be faced with its own dissi-
dents in one form or another, that it may have to
enforce or defend its values by the use of sheer
force, or that there may be difficult choices between autarchy and dependence (1). This sense of all
round, closed, all encompassing solution can limit
rather than provokes further discussion on the question, whatever the explicit and provocative utopian

overtones of his later writings.

More important, however, is perhaps the virtual absence of any consideration for the ways and means by which such a society may come about. The contrast with Marx is again striking. The latter was never entirely fixed upon the modalities of a transition of socialism, alternatively favourising an armed revolution, or a mass uprising similar to the 1870 Paris commune, or again some more peaceful means to the same end. It was nevertheless always to be prepared by a series of concrete steps, involving the creation of parties and organizations, political agitation, mass education, the organization of the proletariat and the development of a common political program. These questions are entirely absent from Marcuse's own project. Marcuse throughout acknowledges the necessity to redefine the original marxist problematic to suit changed circumstances. He even suggests that the issue of revolution versus status quo should constantly be taken up anew in a broad calculus of the human costs involved against the possibilities that a co-operative society will provide. Yet concerning the character of this society, the arguments for a revolutionary option or the possible forms of a transition, Marcuse remains at the level of general considerations rather than specific analyses or detailed arguments. Even the controversial essay on "Repressive Tolerance" is highly ambiguous in its practical implications (2). The detailed economic and historical analyses that he throughout advocates as necessary for the revolutionary cause find little place in his own works. In contrast to Marx, Sartre, or even Kierkegaard, which all at various points are commended for their ability to convey the essentials of a given situation in clear and concrete analyses, Marcuse himself is often abstract, elusive, ambiguous. The project of liberation and the idea of freedom which animates his work, and gives force to his critique of contemporary society is clear, constant and solid throughout his writings, as to the main lines; yet it lacks the vividness and sensuality of other utopian writers, or again the living, contradictory but tremendously vital force characteristic of Marx's own works (3).

There is one set of explanations which may help to explain the paradox. It also points to what is Marcuse's main force. His position has always been that of an exile, and not only in the USA. His early commitment to the marxism advocated by figures such as Rosa Luxembourg and Karl Liebknecht found no

outlets in politics after the failure of the German
revolution of 1921. The difficult and confused years
of late Weimar Germany, followed by 12 years of Nazi
rule, itself leading to a divided Germany certainly
did not help to make the marxist project as Marcuse
understands it a very real issue. Post-war America
did not itself offer much in terms of concrete
analyses; the nearest to such an analysis was Soviet Marxism, which is as much an indictment of
capitalist America as of the Soviet interpretation
of the marxist legacy (in fact Soviet Russia is at
least credited with a rational political ideology,
which leaves open the possibilities for a true marxist revolution). Eros and Civilization and One Dimensional Man in very different ways, were both
answers to the utter lack of revolutionary prospects
or even hopes in the US of the fifties and early
sixties. Even the student movement and the various
upheavals of the sixties did not fundamentally change this situation, as the involvement of large masses of people remained axiomatic for Marcuse's revolutionary project, just as it had with Marx. The
renewed optimism of these years did not in fact
imply that Marcuse was any more sanguine about the
immediate prospects for the co-operative society.

    In the circumstances Marcuse's approach is not
to present a detailed picture of the good society or
a specific program of political action. The latter,
when taking Marcuse's radicalism into account, was
either impossible or impracticable. As for the vision of the co-operative society, if it is not more
visible or detailed, it is surely in part due to the
traditional marxist rejection of utopian thinking.
Yet in part it must also be attributable to Marcuse's understandable desire to avoid outright rejection from an environment where marxist ideas and
the marxist tradition as a whole (i.e. left wing
parties, organizations, newspapers, periodicals,
militants, etc..) never has played the role it does
in Western Europe. The hopelessness and pessimism of
One Dimensional Man is thus a measure of this isolation; the lack of such a continuous socialist tradition could also help to explain the impact Marcuse's
own writings has had in terms of its revival in
later years (4). The abstract and elusive quality of
Marcuse's thought would thus primarily be a reflection of the tremendous distance between his radical
interpretation of Marx, with its emphasis upon an
all round revolution in man's entire existence, and
the social and political realities in which he
lived.

To this first explanation could be added another one, which uses the same terms, but in reverse order. Marcuse throughout remains faithful to his grand project of human liberation. The lack of immediate prospects for any such liberation entails that the first task is not the further definition of a free society or a specification of the modalities of political action. It must be to force readers to reflect upon the world in which they live. In a way similar to Brecht's "estrangement effect", Marcuse deliberately aims to create a distance from the prevailing realities by restating what are obvious and commonly accepted facets of these realities in terms which show them to be no longer natural, or given, or self-evident. The distance is obtained through a high level of abstraction, by imposing an almost planetary perspective upon social issues or cultural currents, by forcing upon the reader or the audience unfamiliar terms or concepts, derived from the German philosophical tradition or coined for the occasion. An elusive, shifting, abstract and general manner of presentation is thus the best tool for provoking reflection, for forcing readers or students to go beyond their usual intellectual world, for demanding that they take up anew for examination what would seem commonsensical knowledge or intractable problems. In this perspective the co-operative society is not so much a picture of the good society - even if is is that also. It is primarily a set of general political and ethical guidelines which helps to direct philosophical inquiries, serve to focus the attention upon the important, if very general issues, and helps to engage an ongoing dialogue with whoever may feel puzzled by Marcuse's radical positions, and/or provoked by the intangibility of his thought.

It is this second explanation that I favour. The co-operative society functions as the "second dimension" to which his work constantly refers.The generality of its central assumptions is understandable when it is considered, not as an utopia in the traditional sense, but as a set of ethical and political ideals, which can help us to better/steer a technological and scientific development, where the importance of individual happiness appears forever subordinated to the imperatives of impersonal economic laws. It re-introduces into the political debate a whole range of human needs, emotions and aspirations which, from being alien to a rational economic and political decision making process, should enter at the heart of such processes and mark the very rationality used to reach whatever may be working solutions. To clarify our ideas about the good society is more rather than less urgent in these times of economic crisis, when new technological advances are in the making which could transform our lives and those of our children.

It is here that I see Marcuse as making a genuine contribution to political theory. Marcuse views are radical, and nothing short of a total revolution in the classical marxist sense make them into realities. There are other ways to promote traditional and untraditional socialist ideals. Our material wellbeing may not yet be fully ensured - it may even be that we are still years behind the level of material and technical development Marx saw as the pre-condition for socialism - it is nevertheless high and will most probably remain so, despite some cutbacks. The concern with other human needs and satisfactions will probably grow rather than abate. This suggest that more vocal demands will be made upon the present or later institutions in terms of clear political choices where the human element, be it in terms of pleasant environment, the provision of social facilities, or full security against illness and accidents, becomes more dominant. The coming age of ordinators will itself bring many changes. The ineptitude of a vast army of unemployed coexisting with ever more demanding job performances for the wages-earning part of the population will not continue for ever. Work is on the way to become a priviledge, and it will have to be shared. The shift toward more creativity, self-reliance and responsability in work situations may again be reflected in a greater participation in the politics of welfare. The problems of leisure, old age, impersonal city life or self-enclosed suburbs may also require imaginative solutions based on technical know how and human concerns.

Exactly what the coming years may bring is impossible to say. The value of Marcuse's research and of his vision of the co-operative society is that he insists that we place our ideas on the good society at the center of our judgement upon society, upon science and upon technological development. His merit is to have constantly fought what could be termed "technological fatalism", i.e. the all too widespread belief that there is an independant entity outside our combined wills and inaccessible to human action. His force lies in his ability to oblige his reader to go beyond the evidence of his socialization into the present society in order to

be able to judge it by standards which are other
than those of common sense or conformity. To the
extent that the co-operative society, as a vision
and a set of standards, can help in this task and
can serve to remind us that it is up to ourselves to
direct and shape the coming technological and economic development, then it makes Marcuse's research
well worth reading and working with. The collective
realisation of the good society is still on the
agenda.

NOTES

1. "On Hedonism", op. cit., p. 193.
2. "Repressive Tolerance", op. cit., passim.
3. There is no lack of such utopias or coun-
ter-utopias. The best known are surely Orwell's <u>1984</u>
or the more ambiguous <u>Brave New World</u> of Aldous
Huxley. A good illustration of what the co-operative
society could look like is provided by Ursula LeGuin
<u>The Dispossessed</u> (London: Victor Gollanz, 1974).
4. See <u>The Revival of American Socialism</u>, op.
cit., see also introduction for a review of the
secondary literature.

BIBLIOGRAPHY OF WORKS BY MARCUSE

Given the importance of the political and historical dimension in Marcuse's works, these will be listed chronologically, and divided into books, collected essays, essays and articles, and interviews. All references will be to the English text when available, next French, next German. The edition used here is indicated last, in parentheses.

Books

1. Der deutsche Künstlerroman, phil diss., University of Friedburg-im-Breisgau, 1922.
2. Schiller Bibliographie unter Benutzung der Tramelschen Schiller-Bibliothek, Berlin: S. Martin Graenkel, 1925, pp. 137.
3. Hegel's Ontologie und die Grundlegung einer Theorie der Geschichtlichkeit, Frankfurt am Main: V. Klostermann Verlag, 1932, pp. 368. also in French: L'Ontologie de Hegel et la Théorie de l'Historicité, Paris: Editions de Minuit, 1972.
4. Reason and Revolution: Hegel and the Rise of Social Theory, New York: Oxford University Press, 1941, pp. xii, 431. Second edition with "Supplementary Epilogue", New York: Humanities Press, 1954, pp.xii, 439. Paperbound edition with new preface, "A Note on Dialectic", Boston: Beacon Press, 1960, pp.xvi, 431 (Routledge and Kegan Paul, 1973).
5. Eros and Civilization: A Philosophical Inquiry into Freud, Boston: Beacon Press, 1955, pp. xii, 277. Paperbound edition with new preface, New York: Vintage Books, 1962, pp. xviii, 256. Second edition with new preface, "Political Preface, 1966", Boston: Beacon Press, 1966 (Abacus, 1973).
6. Soviet Marxism: A Critical Analysis, New York: Columbia University Press, 1966, pp.271. Paperbound edition with new preface, New York: Vintage

Russian Library, 1961, pp.xvi, 252 (Pelican, 1971).
    7. One Dimensional Man: Studies in the Ideology of Advanced Industrial Society, Boston: Beacon Press, 1964; paperbound edition, 1966, pp. xvii, 260 (Abacus, 1972).
    8. An Essay on Liberation, first published USA, Boston: Beacon Press, 1972. (Allen Lane, The Penguin Press, 1972).
    9.Counter-Revolution and Revolt, first published USA, Boston: Beacon Press, 1972. (Allen Lane, The Penguin Press, 1972).
    With K. Popper: Revolution or Reform: A Confrontation, edited by A. T. Fergusson, Chicago: New University Press, 1976. Translated from Revolution oder Reform?, edited by Franz Stark, Munich: Kosel-Verlag, GmbXH & Co., 1972.
    10. The Aesthetic Dimension: Toward a Critique of Marxist Aesthetics, Boston: Beacon Press, 1978. Revised translation from Die Permanenz der Kunst: Wider eine Bestimmte Marxistische Aesthetik, Munich: Carl Hanser Verlag, 1977.

A complete edition of the writings of Herbert Marcuse is under publication by Suhrkamp Verlag, Frankfurt-am-Main.

COLLECTED ESSAYS AND ANTHOLOGIES

    A. Negations, translated by J. Shapiro, first published USA, Boston: Beacon Press, 1968. Republications of entries 26, 29, 30, 31, 32, 58, 76, 81. (Allen Lane, The Penguin Press, 1972).
    B. Five Lectures, translated by J. Shapiro and S. M. Weber, first published USA, Boston: Beacon Press, 1970. Republications of entries 46, 47, 59, 83, 84. (Allen Lane, The Penguin Press, 1970).
    C. Studies in Critical Philosophy, translated by Joris de Breis, first published London: NLB, 1972. Republications of entries 22, 27, 36, 49, 92.
    D. The Essential Frankfurt School Reader, edited by Arato, A. and Gebhardt, E., New York: Unizen Books, 1978. Reprints of entries 34, 70 and 51a.
    E. Philosophie et Révolution, Paris: Denoël-Gonthier, 1969. Republication of entries 11, 15, 22.
    F. Culture et Societé, Paris: Editions de Minuit, 1970. Republication of entries 23, 26, 30, 31, 32, 46, 47, 58, 59.
    G. Pour une théorie critique de la societé, Paris: Denoël-Gonthier, 1971, Republication of en-

tries 27, 75, 82.

H. <u>La fin de l'Utopie</u>, Paris: Editions du
Bevil, 1968. Publication of entries 83, 84, as well
as two seminars on "Morality and Politic in an
affluent society" and on "Vietnam, the third world
and the opposition in the major industrial countries".

I. <u>Kultur und Gesellschaft II</u>, Frankfurt am
Main: Suhrkamp Verlag, 1965. Republication or publication of entries 23, 36, 58, 59, 59a, 61.

K. <u>Das Ende der Utopie</u>, Berlin: Peter von
Maikowoki, 1968. (See <u>La Fin de l'Utopie</u>, above).

L. <u>Philosophy und Revolution</u>, Berlin: Verlag
Philosophy und Revolution, 1967. Republication of
entries 11, 15, 25.

M. <u>Ideen zu einer kritischen Theorie der Ge-</u>
<u>sellschaft</u>, Frankfurt am Main: Suhrkamp Verlag,
1969. Republication or publication of entries 27,
75, 82.

Essays, Articles and Book Reviews

10. "Contributions to a Phenomenology of Historical materialism", in <u>Telos</u>, No.4, Fall 1969, pp.
3-4. First published as "Beiträge zur Phänomenologie
des Historischen Materialismus", in <u>Philosophische</u>
<u>Hefte</u>, No. 1, July 1928, pp. 43-68.

11. "Uber konkrete Philosophie" (On Concrete
Philosophy), <u>Archiv für Sozialwissenschaft und So-</u>
<u>zialpolitik</u>, vol.62 (1929), pp. 11-128. Also publi-
shed as "Sur la philosophie concrète" in <u>Philoso-</u>
<u>phie et Révolution</u>, Paris: Denoel_Gonther, 1969.

12. "Besprechung von Karl Vorlander: Karl
Marx, sein Leben und sein Werk", <u>Die Gesellschaft</u>,
vol. VI, 1929, part II, pp. 186-209.

13. "Zur Wahrheitsproblematik der Soziologischen Methode" (On the Problem of Truth in the
Sociological Method), <u>Die Gesellschaft</u>, vol.VI,
1929, part II, pp. 356-369.

14. "On the Problem of the Dialectic", in
<u>Telos</u>, No.27, Spring 1975, pp.12-39. Part I was
translated from "Zum Problem der Dialektik I", <u>Die</u>
<u>Gesellschaft</u>, vol.VI, 1929, pp.356-369.

15. "Transzendertaler Marxismus?" (Marxisme
Transcendental?), <u>Die Gesellschaft</u>, Vol.VII, 1930,
part II, pp.304-326. Also published in French as
"Marxisme Transcendental?" in <u>Philosophie et Révo-</u>
<u>lutions</u>, Paris: Denoël-Gonthier, 1969.

16. "Besprechung von H. Noack: Geschichte und
System der Philosophie", <u>Philosophische Hefte</u>, Vol.

II, 1930, pp.91-96.

17. "Das Problem der geschichtlichen Wirklich-
keit: Wilhelm Dilthey" (On the problem of Historical
Reality: Wilhelm Dilthey), Die Gesellschaft, Vol.
VIII, 1931, pp.350-368.

18. "Zur Kritik der Soziologie" (Toward a
Critique of Sociology), Die Gesellschaft, Vol. VIII,
1931, part II, pp. 270-280.

19. "On the Problem of the Dialectic", in
Telos, No. 27, Spring 1975, pp. 12-39. Part II was
translated by Duncan Smith from "Zum Problem der
Dialektik II", Die Gesellschaft, Vol.VIII, 1931,
part II, pp.541-557. See entry 14 above.

20. "Zur Auseinandersetzung mit Hans Freyers
Soziologie als Wirklichkeitswissenschaft", Philosophische Hefte, Vol.III, Nos.1/2, 1931, pp. 83-91.

21. "Besprechung von Heinz Heimsoth: die Errungenschaften des Deutschen Idealismus", Deutsche
Literaturzeitung, Vol.53, No.43, 1932, pp.2024-2029.

22. "The Foundation of Historical Materia-
lism", Studies in Critical Philosophy, London: New
Left Books, 1972. First published as "Neue Quellen
zur Grundlegung des Historischen Materialismus",
Die Gesellschaft, Vol. IX, 1932, part II, pp.136-
174. Also published in French as "Les Manuscrits
Economico-Philosophiques de Marx" in Philosophie et
Révolution, Paris: Denoël-Gonthier, 1969.

23. "On the Philosophical Foundation of the
Concept of Labour in Economics", translated by Douglas Kellner, Telos, No.16, Summer 1973, pp.9-37.
First published as "Uber die philosophischen Grund-
lagen des Wirtschaftswissenschaftlichen Arbeitsbe-
griffs", Archiv für Sozialwissenschaft und Sozial-
politik, Vol.69, 1933, pp.257-292.

24. "Philosophie des Scheiterns: Karls Jaspers
Werk", Unterhaltungsblatt der Vossischen Zeitung,
No.339, December 1933.

25. "Besprechung von Herbert Wacker: Das Ver-
haltnis des junger Hegel zu Kant", Deutsche Literaturzeitung, Vol.55, No.14, 1934, pp.629-630.

26. "The Struggle Against Liberalism in the
Totalitarian View of the State", Negations, Boston:
Beacon Press, 1968. First published as "Der Kampf
gegen den Liberalismus in der totalitären Staatsauffassung", Zeitschrift fur Sozialforschung, Vol.III,
1934, pp.161-195.

27. "A study on Authority", Studies in Critical Philosophy, London: New Left Books, 1972. First
published as "Theoretische Entwurfe über Autorität
und Familie: (Ideengeschichtlicher Teil)", Studien
über Autoritat und Familie: Forschungsberichte aus

dem Institut für Sozialforschung, Paris: Felix Alcan, 1936, pp.136-228.

28. "Autorität und Familie in der deutschen
Soziologie bis 1933", ibid, pp. 737-752.

29. "The Concept of Essence", Negations, Boston: Beacon Press, 1968. First published as "Zum
Begriff des Wesens", Zeitschrift für Sozialforschung, vol.V, 1936, pp.1-39.

30. "The Affirmative Character of Culture",
Negations, Boston: Beacon Press, 1968. First published as "Uber den affirmativen Charakter der Kul-
tur", Zeitschrift für Sozialforschung, Vol.VI, 1937,
pp.54-59.

31. "Philosophy and Critical Theory", Negations, Boston: Beacon Press, 1968. First published
as "Philosophie und kritische Theorie", Zeitschrift
für Sozialforschung, Vol.VI, 1937, pp.54-59.

32. "On Hedonism", Negations, Boston: Beacon
Press, 1968. First published as "Zur Kritik des
Hedonismus", Zeitschrift für Sozialforschung, Vol.
VII, 1938, pp.55-89.

33. "An Introduction to Hegel's Philosophy",
Studies in Philosophy and Social Science, Vol.VIII,
1940, pp.394-412. (Forstudy to Reason and Revolution).

34. "Some Social Implications of Modern Technology", in Studies in Philosophy and Social Sciences, Vol.IX, 1941, pp.414-439. Reprinted in Arato,
A. and Gebhart, B. (editors) The Essential Frankfurt
School Reader, New York: Unizen Books, 1978.

35. "A Rejoinder to Karl Lowith's review of
Reason and Revolution", in Journal of Philosophy and
Phenomenological Research (Buffalo 1941-42), vol.
II, pp.560-3.

36. "Some Remarks on Aragon: Art and Politics
in the Totalitarian Era", (unpublished, Washington
DC, September 1945).

37. "Existentialism: Remarks on Jean-Paul
Sartre's L'Etre et le Néant", Journal of Philosophy
and Phenomenological Research, Vol.VIII, No.3, March
1948, pp.309-336. German translation in Sinn und
Form, Vol.II, No.1, 1950, pp.50-82.

38. "Lord Acton: Essays on Freedom and Power",
American Historical Review, Vol.LIV, No.3, April
1949, pp.557-559.

39. "Review of Georg Lukács' Goethe und seine
Zeit", Journal of Philosophy and Phenomenological
Research, vol. IX, No.1, September 1950, pp.142-142.

40. "Anti-Democratic Popular Movements", in
H. Morganthau, (ed.), Germany and the Future of Europe, Chicago 1951, pp. 108-13.

BIBLIOGRAPHY OF MARCUSE

41. "Recent Literature on Communism", World Politics, Vol.VI, No.4, July 1954, pp.515-525.
42. "Dialectic and Logic Since the War", Continuity and Change in Russian Thought, edited and with an introduction by Ernest J. Simons, Cambridge, Mass.: Harvard University Press, 1955, pp.347-358. Reissued by New York: Russell and Russell, 1967.
43. "Eros and Culture", The Cambridge Review, vol.I, No.3, Spring 1955, pp. 107-123.
44. "The Social Implications of Freudian 'Revisionism'", Dissent, Vol.II, No. 3, Summer 1955, pp.221-240. Reprinted as epiloque to Eros and Civilization and in Voices of Dissent, New York: Grove Press, 1958. German translation in Psyche, Vol.II, 1957, pp.801-820.
45. "A Reply to Erich Fromm", Dissent, Vol.III, No.1, Winter 1956, pp.79-81.
46. "La Théorie des Instincts et la Socialisation", La Table Ronde, No.108, 1956, pp.97-110. Also in Eros and Civilisation, Boston: Beacon Press, 1955, 1966.
47. "Theory and Therapy in Freud", The Nations, Vol.CLXXXV, September 1957, pp.200-202.
48. "Freedom and Freud's Theory of Instincts", Five Lectures, Boston: Beacon Press, 1970; Toronto: Saunders, 1970; London: Allen Lane, The Penguin Press, 1970; First published as "Trieblehre und Freiheit", in Freud in der Gegenwart: ein Vortragszyklus der Universitaten Frankfurt und Heidelberg zum hundertsten Gevurtstag ("Frankfurter Beiträge zur Soziologie", Vol.VI, (Frankfurt am Main: Europäische Verlagsanstalt, 1957)), pp.401-424.
49. "Progress and Freud's Theory of Instincts", Five Lectures, London: Allen Lane, The Penguin Press, 1970, pp.28-43. First published as "Die Idee des Fortschritts im Licht der Psychoanalyse", in Freud in der Gegenwart:, op. cit., pp.425-441.
50. "Preface" to Marxism and Freedom, by Raya Dunayevskaya, New York: Twayne Publishers, 1958, pp.15-20.
51. "Notes on the Problem of Historical Laws", Partisan Review, No.26, Winter 1959, pp.117-129.
52. "The Ideology of Death", The Meaning of Death, edited by Herman Feifel, New York: McGraw-Hill, 1959, pp.66-76.
53. "Karl Popper and the Problem of Historical Laws", Partisan Reviews, 1959. Also published in Studies in Critical Philosophy, London: New Left Books, 1972.
54. "De l'Ontologie à la téchnologie: les tendances de la société industrielle", Arguments,

294

Vol.IV, No.18, 1960, pp.54-59.

55. "A Note on the Dialectic", new preface to 1960 paperbound edition of Reason and Revolution. Reprinted in The Essential Frankfurt School Reader, edited by Arato, A. And Gebhardt, E., New York: Unizen Books, 1978.

56. "Language and Technological Society", Dissent, Vol.VIII, No.1, Winter 1961, pp.66-74.

57. "The Problem of Social Change in Technological Society", lecture presented to a Unesco Symposium on Social Development. Printed for limited distribution under the auspices of Raymond Aron and Bert Hoselitz, Paris, 28 April 1961, pp. 139-60.

58. "Ideologie et société industrielle avancé", Mediations, No.5, Summer 1962, pp.57-71.

59. "Zur stellung des Denkens heute", in Zeugnisse: Theodor W. Adorno zum 60. Geburtstag, ((Im Auftrag des Instituts für Sozialforschung herausgeben von Max Horkheimer) Frankfurt am Main: Europäische Verlagsanstalt, 1963), pp.45-49.

60. "Dynamismes de la société industrielle", in Annales: Economies, Sociétés, Civilizations, Paris,1963,vol.18, pp.90632.

61. "World Without Logos", Bulletin of the Atomic Scientists, Vol.20, January 1964, pp.25-26.

62. "Industrialization and Capitalism in the Work of Max Weber", Negations, Boston: Beacon Press, 1968.

63. "The Obsolescence of the Freudian Concept of Man", Five Lectures, London: Allen Lane, The Penguin Press, 1970, pp.44-61. First published as "Das Veralten der Psychoanalyse" (Obsolescence of Psychoanalysis), paper for the 1963 Annual Conference of the American Political Science Association, in New York.

64. "Ethics and Revolution", Ethics and Society, edited by Richard T. deGeorge, New York: Anchor, 1966, pp.130-146.

65. "Socialism in the Developed Countries", International Socialist Journal, Vol.II, No.8, April 1965, pp.139-152. First published as "Perspektiven des Sozialismus inder entwickelten Industriegesellschaft", Praxis, Nos. 2/3, 1964, pp.260-270. (Address presented at the Conference on Socialist Perspectives in Korcula).

66. "Remarks on a Redefinition of Culture", Daedalus, vol.XCIV, No.1, Winter 1965, pp.190-207. Reprinted in Science and Culture, edited by Gerald Holton, Cambridge, Mass.: Houghton Mifflin, 1965. Second edition, Boston: Beacon Press, 1967, pp.218-235.

67. "A Tribute to Paul A. Baran", Monthly Review, Vol.XVI, No.2, March 1965, pp.114-115.

68. "Nachwort" to Walter Benjamin's Zur Kritik der Gewalt und andere Aufsarze, Frankfurt am Main: Surhkamp Verlag, 1965, pp.99-106.

69. "Repressive Tolerance", A Critique of Pure Tolerance, by H. Marcuse, R. P. Wolff and Barrington Moore, Jr., Boston: Beacon Press, 1965, pp.81-117. German translations: Frankfurt am Main: Surhkamp Verlag, 1966. (With 1969 postscript, London: Jonathan Cape Ltd., 1969). Reprinted in Critical Sociology, edited by P. Connerton, London: Penguin, 1976.

70. "Epilogue to the New German Edition of Marx's 18th Brumaire of Louis Napoleon", Radical American, Vol.III, No.4, July/August 1969, pp.55-59. First published as "Nachwort" to Karl Marx's Der 18 Brumaire des Louis Bonaparte, Frankfurt am Main: Insel-Verlag, 1965, pp.143-150.

71. "Der Einfluss der deutschen Emigration auf das amerikanische Geistesleben: Philosophie und Soziologie", Jahrbuch fur Amerikastudien, Vol.X, Heidelberg: Carl Winter Universitatsverlag, 1965, pp.27-33.

72. "Socialist Humanism?", Socialist Humanism, edited by Erich Fromm, New York, Doubleday, 1965, pp.96-106. Paperback edition, New York: Anchor, 1966, pp.107-117.

75. "Comes the Revolution" (reply to Mr. Berman's Review of One-Dimensional Man), Partisan Review, Vol.XXXII, No.1, Winter 1965, pp.159-160..

76. "Statement on Vietnam", Partisan Review, vol.XXXII, No.4, Fall 1965, pp.646-649.

77. "On Science and Phenomenology", Vol.II of Boston Studies in the Philosophy of Science, edited by Robert Cohen and Marx W. Wartofsky, New York: The Humanities Press, 1965, pp.279-291. Also published in Arato, A. and Gebhardt, E. (editors), The Essential Frankfurt School Reader, New York, Unizen Books, 1978.

78. "Sommes-nous déja des hommes?", Partisans, No.28, April 1966, pp.21-24.

79. "Role of Conflict in Human Evolution", Discussion in A. de Reuk and J. Knight (editors), Conflicts in Society: A CIBA Foundation volume, Boston: Little, Brown and Co., 1966.

80. "Vietnam - Analyse eines Exempels", Neue Kritik, Frankfurt am Main, No. 26-37, July-August 1966, pp.30-40.

81. "Zur Geschichte der Dialektik", Sowjetsystem und Demokratische Geselschaft, Freiburg: Herder Verlag, 1966, Vol.I, pp.1192-1211.

82. "The Individual in the Great Society", Part I, _Alternative_, Vol.I, No.1, March/April 1966, Part II, _Alternative_, vol.I, no.2, Summer 1966.

83. "Love Mystified", _Commentary_, Vol.XLIII, No.2, February 1967, pp.71-76. Reprinted as "Love Mystified: A Critique of Norman O. Brown and A Reply to Herbert Marcuse by Norman O. Brown", _Negations_, Boston: Beacon Press, 1968.

84. "The inner logic of American Policy in Vietnam", _Teach-ins_, USA, New York: Praeger, 1967, pp.65-67.

85. "The Obsolescence of Marxism", _Marx and the Western World_, edited by Nicholas Lobkowics, Notre Dame, Ind.: University of Notre Dame Press, 1967, pp.409-418.

86. "Thoughts on the Defense of Gracchus Babeuf", in _The Defense of Gracchus Babeuf_, edited by J. A. Scott, Boston: University of Massachusetts Press, 1967, pp.96-105.

87. "Aggressiveness in Advanced Industrial Society", _Negations_, Boston: Beacon Press, 1968. First published as "Agressivität in der Gegenwartigen Industriegesellschaft", in _Neue Rundschau_, No.1, 1967.

88. "The Concept of Negation in the Dialectic", _Telos_, No.8, Summer 1971, pp. 130-132.

89. "The End of Utopia", _Five Lectures_, op. cit., pp.62-82. First published as "Das Ende der Utopie", lecture delivered at the Free University of Berlin, July 1967.

90. "The Problem of Violence and the Radical Opposition", _Five Lectures_, op. cit., pp.83-108. Lecture first delivered at the Free University of Berlin, July 1967.

91. "Ist der Idee der Revolution eine Mystification", _Kursbuch_, Frankfurt am Main, No.9, pp.1-6.

92. "On Changing the World: A Reply to Karl Miller" (a reply to a review of _One Dimensional Man_), in _Monthly Review_, LXI, October 1967, pp.3-7.

93. "The Question of Revolution", _New Left Review_, No.45, September-October 1967, pp.3-7.

94. "The Responsibility of Science", in L. Krieger and F. Stern, _The Responsibility of Power. Historical Essays in Honor of Hajo Holborn_, New York: Doubleday and Company, 1967.

95. "Die Zukunft der Kunst", in _Neues Forum_, XIV, November-December 1967, pp. 863-866.

96. "Re-examination of the Concept of Revolution", _New Left Review_, No.56, July/August 1969, pp.27-34.

97. "Liberation from the Affluent Society", in

David Cooper (ed.), <u>The Dialectics of Liberation</u>,
London 1968,pp. 175-92.
    98. "Friede als Utopie", in <u>Neues Forum</u>, Vien-
na, November-December 1968, vol.XV, no.179-180,pp.
705-7.
    99. "Varieties of Humanism", <u>Center Magazine</u>,
I, July 1968, pp. 13-15.
    100. "Freedom and the Historical Imperative",
<u>Studies in Critical Philosophy</u>, London: New Left
Books, 1972. Also published as "La Liberté et les
impératifs de l'Histoire" (speech; also scattered
discussion with participants in <u>La Liberté et l'Or-
dre Social</u>, Textes des conférences et entretiens
organisés par les Rencontres Internationales de
Genève, 1969. Boudry (Neuchatel): Editions de la
Baconnière, 1969.
    101. "Nicht enfach zerstoren", in <u>Neues Forum</u>,
XVI, August-September 1969, pp. 485-488.
    102. "On the New Left" (a talk at the twen-
tieth anniversary of the <u>Guardian</u>), in <u>The New Left:
A Documentary History</u>, by Massimo Teodori (ed.),
Indianapolis: Bobbs-Merill Company, 1969.
    103. "The Relevance of Reality", Presidential
Address at the annual meeting of the Pacific Divi-
sion of the American Philosophical Association,
published in <u>Proceedings and addresses of the APA</u>
(College Park, Md., 1969), pp. 39-50.
    104. "The Realm of Freedom and the Realm of
Necessity: A Reconsideration", <u>Praxis</u>, Zagreb,
No.1/2, 1969, pp.20-25.
    105. "Revolutionary Subject and Self-Gover-
ment", <u>Praxis</u>, Zagreb, No.1/2, 1969, pp.326-329.
    106. "Humanismus - gibt's den noch?" <u>Neues Fo-
rum</u>, XVII, Anfang April 1970, pp.39-53.
    107. "Marxism and the New Humanity: An Unfi-
nished Revolution", in <u>Marxism and Radical Religion: Essays Toward a Revolutionary Humanism</u>, by J.
C. Raines and T. Dean, Philadelphia: Temple University Press, 1970.
    108. "Dear Angela", letter to Angela Davis,
published in <u>Ramparts</u>, 9, (Berkeley,February 1971),
p.22.
    109. "Charles Reich as Revolutionary Ostrich",
in Philipo Nobile, ed., <u>The Con III Controversy</u>, new
York 1971,pp. 15-7.
    110. "The Movement in a new Era of Repression:
An assessment", speech delivered at the University
of California at Berkeley, 3 February 1971, published in the <u>Berkeley Journal of Sociology</u> (Berkeley 1971/72), vol. XVI,pp. 1-14.
    111. Letters to Chicago Surrealists, october

1972, untitled and unpublished, among private papers
Herbert Marcuse.
    112. "When Law and Morality Stand in the Way",
Society, (New Brunswick, September-October 1973),
vol. 10,no.6,pp.23-4.
    113. "Some General Remarks on Lucien Gold-
mann", in Lucien Goldmann et la sociologie de la
littérature, Brussels 1973-74,pp.51-2.
    114. "Marxism and Feminism", lecture delivered
at Stanford University,7 March 1974, published in
Women's Studies (old Westbury 1974),pp. 279-88; also
in North Star (1-15 April 1974), vol.4,no. 15,pp.34-
41; reprinted as "Socialist Feminism: The Hard Core
of the Dream", in Eccentric (Eugene,November 1974),
pp.7-47.
    115. "Theorie und Praxis", lecture delivered
in Frankfurt, 28 June 1974, published in Zeit-Messungen, pp.21-36.
    116. "Failure of the New Left?" lecture, Uni-
versity of California at Irvine, April 1975, first
published in German("Scheitern der Neuen Linken?")
in "Zeit-Messungen", pp. 37-38 (translated in New
German Critique, 18, Milwaukee,fall 1979,pp.3-11.
    117. "Un nouvel ordre", in Le Monde Diplomatique,
juillet 1976,no.268.
    118. "Enttauschung", in Gunther Neske, ed.,
Erinnerung an Martin Heidegger, Pfullingen 1977,p.
162-3.
    119. "Mord darf keine Waffen der Politik
sein", in "Die Zeit", 39 (Hamburg, 23 September
1977), pp. 41-2; (translated in New German Critique,
12, Milwaukee, fall 1977,pp. 7-8).
    120. "Protosozialismus und Spatkapitalismus.
Versuch einer revolutionstheoretischen Synthese von
Bahros ansatz", in Zeitschrift fur Sozialdiskussion
19 (1978), pp. 5-27; ("Protosocialism and Late Capitalism: Toward a Theoretical Synthesis Based on
Bahro's Analysis"), in Ulf Wolter, (ed.), Rudolf
Bahro, Critical Response, White Plains, 1980, pp.
25-48.
    121. "The Reification of the Proletariat", in
Canadian Journal of Political and Social Theory
(Winnipeg 1979), vol.3,no. 1,pp. 20-3.

Interviews

    Emanzipation der Frau in der repressiven Ge-
sellschaft: Ein Gesprach mit Herbert Marcuse und
Peter Furth: Das Argument, IV, No.23, 1962, pp. 2-
11.

Professoren als Staats-Regenten?: <u>Der Spiegel</u>, August 21, 1967, pp.112-118.

Gesprach Herbert Marcuse - Peter Merseburger in der Panorama-Sendung des NDR (Neue Deutsche Rundfunk) am 23.10.1967: <u>Weltfrieden und Revolution: Neue politischtheologische Analysen</u>, edited by Hans-Eckehard Bahr. Hamburg: Rowohlt Taschenbuch Verlag, 1968.

Credo nel progresso, nella scienza, nella technologia ma usati al servizio del'uomo: Interview with Franco Vegliani, <u>Tempo</u>, Milan, July 2, 1968. pp.16-23.

<u>L'Express</u> va plus loin avec Herbert Marcuse: <u>L'Express</u>, 23-29 September 1968, pp.54-62.

Revolution 1969: Interview with Henrich von Nussbaum, <u>Neues Forum</u>, XVI, January 1969, pp.26-29.

Revolution Out of Disgust: <u>Australian Left Review</u>, December 1969, pp.36-47. First published as "Revolution aus Ekel", <u>Der Spiegel</u>, July 28, 1969, pp.103-106.

A Conversation with Herbert Marcuse, by S. Keen and J. Raser: <u>Confrontation</u>, No.6, Summer 1971, pp.7-18.

Heidegger's Politics: An Interview with Herbert Marcuse by Frerderick Olafson: <u>Graduate Faculty Philosophy Journal</u>, Vol.6, No.1, Winter 1977, pp. 28-40.

Herbert Marcuse on the Need for an Open Marxist Mind: <u>The Listener</u>, Vol.99, No.2546, February 9, 1978, pp.169-171. Reprinted in B. Magee, (editor), <u>Men of Ideas</u>, London: BBC, 1978.

Theory and Politics: A Discussion with Herbert Marcuse, Jürgen Habermas, Heinz Lubasz and Telman Spengler: <u>Telos</u>, No.38, Winter 1978, pp.124-153. First published in J. Habermas, S. Bovenschen (eds.), <u>Gespräche mit Herbert Marcuse</u>, Frankfurt am Main, pp. 9-62.

A review of the secondary literature can be found in the Introduction and notes. A number of useful works on freedom are cited in the notes to the Introduction and to chapter four. Additional references to interviews can be found in Barry Katz, op.cit., whose entries on recent unpublished materiale are reproduced here.

Piccone P., 19, 22, 37n,
39n, 206, 273n
Plekhanov G.V., 45, 117,
142, 236
positivism, 11, 17, 45,
46, 75, 108, 143, 148,
157, 236, 246, 255-
56t, 273
progress, 195, 255-56t

reason, 109, 124-25,
128t, 137n, 146t, 153-
59, 173-74n, 184t,
209-11, 219-20, 229t,
251t, 255-56t, 259,
266, 273, 279
instrumental, techno
logical, 124, 155-56,
173-74n, 196, 229t,
252t, 255-56t, 261
reification, 53-5t, 64,
84t, 86-92, 98-9, 101,
154, 191-200, 229t,
239, 253t, 256t, 259-
61, 263-64, 266, 268,
271, 278n   see also
objectification
revolution, 48, 51, 54t,
57, 59, 67, 79, 99,
101, 106n, 110-11,
121, 126, 147, 149,
156, 167, 178, 180,

revolution (cont'd)
220-21n, 238, 250,
284-888
Rhodes J.M., 38n, 109,
132n, 216n
Robinson P.A., 9, 35n,
103n, 198-99, 216n

Sartre J.P., 4, 31n, 36n,
44, 239, 244, 247n,
264-65, 273, 276n, 284
Schiller F., 186, 208
Schmidt A., 19, 37n, 112,
133n
Schoolman M., 12, 19,
35n, 38n, 96-7
Shakespeare W., 162
Slater P., 10, 21, 35n
species being, 81-2t, 84-
5t, 88-91, 94, 99-100,
124, 136n, 149, 158-60
Stendhal, 165

Therborn G., 37n, 39n
60n, 131n, 176n, 206,
218n
truth, see knowledge

Weber M., 66, 143, 149
243-44, 247n, 259,
261, 262, 265, 276n

Note: as Marx is mentioned on almost every page, he
is not included in the index - n after a page number
refers to the notes - t after a page number refers
to the tables. See "editorial notes" for references
to other matters of notation.